"This book is for anyone interested in the front-lines of education. Most chapters center on an exciting learning environment, on particularly well done descriptions of real live kids with a real live teacher, or on certain theories of instruction relevant to the generally acknowledged problems of our schools.

"Most parents are extremely interested in the quality of their children's education, and they can be counted upon to support any teacher who seems to be effective according to their frames of reference. But so often parents are left in the dark about what it is that good teachers do and others do not. Sensing vaguely that something ought to be different or that there are areas for improvement, they are left high and dry without concrete suggestions once they have protested the status quo. This book offers no panaceas for dull teaching or repressive schools, but it does offer a series of examples of what some good teachers do and how they do it."

—From the Introduction

THE CHANGING
CLASSROOM

Edited by

Carol Goodell

BALLANTINE BOOKS • NEW YORK

Grateful acknowledgment is made to the contributors of selections in this book for use of copyrighted material:

How to Survive in Your Native Land, by James Herndon. Reprinted by permission of Simon and Schuster. Copyright © 1971 by James Herndon.

Tolstoy on Education, edited by Leo Weiner. Reprinted by permission of the University of Chicago Press.

An Empty Spoon, by Sunny Decker. Reprinted by permission of Harper & Row, Publishers, Inc. Copyright © 1969 by Sunny Decker.

The Lives of Children, by George Dennison. Reprinted by permission of Random House, Inc. Copyright © 1969 by George Dennison.

"A Place in Space," by Gordon Ashby, a selection from *Big Rock Candy Mountain* by permission of the author.

Summerhill: For and Against, edited by Harold H. Hart. Reprinted by permission of the publisher. Copyright © 1970 by Hart Publishing Co., Inc.

Teaching for Survival, by Mark Terry. Reprinted by permission of the author and Ballantine Books, Inc. Copyright © 1971 by Mark Terry.

Self-Renewal: The Individual and the Innovative Society, by John W. Gardner. Reprinted by permission of Harper & Row, Publishers, Inc. Copyright © 1964 by John W. Gardner.

Pygmalion in the Classroom: Teacher Expectation and Pupils' Intellectual Development, by Robert Rosenthal and Lenore Jacobson. Reprinted by permission of Holt, Rinehart and Winston, Inc. Copyright © 1968 by Holt, Rinehart and Winston, Inc.

Piaget for Teachers, by Hans G. Furth. Reprinted by permission of Prentice-Hall, Inc. Copyright © 1970 by Prentice-Hall, Inc.

Hooked on Books, by Daniel N. Fader and Elton B. McNeil. Reprinted by permission of G. P. Putnam's Sons. Copyright © 1968 by Daniel N. Fader and Elton B. McNeil.

The Open Classroom, by Herbert Kohl. Reprinted with permission from The New York Review of Books. Copyright © 1969 by Herbert Kohl.

Yellow Pages for Learning Resources, edited by Richard Saul Wurman. Reprinted by permission of the editor. Developed under a grant from Educational Facilities Laboratories, Inc. and published by the MIT Press. Copyright © 1972 by GEE! Group for Environmental Education Inc.

On the Outskirts of Hope, by Helaine Dawson. Used by permission of McGraw-Hill Book Company. Copyright © 1968 by McGraw-Hill, Inc.

Teacher, by Sylvia Ashton-Warner. Reprinted by permission of Simon and Schuster, Inc. Copyright © 1963 by Sylvia Ashton-Warner.

Role Playing for Social Values: Decision-Making in the Social Studies, by Fannie R. Shaftel and George Shaftel. Reprinted by permission of Prentice-Hall, Inc. Copyright © 1967 by Prentice-Hall, Inc.

What Do I Do Monday? by John Holt. Reprinted by permission of E. P. Dutton & Co., Inc. Copyright © 1970 by John Holt.

Schools Where Children Learn, by Joseph Featherstone. Reprinted by permission of Liveright, Publishers. Copyright © 1971 by Joseph Featherstone.

Push Back the Desks, by Albert Cullum. Reprinted by permission of Citation Press, a division of Scholastic Magazines, Inc. Copyright © 1967 by Scholastic Magazines, Inc.

Abridgement of "Classroom Meetings," by William Glasser, reprinted from *Schools Without Failure* by permission of Harper & Row, Publishers, Inc. Copyright © 1969 by William Glasser.

Teaching as a Subversive Activity, by Neil Postman and Charles Weingartner. Reprinted by permission of Delacorte Press. Copyright © 1969 by Neil Postman and Charles Weingartner.

SBN 345-24891-0-195

First Printing: May, 1973
Third Printing: September, 1975

Printed in the United States of America

Cover photo by Phoebe Dunn

BALLANTINE BOOKS
A Division of Random House, Inc.
201 East 50th Street, New York, N.Y. 10022

*For Bill, my husband,
and Beth and Douglas,
our children*

Education is what you learn in books, and nobody knows you know it but your teacher. I
asked Mrs. Harris when we were plaiting rags
for her kitchen rug what good Marco Polo would
ever do me, and Mrs. Harris said education gave
you satisfaction, but I had rather be ignorant and
have fun than be educated and have satisfaction.
—V. C. Hudson: *O Ye Jigs and Juleps*

In Memory of
Jack Michael Baer
3-11-64 to 11-28-69
and all the other children who
have been stricken with leukemia

Contents

TOPICS

If you're interested in a particular topic, you might use this listing as a reading guide.

A brief annotated fan letter to people I'd like to thank for having helped:

William Goodell
George Young
Laura Jamison
Stewart Brand
Christine Conaway
Dick Raymond
Margaret and
  Bob Guyton

People whose expectations were high and who provided early encouragement.

Nan Gjestland
Priscilla Larsen
Elizabeth Ellis

Friends who read and commented intelligently, especially when they didn't agree.

Nancy Lange
Peggy Slajchert

Young friends who did the same while acting in the capacity of students.

Fannie and George
  Shaftel

General mentors.

Helen Hockabout
Precious Warren
Priscilla Larsen

Each of whom, in her own way, kept the home fires burning when I got my most frantic.

Douglas Goodell
Beth Goodell

Who are such neat flexible kids that they think it's perfectly normal to have a mom typing or reading in the center of their playroom while they set up an electric train under the typewriter table.

The Changing
Classroom

Introduction

I have more hope for the American school mess now than I did before the research for this book began. At least we recognize that there is a need for alternatives and personally I have been astounded by discovery of exciting and interesting learning environments all over the country, often in the most unlikely places.

This book is for anyone interested in the frontlines of education. Most chapters center on an exciting learning environment, on particularly well done descriptions of real live kids with a real live teacher, or on certain theories of instruction relevant to the generally acknowledged problems of our schools.

Most parents are extremely interested in the quality of their children's education, and they can be counted upon to support any teacher who seems to be effective according to their frames of reference. But so often parents are left in the dark about what it is that good teachers do and others do not. Sensing vaguely that something ought to be different or that there are areas for improvement, they are left high and dry without concrete suggestions once they have protested the status quo. This book offers no panaceas for dull teaching or repressive schools, but it does offer a series of examples of what some good teachers do and how they do it.

One of the more telling arguments about teaching as a profession versus its interpretation as a job is that teachers cannot be sued for malpractice. This is not true for any other profession. Indeed most teachers cannot even be fired for poor teaching. So the burden of retraining and increased education is immense, and can and is being partially done by parents and writers as well as through more established channels. Pressure, loving or abrasive, has been brought on the American education system and it is slowly responding.

Research for this book began in an orderly way. I read and read and kept selecting for possible use what I liked as a mother and as a teacher, always delaying the development of some hard criteria for elimination until some mythical time when all of the reading would be done and then somehow I could get objective. Well, that time just never came. The reading came to an end due to deadlines and eyestrain, rather than to an end of worthwhile books. And I am more emotionally responsive than ever to what should go into this book. It becomes clear that I have consistent biases for what is worth reading about education, and these preferences center around:

1. teachers who clearly love children and teaching
2. teachers who can convey their personal involvement with a class through descriptions of specific projects that did or did not do what they had hoped
3. teachers who hold themselves primarily responsible for what happens in their classrooms although they may be most articulate about conditions which constrain them
4. teachers who skirt the feeling that there is one right way
5. teachers who are good bitchers
6. teachers who have a sense of humor, particularly in relation to themselves
7. teachers who have alternatives to educational jargon. Final selections are based upon these biases with an emphasis on materials which can be of immediate use to teachers looking for specific techniques.

Recognizable common themes emerged as a result of my reading. Without laboring the points, I thought you might be interested. The theme of changing perceptions of themselves as teachers is the strongest, and is explored in a number of ways in the anthology and in the books from which this anthology is taken. Changes in the way they perceive themselves and their classes are developed in the space of a single school year in the books by Dennison and Decker, while Holt, Tolstoy and Cullum reflect over much longer periods. Herndon's classics *The Way It Spozed to Be* and *How to Survive in Your Native Land* were written ten years apart. They are reports from the same witty, perceptive man exploring his feelings about himself and learning and kids and our country, but he sees these roles in a different light. Yet the latter book is not meant to be the announcement of a conversion to a right way of living or teaching, but a statement of where Herndon is now and how he thinks he got there. Herb Kohl's books represent changes in his role as the teacher traced from his emotional description of *36 Children* to thoughts on how to effect a more non-authoritarian class in *The Open Classroom*.

A second common theme was the frequent and excellent use made of anecdotal child-centered stories. If teachers share a common trait, it is empathy for classroom situations, which certainly isn't surprising. But it is surprising and exciting that so many of the teachers who write well can recall and make use of revealing and insightful incidents to illustrate their concepts. This makes it easy for other teachers to identify, helps those who are about to begin teaching to understand what running a real classroom with real kids is like, and gives others unfamiliar with the wide variety of types of classroom situations a broader perspective that is pleasant to read about.

A sense of professional isolation is profound. And it's no wonder. It's hard for teachers to find out what is happening next door, let alone in other school districts. Official once-a-year visitation days are stilted ocasions planned for with the precision of dinner at the White House. Such formalized experiences are in no way representative of the continuum of what is a classroom day to day. Educational conferences are frequently sterilized experiences based more on materials and methods than on kids, and indeed it is rare to have a child involved in a teacher's conference at all. And the isolation extends beyond that to a feeling that the conferees are sort of talking to themselves professionally; that parents and other teachers who agreed were rather sparse or too scared or just not talking.

Guilt keeps creeping in. Teachers are assailed professionally on all sides, and they seem to believe much of the worst that they read and hear about themselves. Is there any other profession where the self-image is so bad? Agony, remorse and doubt are the secret companions of many teachers. They lack objective feedback on their own or their peer efforts because their peer reflectors are second-handers—parents, teachers' room gossips, or administrators who are not really part of the classroom. By comparison I read somewhere that surgeons have a committee of peers for hospital performance reviews; attorneys have trial transcripts; but teachers really aren't sure of what is happening in other classes. So they continue to harbor doubts as to their own performance, measured as it is only against some impossible sterilized image of what the norm is.

A problem of publicizing any particular teacher's work is the natural tendency to try to exactly duplicate that work. As a result, we end up practically carving in stone ideas or concepts that person had. We cut ourselves off from adapting those techniques to different situations as undoubtedly the original innovator would have, and tend to introduce yet another inflexible system. We get bogged down into discipleship of varying proportions, some of which end up nearly completely contrary to the basic premises of the originators' initial ideas.

The importance of the personality of the teacher is hard to overestimate. I agree with Herb Kohl's idea that if you are happy with the way you are doing things, if whatever style you have seems right for you as a teacher, then it would be damaging for you to try to change. Change is no panacea by itself. It's the recognition of the need for change and then its implementation that can cause good things to happen.

None of the excerpts from books that make up this anthology is chosen as a total solution to any problem. All are presented as examples that I think are interesting, useful and valuable in an educational and personal sense, and together they constitute notice of redirections of the educational wind. In the first section of this book are cross-referenced suggestions for the reading for specific interest areas. Other than that it really doesn't matter. Take your pick. Start anywhere. It's strictly an à la carte reading menu.

Bon appétit
Carol Guyton Goodell

San Carlos, California
December, 1972

I. View from Within

View from Within

Teachers who love teaching and either love or lament their current teaching situation are legion, thank heavens; those who can write well enough about it to let the rest of us emphathize are rare. These selections were made because they reveal real classrooms with real kids. You can feel a part of their situations and you feel you know the kids involved too.

Christopher Columbus

James Herndon

from *How to Survive in Your Native Land*

Thus: about a month before the end of one school year, Frank Ramirez and I invented a course for the next year. We thought up a simple notion. We wanted a two-hour class, and we wanted to both be there at the same time. We wanted the class to be free of certain restrictions —those regarding curriculum, those regarding grades and those regarding school behavior rules, mainly the ones about leaving the classroom.

We didn't think there ought to be any difficulties in arranging it, and at the same time we prepared to answer all the difficulties logically. The two-hour class was O.K. because the eighth grade kids had two electives anyway; they could just choose to take our class instead of two others. We would arrange to have the class the last two periods in the day (seventh and eighth); since all teachers got a preparation period (a free period, but you weren't supposed to call it *free*), we'd take ours seventh and eighth respectively and spend our *free* time teaching together in the classroom in our new class. We were making, we planned to point out, a sacrifice. The kids would enroll voluntarily and we'd notify parents about what kind of course it was. We sent out notices and held a meeting of kids who thought they might want to enroll.

Everything worked out fine. There was no trouble. We were perhaps a bit disappointed. The principal agreed. The vice-principal agreed. The counselors agreed. Perhaps the parents agreed; they abstained at least, since none sent back comment. There were really only two difficulties. First, the schedule didn't work out. When we got back to school in the fall, we found out that Lou had forgotten to schedule our prep periods right, so that we couldn't work the class in the same room at the same time for two hours. Lou merely said he was sorry he forgot it, and declined to make any changes then, at the beginning of school. He couldn't see why we were pissed off; he considered it a minor matter. We felt the whole course had been sabotaged.

The other difficulty was with the kids. About twenty-five kids showed up, clearly divided in their intentions. A few were really looking forward to having two periods of time to do stuff in—our emphasis had been on the arts, generally, and they planned to paint and write and put on plays. The rest had only been attracted by the *no assignment* and *no grade* promise in our presentation; they came in wising off and horsing around, equally clearly prepared to disbelieve and test us out. As for that great rest of the school kid population who weren't in fact there, it's clear they just considered the whole thing a trap or a shuck. They knew they could put up with the ordinary school routine, having done it seven years already, but who knew what might happen to them if they risked something new?

Besides the intentions of the kids, of course, there was also the fact of our intention—Frank's and mine. I think that is best expressed by this: we would do, as the main thing, all the stuff we did in our regular classes as a sideline when the regular "work" was finished.

Frank had been working at the school for perhaps eight or nine years. In the two or three years I'd been there, I learned from watching him how to conduct yourself as a regular teacher in regular classes in a regular school. How you could teach and work there without driving yourself nuts with boredom, rage, a sense of your own hypocrisy, without unending uproars with the administration and parents and without getting fired, which was important to me. Frank was the best at this I ever saw. He filled his room with art materials, even though he was supposed to be teaching English and social studies to seventh graders. While other teachers were complaining publicly how difficult it was in the short time of nine months to "get through" the "material" in the texts, Frank announced that the stuff you were supposed to teach in a year could be handled easily in six weeks or so, and you had the rest of the time to do other things you might care to do. He figured the other teachers dragged out the teaching of Egypt or math all year because they didn't have anything else they wanted to do or cared about, or because they were afraid of the kids once the threat of the curriculum was called off.

In Language Arts, he showed the kids how to diagram sentences, pointed out the parts of speech, showed them where to put commas and semicolons—all in quite a short time. He was the only man I've ever heard give a good answer to that old kid question, Why do we have to make these diagrams?

Why? Because they are beautiful, said Frank. What Frank understood, or knew how to work, or knew how to involve the kids in, or something . . . was a kind of interrelationship between studies, which were supposed to be real, and fantasy, which was supposed to be not-real. So that if they were "studying" some place which was an island, they studied it O.K., read the book, answered them questions on ditto sheets, and then the kids would find themselves with big pieces of paper inventing an island, drawing and painting in its geography, describing its people, its kings and rulers, the way the people ate, or what they lived in, or how they celebrated Christmas. Or they went to the library and got books and wrote to the authors, and put the authors' answers up on the board, telling where they were born and how they got the idea of writing such and such a kid's book. Then Frank might give some letters to other kids, who would write secret answers as if they were the authors and these would go up on the board too. He took kids to the Golden Gate Bridge, where they dropped off bottles with fake notes in them into the outgoing tide and the answers to these notes, from points up and down the California coast, went up on the board too, along with "environments" made from junk in cigar boxes and illustrations from books or stories which he made the kids paint left-handed with big brushes on small pieces of paper so their technique or lack of it wouldn't get in the way.

I joined him in this kind of work. In my class we wrote to the Peace Corps and got real information about the problems of various countries and the straight dope on what the Corps hoped to do in these countries, how they would work, and so on. The kids, pretending to be Peace Corps workers themselves, wrote imaginary journals of stays in Africa and South America; the idea was that they would use the official information in their writing and would solve a lot of problems. In fact, though, their journals were full of first-class air travels to and from the countries, drinking cocktails and making it with stewardesses or *white hunters* in the *bush,* torture by *natives,* escapes, liaisons with chiefs' daughters, buried treasures and elephants' graveyards. Little attention was given to the raising of chickens, the building of irrigation systems, or the growing of flax. Medical care was brought in only as accessory to a needed miracle—the chief's son cured by a shot of penicillin just when the Corpsman was about to be eaten up by head-hunting pygmies.

In English, I had the kids begin inventing languages. They wrote down lists of common words and when we had the lists we'd start making a picture or symbol to stand for it, just like them Egyptians did. Then we'd choose the best symbol and make lists of those and after we had a couple of hundred or so we'd start translating simple fairy tales into our new language, or making up stories to write in it, and put the stories on huge decorated pieces of paper and send them over to Frank's class to see if they could decipher them, as if they were Linear B.

Sooner or later there would be an item in the school newspaper about it:

The kids in Rooms 45 and 31 are making up their own languages in their class. Here is an example of it; can you figure it out?

A couple of teachers would say That sounds like an interesting project and point out its relationship to Egypt to me. But, like the fake Peace Corps, where other teachers were always faintly disappointed when these journals, put on display in the library, failed to follow the government plans (the kids weren't using the information from official sources, and so it followed that they weren't learning anything, and so it wasn't social studies, but only fantasy)—the article failed to display the real point of such an activity. It failed to show the tremendous uproar when twenty kids rushed to the board to put up their symbols, the arguments of kids about which was best, and the fine look of the decorated pages when they were done. It also failed to show my pleasure at symbols which I thought just right, like these:

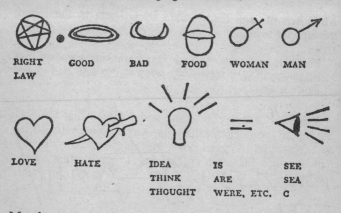

RIGHT LAW   GOOD   BAD   FOOD   WOMAN   MAN

LOVE   HATE   IDEA THINK THOUGHT   IS ARE WERE, ETC.   SEE SEA C

My pleasure was also in the process of the symbols working out. *Right* started out as a complicated drawing of a sheriff, *good* as an angel, *bad* as the devil—then they were refined into the star, horns and halo. We talked about the necessity of briefer, less complicated forms, since we wouldn't want to do all that drawing every time we Egyptians sent a note to a friend. Later on we learned from ourselves, and the symbols became simpler right away, as in *think* and *is*. We went on and made certain kinds of words different colors when we made posters, blue for things, red for actions, green for descriptions and so on, following the familiar pattern of seventh-grade pedants. I pushed it a bit further, trying to make the changeover from ideograph to alphabet, so that a symbol which once meant only *good* came to represent *G* while retaining the meaning of good.

We went on and on with it. Too much! I thought to myself all the time, full of excitement and pride, it is a great lesson. We are inventing, we are learning parts of speech and puns and structure of language and intricacies of grammar—all participating, with fun, uproar, excitement, consultant approval, letters from the superintendent saying as how Frank and I were creative teachers, A's for the kids, Frank and I coming to work feeling good and ready to go, happy parents—and we all lived through a kind of Golden Age of Rooms 31 and 45 at Spanish

Main School. I mean we were a big success—more importantly *I* was; Frank had already been one for some time.

In this marvelous confident mood we approached the beginning of the year in Creative Arts. We had more ideas than you could shake a stick at.

For most of that year Frank and I agreed that CA—as the school soon began calling it—was absolutely the worst class we could have imagined. Nothing worked right. We had a lot to blame it on, griping to each other, commiserating together, telling each other it wasn't our fault. It was the administration's fault for one thing, scheduling things wrong. Then it was the kids' fault, for not being the right kind of kids. It was also the school's fault, for manifesting an atmosphere in which you wouldn't do anything unless you were made to.

In fact, another two main things—of a quite different nature, and yet quite firmly connected—were at fault. The first was what had seemed to us a detail and concerned leaving class. On the very first day we issued Permanent Hall Passes, each with a particular kid's name on it, and told the kids they could come and go in and out of our classrooms at any time, without asking permission or leave, and they could go anywhere around the school grounds. If stopped they had only to show their passes. We announced this casually; it seemed simple and obvious to us. One of the biggest drags in a school is the fact that whenever a kid wants to go anywhere, or whenever you want to send a kid somewhere to get something or do something, you have to stop and write out a pass, sign it, date it, put down the time and his expected destination. If you didn't, then the kid was sure to get stopped by some adult in the halls or wherever he was and get in trouble for being in the halls without a pass. Then the kid would come back to you, sometimes with the adult in question or with some goofy Rally Boy or Rally Girl who was On Duty at the time, and demand that you save him from detention or calling his mom for this sin, and you'd have to say Yeah, I sent him out, or

Yeah, I said he could go . . . then like as not the kid hadn't gone where you said for him to go or where he said he was going, and so you had to go into that, and in the end everyone was mad and nothing had been accomplished, except maybe the kid had gotten his smoke in the bathroom, supposing that was what he wanted.

Being smart, we got around all that with the Permanent Hall Passes. The kids were ecstatic, and spent quite a bit of time that first day interrogating us as to what we really meant. They kept it up so long I finally got mad and yelled that it meant they could leave anytime, go anywhere on the grounds, that yes, once and for all yes, that was what it meant and if anyone said another word about it I was pulling back these passes and it was all off. Then they believed it.

The second thing was that all the great notions we had, all the ideas for things to do, all our apparatus for insuring a creative, industrious, happy, meaningful class didn't seem to excite the kids all that much. Most of the kids didn't want to do any of them at all, anytime. They didn't want to write to the Peace Corps, they didn't want to bring cigar boxes and make avant-garde environments, they didn't want to make plaster statuary, they didn't want to write stories, they didn't want to paint left-handed or make up new languages . . . they didn't want to do a fucking thing except use that fucking Permanent Hall Pass in the way it was supposed to be used, namely to take it and leave the class, roam around, come back in, leave again, roam around and come back in. When they went out they would say *There's Nothing To Do Around Here,* and leave, and when they came back they would say *There's Nothing To Do Out There,* and everyone would agree and say that awhile and bitch about the number of adults and narc Rally Boys who made them show their pass and brag to each other about how they told off the chickenshit narcs of all sorts . . . and for the first few days we were besieged by teachers and Rally Boys asking were those unbelievable *Permanent Hall Passes* valid and we'd say yes, and then for a few more days we were visited by kids who had invented excuses to get out of class in order to drop by and ask us urgently if it were really true that we had given out *Permanent Hall Passes* to *Every Kid* in our *Class,* and we'd say Yes! . . . and after those gripes and narratives had run out of interest someone would remember to say There's Nothing To Do In Here again, and out most of the kids would go.

Well, as a lesson plan, there is nothing I can recommend quite so highly as a Permanent Hall Pass. After a while, Frank and I, on the edge of complete despair, began to figure out what was wrong with the ideas that had worked so well in our regular classes. It was very simple. Why did the kids in regular class like to do all that inventive stuff? Why, only because it was better than the regular stuff. If you wrote a fake journal pretending to be Tutankhamen's favorite embalmer, it was better than reading the dull Text, answering Questions on ditto sheets, Discussing, making Reports, or taking Tests. Sure it was better—not only that but you knew the teacher liked it better for some insane reason which you didn't have to understand and you would get better grades for it than you were used to getting in social studies or English. But that only applied to a regular class where it was clear you had to (1) stay there all period and (2) you had to be doing something or you might get an F. Take away those two items, as Frank and I had done in all innocence, and you get a brief vision of the truth.

We were in a new world. Nothing can be worse than that. We had to face the fact that all the stuff we thought the kids were dying to do (if they only had time away from the stupefying lessons of other teachers) was in fact stuff that *we* wanted them to do, that *we* invented, that interested *us*—not only that but it interested us mainly as things to be doing during periods of time when something had to be going on, when no one was supposed to be just sitting around doing nothing. And not only things to be doing—it was things for *them,* the kids, to be doing. Things we wanted to see them do, the results of which we wanted to see. We wanted to see what symbols the kids would invent for English words; we didn't have much curiosity about the symbols we ourselves would invent. We didn't write fake Peace Corps journals ourselves; we only told the kids to do it. I don't mean to criticize us harshly on these points; that is, by and large, the attitude of teachers and it's a normal rationale for teaching. You want to see what the kids can do, you want to get some idea of their abilities, their intelligence, their cleverness, their ingenuity, their—creativity. You want to have something interesting to do during the class time. It was clear that many kids rather liked the writing or the painting or constructing or whatever it was, once they got started (since they had to do something) and once it was finished, once the other kids expressed admiration, once they got a A, once their work was shown in the room on Back to School Night. Looked at that way, we were able to decide that we had a lot more ideas than the kids and the kids never knew what they wanted to anyway, and if we made them do stuff we knew was interesting and exciting and all, they would be better off for it. About the sixth week of CA, we laid that out to the kids and tried to establish a hard line.

Since no one is doing anything, *then therefore,* we told them, sat down in their seats and quiet, you'll have to do assignments. We told them how great the assignments would be. That was going to be that.

Indignation, disappointment and sneers greeted my own pronouncement. I was told in plain words that I was being chickenshit. I was reminded of my brave words *when I talked them into taking this lousy course last year* (I'd thought no one was listening) and quite clearly informed that it was the same old thing—teachers promising "class participation in decision making" and then if it didn't work out just like the teacher wanted, the teacher then unilaterally changed his fucking mind. (I remind myself how things change when you give up your authority, officially, even if you really want to keep it, privately. The kids begin to talk to you just as if you are a real person, and often say just what they mean.) I was informed that the only virtue of the class was its freedom to do (to come and go) and not-do; take away that and they all planned to see their counselors and ask for transfers.

I think I would have weathered that storm, stuck to the new hard line if it hadn't been for Meg, Lily, and Jane. Meg, Lily, and Jane were our heroes. They were doing just exactly what Frank and I had figured everyone would be doing in CA, namely, they were doing stuff all the time. The first day or so, one of the things the kids had in mind was to make a newspaper, a kids' newspaper (underground papers not having been invented yet) as opposed to the boring, tendentious adult-oriented official school paper which was mostly written by the teacher in charge anyway. Having decided that, most of the kids then made use of their passes to come and go and talk about nothing to do; Meg and Lily started off immediately to make the newspaper. Meg would get the material and edit it, Lily would type and run it off and figure how to distribute it, and Jane would do the illustrations. In the end, receiving absolutely no cooperation from anyone else, they had done it all themselves, Meg not only edited but wrote all the stories (no one else could stop coming in and out long enough to do so) and Lily talked the office into letting her use the mimeograph machine which was unheard of and Jane drew all sorts of stuff for it. Since that time, they had begun plans for a literary magazine to be called *Infinity,* and spent their time trying to persuade the other members of the class to write something for it. Having no luck whatsoever, they complained bitterly during that first six weeks about the other kids, how they wouldn't do anything, and how it was supposed to be a class project, and Frank and I would try to talk to the kids about writing, and about class solidarity and so on, but no use.

The point is, I had counted on support from these three in our new, reactionary notion of class. Surely they would be in favor of making the other kids write and paint and draw and so on, thus supplying them with material—but in fact, they weren't. They too threatened rebellion. Jane announced she would draw or paint nothing else that year if required to. Meg agreed that it was too bad that no one else wanted to write for the magazine, but that it was obvious that "enforced writing" (she said) wasn't going to be any good. She might as well be taking *Journalism,* she said, with noticeable disgust.

I tried arguments. How about the fact that they wanted to work and couldn't get anything done because everyone else was just screwing around? Wouldn't it be better if everyone wrote and drew for the magazine? Yes, they said, but only if they really wanted to. We went thus round and round. Meg, most brilliant and articulate of girls, told me that even in the regular journalism class there were only two or three people who really wanted to write for the paper and had any talent for it; the rest of the students, being forced to do so in order not to flunk, wrote only boring and rather stupid stuff. That, she said, was probably what caused the journalism teacher to have to rewrite most of the dull, boring stuff, and what made the whole paper thus sound like it had been written by a teacher, and after all, dull, boring stuff rewritten was still dull, boring stuff. Not only that, she said, isn't it so that good magazines are really put out by these very people who have talent and the desire to put them out? And isn't it so that most people in the world do not write, don't put out magazines, maybe don't even read them? But the magazines are good, sometimes, which was the point. Why should it be different in a class?

The fact that a magazine was good was the point. The desire of the teacher that everyone "participate" was beside the point and would surely result in a bad magazine. You couldn't have both, she was trying to tell me, and so you had to decide which you wanted.

Well, Frank and I decided without no trouble. Reaction would have to wait. Perhaps we only wanted to be reassured. The hall passes remained, and *Infinity* came out regularly. The class remained in a state of chaos, measured by ordinary school standards. Yet if I select *Infinity* as a measure (I think now), the class takes on a surprising aspect of solidarity. When an issue was ready to be put together, for instance, everyone knew it. They came that day prepared to collate the pages, staple them, serve as runners to bring twenty copies or so to every classroom (using Permanent Hall Passes to do so) and when all that was over they sat down to look at and read and comment on *Infinity* and criticize it and decide if this new issue was as good or better or worse than some previous issue just as if they were really involved in it. After the first issue, in any case, Meg didn't have to write at all and Jane didn't have to do all the drawings and Lily had more offers of help with the mimeograph machine than she could handle. The offers came from other kids in other classes. They did exist. Stories poured in. There were secret writers all over the place. Kids in CA read them and judged them. *Infinity* kept coming out. The whole class took credit for it, time and time again, and they were right. *We* are doing it, they said. After all, who else was?

Well. It was the class of Piston and the kite. I think that has already told most everything else. Frank and I continued to run between joy and desperation, constantly hassled because Egypt teachers complained to us about the Permanent Hall Pass kids giving their kids the finger seventh and eighth period as they passed by, because the secretaries were complaining that the kids were using too many mimeograph blanks and cluttering up the office and arguing with them about which should have priority, page fourteen of *Infinity* or some announcement from the administration about PTA meetings, continually anxious because it always looked like no one was doing anything, and because, for example, a marvelously bright girl like Marcia should have decided to use all her free gift of time in CA doing nothing all year except going around to the boys asking them stuff like *Have you seen Mike Hunt?* (a nonexistent person whose name, translated into quick speech, turns out to be My Cunt)—a question which I'd heard asked myself a time or two when I was in the eighth grade and which had interested me then more than anything else in the entire whole wide world. We were bothered and confused and upset because the kids who never would do anything we suggested they might do were always the very kids who kept complaining to us that they were

bored, that there was Nothing To Do In Here (and Out
There), that We Never Do Anything In This Class
and We Don't Learn Anything In Here. When we heard
that complaint, we'd haul out some idea (figuring we had
the kid this time!) and say *Then why don't you do* this
or that? Then the complaining kid would say triumphantly,
Naw, I don't want to! Well, what about doing this or that
other thing, we'd say, and the kid would say *Uh-uh,*
and then we'd say *O.K., what about . . .* and the kid got
to say *No Good* and then cut out and go to the bathroom
and arrive back later saying *There's Nothing Going On.*

This drove us out of our minds, and it drove us out of
our minds every day. We tried to figure it out, and couldn't
do it. All we could see was that the fucking kids were
trying to drive us out of our minds. We did see that
somehow this was the crucial issue of the course. Un-
accountably, the course was not, as we'd thought, a course
where students would get to do all the things we'd
thought up for them to do, but instead a course where
they could steadfastly refuse to do everything and then
complain that there was nothing to do.

Christopher Columbus schemed and made a lot of plans
and talked the principal into it and finally set sail for India,
figuring that if he could get there by this new route he
would become rich and famous. Unfortunately he ran into
the New World first. Columbus' plans were all predicated
on it being India, so he didn't know what to do with it,
didn't understand it, and ended up convinced that everyone was trying to drive him out of his mind. Since there
weren't going to be any spices or silks, he became obsessed with the only thing left to insure riches and fame.
He thus tortured Carib and Arawak chiefs from all over,
figuring from Old World premises that they knew where
the gold was but naturally wouldn't tell him. It never
penetrated his mind that they really didn't have any.
Columbus sailed North and South and East, gold and
the Old World reinforcing a vertical logic which prevented
him from sailing West long enough to actually run into
gold.

On one of his sailing trips, he came across several very large canoes, way out of sight of land. The canoes seemed to be full of richly dressed native businessmen, all painted and befeathered and going somewhere definite and purposive. But Columbus knew that the natives of the New World didn't go out of sight of land. He mentioned them in dispatches as an oddity, something else trying to drive him out of his mind, intimated that they were crazy, and forgot them. He didn't try to find out where they lived, or where they were going. He didn't follow them, or torture them, or try to get rich and famous from them. They didn't fit into his notion of how things were, didn't make any sense in view of his idea of what he was doing. It was too bad. I don't think Columbus ever found out that those seagoing businessmen were most likely Aztecs, possessors in nearby Mexico City of all the gold in the world. Columbus invented the New World, but its terms lay apart from his Old World logic and he just couldn't take any advantage from it.

Frank and I did a little better than Columbus. If we never quite accepted the notion that the real curriculum of the course was precisely the question What Shall We Do In Here? and that it was really an important question and maybe the only important question, we did finally understand that there was no gold in CA. We did see that if you agreed beforehand not to threaten the kids with grades, and if you agreed that everyone could leave the room at any time without asking you, that you had just entered a New World.

But quite late in the year, we did get some idea of where we were. There was a big blond kid named Greg in the class, and Greg had maddened us all year. He wouldn't do anything at all, he complained all the time about there was nothing to do, he scoffed at all our ideas, he gave the finger to Egypt classes every day, he Took Advantage of Freedom, he smoked in the bathroom, he encouraged Marcia and Mike Hunt, he was the original big lump of a thirteen-year-old in a canoe way out of sight of land, just trying to drive us crazy. That goddamn purposeless Greg, Frank and I often told each other, thinking frankly that if we could just get rid of him, transfer him out into some other class, then things might go right . . . Well, one day the roof finally fell in on Greg and he reaped the rewards of all his fucking around all year. The counselors, taking note of all his F's and Unsatisfactories for Citizenship, sent out forms to his teachers, asking them to comment. Of course they all wrote that he was no damn good. So the counselors called his parents and they had to come in, and there they were with the principal and the vice-principal and the counselors and the teachers and there was Greg, faced with all those adults come to deal with the fact that he was no good. There in the office, hearing all the teachers tell Greg's parents that he wouldn't do Spelling, wouldn't do Science, wouldn't do this and that (wouldn't even do Shop, for Christ's sake!), in the face of all those helpful, frowning adults, Frank and I suddenly saw that Greg was really O.K. We remembered that he always helped out collating the magazine; we remembered he'd gotten the ladder and fixed up the lights for the play I'd insisted on putting on; we remembered that he always knew how many kids were in each class when we needed to know in order to distribute *Infinity;* we remembered that he'd helped Piston carry the kite down to the field, and we just remembered that he was usually around when something really needed to be done—in short, we all of a sudden realized that he was a pretty helpful, alert, responsible kid, and we said so. Everyone was astonished. Could he spell? Did he do Egypt? Did he make book ends? We insisted. He was an O.K. kid. We convinced ourselves because we knew it was true. It was a big step for us. We left realizing that we had just realized that this fuck-up kid who drove us crazy was really O.K. and that, far from the class being better if he was gotten rid of, he was actually needed in CA. Therefore, we had to admit, in some way, somehow, our New World class was O.K. too. I mean, if the most fucked-up kid in the class was O.K., as we quite clearly *felt* he was O.K., (although our Old World logic told us he wasn't), and if we were willing to say out loud that he was O.K., if we were going to tell his parents that their kid was O.K. . . . well, it means that even if we had to admit we weren't going to find gold, that anyway discovering the New World was something in itself, and was probably enough for us to do that year. Frank and I came out of the meeting looking at each other strangely, wondering what had happened to us. . . .

One Sunday afternoon towards the end of the year Frank and I went one step further. At the time we didn't know or care that we were going One Step Further—that is only how I see it now. We were up in the country having a picnic and talking along the way about movies and it occurred to us that you could make a movie very well at a school and we began to make it up. We made up an entire movie then and there and since Frank knew about cameras and film and since he had a Sears and Roebuck movie camera we made up our minds to do it. We figured out a great script about a mad kid who murders everyone in a school.

The only thing I had to offer was a marvelous Hawk mask which a painter had made for [my son] Jay one Halloween. We decided to use that mask as the main image of the movie—the costume the murderous kid would put on when he felt murderous. See, he would be a respectable kid, Student-Body President perhaps, whose daddy or older brother or something (I forget) would have been The Hawk a while back and killed a lot of people and then disappeared, but the kid remembered. No one else knew about it or knew that the kid's father or brother had been The Hawk.

Frank and I showed up at school on Monday feeling great. Were we planning to suggest to the kids in CA *How About Making A Film?* and hear them say No We Don't Want To, or There's Nothing To Do Around Here, and then we'd try to persuade them into it and they'd say Have You Seen Mike Hunt? Hell no. It never occurred to us to wonder whether they wanted to make a film at all. We wanted to make a film ourselves and spend the rest of the year doing it. We didn't want to find out what the kids' notions of films were. We didn't want to see what they would do with the film. We didn't want to inspect their creativity.

Had we wanted to See What The Kids Would Do With Film, we'd have no doubt come up with something more constructive—a film about Attitudes And Relationships or The Question of Authority and/or Democracy In The Classroom . . . as it was, we really wanted to make a Tarzan film but couldn't quite see how it could be done and settled for The Hawk.

Let me make the point, before I forget it and breeze on, remembering the movie. If, in the New World, the role of the teacher as giver of orders didn't work out (no one had to follow them orders) it was also true that the other role (the one Frank and I had imagined)—the teacher as Provider Of Things To Do, the teacher as Entertainer— didn't work out either. For wasn't that just what the kids had been telling us all year in their oblique, exasperating way? What did all that Nothing To Do In Here mean, if not that the kids didn't want entertainers, wouldn't accept them if they didn't have to, wanted the teachers to be something else entirely?

Wanted them to be what? What was the difference between all the grand things we'd thought up for the kids to do and The Hawk? Why, merely that we didn't want to do any of the former ourselves and we did want to do the latter. Why should we have assumed that the kids would want to do a lot of stuff that we didn't want to do, wouldn't ever do of our own free will? It sounds nonsensical, put that way. Yet that is the assumption under which I operated, Frank operated, for many a year, under which almost all teachers operate, and it is idiotic. (Does the math teacher go home at night and do a few magic squares? Does the English teacher go home and analyze sentences? Does the reading teacher turn off the TV and drill herself on syllables and Reading Comprehension? Or do any of us do any of those things, even in the classroom?)

Wanted them to be human. Men. Wanted them to define themselves. (Do I define myself as a person who writes fake Peace Corps journals?) Wanted them to stick by Harry Sullivan's rule: Human beings are more alike than not. What you don't do, we probably don't want to do. What you learn from, we probably learn from.

We fired right off on Monday afternoon with the movie. Our main location was the tennis courts next to the field below the school. It was a huge field of grass which was never used by anyone except for girls' PE for softball, two or three weeks out of the year, although the school was overcrowded. Everyone complained about the fact that the other field—the one the kids were allowed to use —was too crowded to play on; at the same time everyone decided not to allow the kids to use the field in question because they would have to be supervised and that would double the duty for teachers and that was out of the question. No one used the tennis courts either, except for the girls' PE about three weeks out of the year and some teachers who played once in a while after school. We went down, Frank and I, seventh period to those tennis courts; a bunch of kids and I watched while Frank filmed the lines running up and down the court very artistically and then I chalked the title *Son of The Hawk* or *Return of The Hawk* (I really don't remember which it was) on the green cement and Frank filmed that and also the legend *A C-Arts Production.* Part of Frank's seventh period class watched too (it was either Social Studies or English) and the rest were—where? It was the same with my own eighth period class who were told by me to either come watch or get into the film or just stay in the room . . . The Hawk made us irresponsible.

By then a lot of kids wanted to be in the film and a lot didn't. We picked who was to be who and divulged the plot. A lot of kids wanted to know why we wanted to call it *Return of The Hawk* (or *Son of*) but we didn't really care to explain. We knew they hadn't seen all them old movies so how were they to know? We were pleased to be authoritarian. Everyone picked a tall, handsome, vain kid named Jon to be the hero and we agreed, mainly because the name was right. We picked Jane to be the heroine; we picked Harvey to be The Hawk, since he was the only one who was brave enough to say he wanted to be The Hawk. We picked Jane, by the way, because she had done all that work all year long and we liked her and because she admitted she wanted to be the heroine. We would have picked Meg and Lily too, except that they said they didn't want to be in the movie. They had other things to do and would be satisfied with bit parts when they weren't busy.

The movie opened. Julie (Jane) and Jon came down the steps holding hands, carrying tennis rackets. They paused for a kiss. Then they went down and started playing tennis. They played a bit. Cut to the fence; a terrible claw (which Jane had spent some time making out of an old rubber glove and cardboard fingernails and green and red paint) was seen shoving a green tennis ball through the fence and rolling it towards the players. The camera followed it rolling along so everyone would know it was important. Show Julie picking up ball and talking. Cut to title which I chalked on the green cement: Oh look, Jon, a green tennis ball! Show Julie holding ball. Then show Julie's hand turning green. Some kid paints Julie's hand a little bit with green paint, Frank films it, the kid paints a little more, he films that—pretty soon Julie's whole arm is green! It is a poison ball! Oh Jon! calls out Julie, and falls over dead. Over by the fence, for a brief instant, the shadow of the hawk mask, then legs running up the stairs. The legs have red tennis shoes on, painted up beforehand. Jon runs over and sees Julie is dead, grinning into the camera all the time.

About that time Frank decided to wait for the "rushes" before shooting any more. When the film was developed and we showed ourselves those rushes, the film became a movie and became real. Everyone saw where the movie was headed, several kids wanted to make suggestions about what to do next, two kids wanted to be cameramen, and everyone wanted to be in it. So that the next day when we started again, there was Jon grinning and saying Poor Julie's dead! and suddenly hundreds (it seemed) of cops rushed from everywhere. There were three authentic cops' jackets and a number of detectives in long raincoats and dark glasses (one leading a dachshund on a leash) —there were also two new cameramen. They filmed Jon, suddenly afraid the cops would think he did it, running to hide in a garbage can, from which half of him stuck out. They filmed the cops and detectives combing the school, climbing over the fences, investigating the office (the principal might have done it!) and Piston as detective snooping around the girls' bathrooms. They took off and filmed The Hawk making an obscure phone call from a booth at the gas station down by the shopping center—the purpose of the call not clear, except for the fact that everyone concerned got to leave the school grounds, and all the kids who watched the movie (they realized that it was a real movie and people would be coming to see it) would know they'd left the school grounds.

Next The Hawk was shown in the darkened science room, mask on, preparing his deadly green poison. Everyone volunteered to smoke cigarettes to produce clouds of smoke and an air of mystery. The Hawk was shown pulling out a lot of junk from an old closet, including an old newspaper, mocked-up by Jane (now, as Julie, dead, and reverting to make-up and prop manager) which told about the old Hawk; the present Hawk swore revenge.

Well, anyway, the plot changed entirely from our original Sunday afternoon conception. It turned out The Hawk's motivation was that he loved the girl Julie, who didn't love him, in spite of the fact he was Student-Body President, but instead that damn conceited Jon. The Hawk had sworn to get her, psychologically twisted as he was, it was implied, by memory of his criminal relative. So there was a lot of panic in the school. Shots showing girls screaming, kids whispering in class (Who is The Hawk?), teachers trying to calm things down, and a splendid burst of paper airplanes flying around and landing to show the legend Watch Out For The Hawk! or The Hawk Is Coming! Hordes of girl reporters besieged the principal (Lou, in dark glasses, was persuaded to look outraged) and he was quoted as saying If we catch The Hawk, he'll be Suspended! Vern the counselor looked serious and allowed as how The Hawk wasn't very well adjusted, or something like that. Julie's mother and father (two kids with Jane-produced gray hair and a mustache) tearfully and cheerfully said We told her not to play with boys! All the time there were shots of those giveaway red tennis shoes walking around here and there, unsuspected.

Frank and I had been edged out as director and cameraman and organizer without any fuss. While everyone had talked about what ought to happen, during the rushes a boy named Phil had written it down and produced a "shooting schedule." He directed from then on because he wanted to direct and knew how to say "shooting schedule." The two cameramen took over as cameramen for the same reasons—they wanted to be, could do it, and did it. The director consulted with Frank, and the cameramen recognized my lust to become a cameraman (never having taken so much as a Brownie photo in my life and afraid of doing so now, while actually dying to) and showed me this and that and let me film a few scenes. Certain kids took over the chalking up of speeches on the tennis court. Other kids took over the organization of crowds when we needed them, bursting into classes and saying We need a crowd! (No one ever suggested filming crowd scenes during lunch, when no classes would have to be interrupted.) Seventh and eighth periods became the time when *The Hawk* was being filmed; the other school considerations—passes, grades, authority, work or not-work, There's Nothing To Do, narcs, complaints—were forgotten. Frank and I, talking things over, found ourselves pleased—not that the Class was going well, but that the Film was going well. When it rained, we all just sat around the classroom content and relaxed, doing nothing without anxiety about doing nothing or should we be doing Nothing or Something or how to tell our parents we weren't doing nothing? and was it educationally sound to do nothing? . . . for we weren't doing nothing, but instead we were sitting around waiting for the rain to stop. It is a big difference.

Well, there were a few shots of Jon, who'd been hiding out from the cops, sneaking around the school trying to find out who The Hawk was. Finally he got into the science room one (simulated) night, and discovered the mask and claws and poison and the old newspapers, hidden away in a cardboard box in a cabinet. Then he knew (reading the name of The Hawk's old man or brother) and there was a dramatic smoke-filled shot of him smearing the Hawk mask with the green poison, grinning into the camera all the time. Phil was upset by now with all that grinning and vanity, but couldn't stop it and there was nothing to be done about it. The next scene showed a poster announcing a Memorial Assembly For Julie and a lot of kids standing around it, girls crying . . . all of this working up to the grand finale.

We filled the multi-use room with kids. Up on the stage came Harvey, the Student-Body President. He began to lead the salute to the flag. All the kids stood up. Cut to his feet. He's wearing red tennis shoes! ". . . with liberty and justice for all," says the title on the green cement. Everyone sits down. Jon gets up in the audience. He comes up to the stage, carrying a cardboard box wrapped with a big ribbon. He presents it to the President. The President is astonished. "For me?" he says. He opens it, unsuspecting. Out of the box he pulls the Hawk mask! His look turns to anger and hatred. Driven mad, he puts on the mask and shakes his fist at the audience. *The Hawk! Our President's The Hawk!* yell some kids. Shots of girls screaming. Then, *Get him!* shout the kids, and The Hawk leaps off the stage. Shots of The Hawk running out of the multi-use room, shots of the crowd chasing him, the last movement of Brahms' Fourth blasting away (later—on tape I mean, at the premiere—I finally got to do something). We had to retake that scene many times because the crowd kept catching The Hawk before he got out the door. They caught him and tackled him and mobbed him over and over again. Fuck this! yelled The Hawk finally, shoving kids off him, these dumb assholes are trying to really kill me! Finally he gets out and flees around the school and then down the steps to the field and the tennis courts, the crowd hot after him. A lot of tricky stuff with speeding up the camera and slow motion. Close-ups of the mask, showing it turning green. Harvey is marvelous; we are all amazed. Staggering, jerking, almost falling (the poison is getting to him), shaking his fist, running in circles, on and on the scene goes, piling up like Brahms . . . he finally collapses in slow motion. The crowd comes up, also in slow motion. Jon reaches down and pulls off the mask. The Hawk's face is green. He is dead. The crowd's fury is over. All look sad. The tape changes to Miles Davis playing "My Funny Valentine." Girls cry. Miles sounds regretful. Everyone starts to go. Jon is all alone with the dead Hawk. The cameramen have learned not to focus on his face, but now it can't be helped. He looks into the camera, grins, and says, "My best friend!" Then he sits down, takes off his shoes and puts on the red tennis shoes. Long shot from above the field, the tennis courts empty except for the dead Hawk, the sitting Jon. Miles plays out the tape to the end.

We put on a grand premiere. We had posters all over, giving the stars' names, the credits; we dittoed off cards for audience reaction, set up chairs in the music room, a white elephant of a building, round without windows, which had been built by some smart architect and which looked modern and which was useless for everything. It was just right for a movie. We showed *The Hawk* over and over, to a hundred kids at a time, watched every showing ourselves, and felt superior to everyone. We spent the rest of the year doing that, and talking about the movie among ourselves when we weren't showing it. We'd spent about two months making it; it was exactly twenty-two and a half minutes long; it had cost just slightly over twenty-five dollars. We asked ourselves just why it was that the hero put on the red tennis shoes at the end? Was he going to turn into another Hawk? Was it just some kind of sentimental gesture? We didn't know. All we remembered was that there at the end someone had called out Put on his shoes! and everyone had felt that was right and so Jon had done it. It was pointed out that no one in the audience had ever asked about it, and so it must be just right, even if we didn't know why.

The School at Yásnaya Polyána

Leo Tolstoy

from *On Education*

GENERAL SKETCH OF THE CHARACTER
OF THE SCHOOL

We have no beginners. The lowest class reads, writes, solves problems in the first three arithmetical operations, and reads sacred history, so that the subjects are divided in the programme in the following manner:

(1) Mechanical and graded reading, (2) writing, (3) penmanship, (4) grammar, (5) sacred history, (6) Russian history, (7) drawing, (8) mechanical drawing, (9) singing, (10) mathematics, (11) talks on the natural sciences, (12) religion.

Before saying anything about the instruction, I must give a short sketch of what the Yásnaya Polyána school is and of what stage of its growth it is in.

Like all living beings, the school not only becomes modified with every year, day, and hour, but also is subject to temporary crises, hardships, ailments, and evil moods. The Yásnaya Polyána school passed through such a crisis during this last summer. There were many causes for it: in the first place, as is always the case, all our best pupils left us, and we met them only occasionally at work in the field, or in the pastures; secondly, new teachers had come to the school, and new influences began to be brought to bear upon it; thirdly, every day of the summer brought new visiting teachers, who were taking advantage of the summer vacation. Nothing is more detrimental to the regular progress of the school than visitors. In one way or another the teacher adapts himself to the visitors.

We have four teachers. Two old ones, who have been teaching in the school for two years, and have become accustomed to the pupils, their work, the freedom and the external disorder of the school. The two new teachers— both themselves fresh from school—are lovers of external precision, programmes, bells, and so forth, and have not yet adapted themselves to the school so well as the first. What for the first seems reasonable, necessary, unavoidable, like the features of a beloved though homely child, that has grown up under one's eyes, to the new teachers sometime appears as a corrigible fault.

The school is held in a two-story stone building. Two rooms are given up to the school, one is a physical cabinet, and two are occupied by the teachers. Under the roof of the porch hangs a bell, with a rope attached to the clapper; in the vestibule down-stairs stand parallel and horizontal bars, while in the vestibule up-stairs there is a joiner's bench. The staircase and the floor of the vestibule are covered with snow or mud; here also hangs the programme.

The order of instruction is as follows: At about eight o'clock, the teacher living in the school, a lover of external order and the administrator of the school, sends one of the boys who nearly always stay overnight with him to ring the bell.

In the village, people rise with the fires. From the school the fires have long been observed in the windows, and half an hour after the ringing of the bell there appear, in the mist, in the rain, or in the oblique rays of the autumnal sun, dark figures, by twos, by threes, or singly, on the mounds (the village is separated from the school by a ravine). The herding feeling has long disappeared in the pupils. A pupil no longer has the need of waiting and shouting: "O boys, let's to school! She has begun." He knows by this time that "school" is neuter, and he knows a few other things, and, strange to say, for that very reason has no longer any need of a crowd. When the time comes to go, he goes. It seems to me that the personalities are becoming more independent, their characters more sharply defined, with every day. I have never noticed the pupils playing on their way, unless it be a very young child, or a new pupil, who had begun his instruction in some other school. The children bring nothing with them, —neither books, nor copy-books. No lessons are given for home.

Not only do they carry nothing in their hands, but they have nothing to carry even in their heads. They are not obliged to remember any lesson,—nothing that they were doing the day before. They are not vexed by the thought of the impending lesson. They bring with them nothing but their impressionable natures and their convictions that to-day it will be as jolly in school as it was yesterday. They do not think of their classes until they have begun.

No one is ever rebuked for tardiness, and they never are tardy, except some of the older ones whose fathers now and then keep them back to do some work. In such cases they come running to school at full speed, and all out of breath.

So long as the teacher has not arrived, they gather near the porch, pushing each other off the steps, or skating on the frozen crust of the smooth road, while some go to the schoolrooms. If it is cold, they read, write, or play, waiting for the teacher.

The girls do not mingle with the boys. When the boys have anything to do with the girls, they never address any one in particular, but always all collectively: "O girls, why don't you skate?" or, "I guess the girls are frozen," or, "Now, girls, all of you against me!" There is only one girl, from the manor, with enormous, all-around ability, about ten years of age, who is beginning to stand out from the herd of girls. This girl alone the boys treat as their equal, as a boy, except for a delicate shade of politeness, condescension, and reserve.

Let us suppose, for example, that according to the programme there is in the first, the lowest, class, mechanical reading, in the second, graded reading, in the third, mathematics.

The teacher comes to the room, where on the floor lie screaming children, shouting, "The heap is not large enough!" or, "You are choking me, boys!" or, "That will do! Don't pull my hair!" and so forth.

"Peter Mikháylovich!" a voice at the bottom of the heap calls out to the teacher as he enters, "tell them to stop!"

"Good morning, Peter Mikháylovich!" shout the others, continuing their game.

The teacher takes the books and gives them to those who have gone with him up to the bookcase; those who are lying on top of the heap, without getting up, also ask for books. The heap becomes smaller by degrees. The moment the majority have books, the rest run to the bookcase and cry: "Me too, me too. Give me yesterday's book; and me the *Koltsóvian* book," and so forth. If there are two left who, excited from the struggle, still keep rolling on the floor, those who have the books cry out to them:

"Don't bother us! We can't hear a word! Stop now!"

The excited boys submit and, out of breath, take hold of their books, and only at first, while sitting at their books, keep swinging their legs from unallayed excitement. The martial spirit takes flight, and the reading spirit reigns in the room.

With the same enthusiasm with which he was pulling Mítka's hair, he is now reading the *Koltsóvian* book (so they call Koltsóv's works with us), almost clenching his teeth, his eyes aflame, and seeing nothing about him but his book. It will take as much effort to tear him away from the book as it took before to get him away from fighting.

They sit down wherever they please: on the benches, the tables, the window-sill, the floor, and in the armchair. The girls always sit down near each other. Friends, of the same village, especially the younger ones (they have greater comradeship), always sit together. The moment one such has decided to sit down in the corner, all his friends, pushing one another and diving under the benches, make for the same place, sit down near him, and, looking about them, express as much happiness and contentment in their faces as though their having taken up those seats would make them happy for the rest of their lives. The large armchair, which somehow found its way into the room, forms the object of envy for the more independent individuals,—for the manorial girl and for others. The moment one of them makes up his mind to sit down in the chair, another guesses his intentions from his looks, and there ensues a struggle. One boy pushes out another, and the victor spreads himself in it, with his head way below the back, and goes on reading like the rest, all absorbed in his work.

I have never noticed any one whispering, or pinching his neighbour, or giggling, or snorting into his hand, or complaining against another. When a pupil who has been studying with a sexton or in a county school comes to us with such a complaint, we say to him: "Why don't you pinch back?"

The two lower classes meet in one room, while the advanced class goes to the next. The teacher comes, and, in the lowest class, all surround him at the board, or on the benches, or sit or lie on the table about the teacher or one of the reading boys. If it is a writing lesson, they seat themselves in a more orderly way, but they keep getting up, in order to look at the copy-books of the others, and to show theirs to the teacher.

According to the programme, there are to be four lessons before noon, but there sometimes are only three or two, and sometimes there are entirely different subjects. The teacher may begin with arithmetic and pass over to geometry, or he may start on sacred history, and end up with grammar. At times the teacher and pupils are so carried away, that, instead of one hour, the class lasts three hours. Sometimes the pupils themselves cry: "More, more!" and scold those who are tired of the subject. "If you are tired, go to the babies," they will call out contemptuously.

All the pupils meet together for the class of religion, which is the only regular class we have, because the teacher lives two versts away and comes only twice a week; they also meet together for the drawing class. Before these classes there is animation, fighting, shouting, and the most pronounced external disorder: some drag the benches from one room into another; some fight; some of the children of the manorial servants run home for some bread, which they roast in the stove; one is taking something away from a boy; another is doing some gymnastics, and, just as in the disorder of the morning, it is much easier to allow them to quiet themselves and resume their natural order than forcibly to settle them. With the present spirit of the school it would be physically impossible to stop them. The louder the teacher calls,—this has actually happened,—the louder they shout: his loud voice only excites them. If you stop them, or, if you can do that, if you carry them away into another direction, this small sea begins to billow less and less until it finally grows calm. In the majority of cases there is no need to say anything. The drawing class, everybody's favourite class, is at noon when, after three hours' work, the children are beginning to be hungry, and the benches and tables have to be taken from one room to another, and there is a terrible hubbub; and yet, in spite of it, the moment the teacher is ready, the pupils are, too, and if one of them should keep them back from starting, he gets his punishment meted out to him by the children themselves.

I must explain myself. In presenting a description of the Yásnaya Polyána school, I do not mean to offer a model of what is needed and is good for a school, but simply to furnish an actual description of the school. I presume that such descriptions may have their use. If I shall succeed in the following numbers in presenting a clear account of the evolution of the school, it will become intelligible to the reader what it is that has led to the formation of the present character of the school, why I regard such an order as good, and why it would be absolutely impossible for me to change it, even if I wanted.

The school has evolved freely from the principles introduced into it by teacher and pupils. In spite of the preponderating influence of the teacher, the pupil has always had the right not to come to school, or, having come, not to listen to the teacher. The teacher has had the right not to admit a pupil, and has had the possibility of bringing to bear all the force of his influence on the majority of pupils, on the society, always composed of the school children.

The farther the pupils proceed, the more the instruction branches out and the more necessary does order become. For this reason, in the normal non-compulsory development of the school, the more the pupils become educated, the fitter they become for order, and the more strongly they themselves feel the need of order, and the greater is the teacher's influence in this respect. In the Yásnaya Polyána school this rule has always been observed, from the day of its foundation. At first it was impossible to subdivide into classes, or subjects, or recess, or lessons; everything naturally blended into one, and all the attempts at separation remained futile. Now we have pupils in the first class, who themselves demand that the programme be adhered to, who are dissatisfied when they are disturbed in their lessons, and who constantly drive out the little children who run in to them.

In my opinion, this external disorder is useful and not to be replaced by anything else, however strange and inconvenient it may seem for the teacher. I shall often have occasion to speak of the advantages of this system, and now I will say only this much about the reputed inconveniences: First, this disorder, or free order, is terrible to us only because we are accustomed to something quite different, in which we have been educated. Secondly, in this case, as in many similar cases, force is used only through haste and through insufficient respect for human nature. We think that the disorder is growing greater and greater, and that there are no limits to it,—we think that there is no other means of stopping it but by the use of force,— whereas we only need to wait a little, and the disorder (or animation) calms down naturally by itself, growing into a much better and more permanent order than what we have created. . . .

We will proceed with the description of the daily order of instruction. At about two o'clock the hungry children run home. In spite of their hunger, they lag behind a few minutes to find out their grades. The grades at the present time amuse them very much, though they give them no privileges.

"I have five plus, and Olgúshka has caught a whopper of a cipher!—And I got four!" they cry.

The grades serve to them as a measure of their work, and disssatisfaction with grades is expressed only when they are not just. There is trouble when a pupil has tried hard, and the teacher by oversight gives him less then he deserves. He will not give the teacher any rest and will weep bitter tears, if he cannot get him to change it. Bad marks, if they are deserved, remain without protest. However, marks are left with us from the old order and are beginning to fall into disuse.

At the first lesson after the dinner recess, the pupils gather just as in the morning, and wait for the teacher in the same manner. It is generally a lesson in sacred or Russian history, for which all the classes meet together. This lesson generally begins at close of day. The teacher stands or sits down in the middle of the room, and the crowd gathers around him in amphitheatrical order, on benches, on tables, on window-sills.

All the evening lessons, especially the first, have a peculiar character of calm, dreaminess, and poetry, differing in this from the morning classes. You come to the school at fall of day: no lights are seen in the windows; it is almost quiet, and only tracks of snow on the staircase, freshly carried in, a weak din and rustling beyond the door, and some urchin clattering on the staircase, by taking two steps at a time and holding on to the balustrade, prove that the pupils are at school.

Walk into the room! It is almost dark behind the frozen windows; the best pupils are jammed toward the teacher by the rest of the children, and, turning up their little heads, are looking straight into the teacher's mouth. The independent manorial girl is always sitting with a careworn face on the high table, and, it seems, is swallowing every word; the poorer pupils, the small fry, sit farther away: they listen attentively, even austerely; they behave just like the big boys, but, in spite of their attention, we know that they will not tell a thing, even though they may remember some.

Some press down on other people's shoulders, and others stand up on the table. Occasionally one pushes his way into the crowd, where he busies himself with drawing some figures with his nail on somebody's back. It is not often that one will look back at you. When a new story is being told, all listen in dead silence; when there is a repetition, ambitious voices are heard now and then, being unable to keep from helping the teacher out. Still, if there is an old story which they like, they ask the teacher to repeat it in his own words, and then they do not allow any one to interrupt him.

"What is the matter with you? Can't you hold in? Keep quiet!" they will call out to a forward boy.

It pains them to hear the character and the artistic quality of the teacher's story interrupted. Of late it has been the story of Christ's life. They every time asked to have it all told to them. If the whole story is not told to them, they themselves supply their favourite ending,—the history of Peter's denying Christ, and of the Saviour's passion.

You would think all are dead: there is no stir,—can they be asleep? You walk up to them in the semi-darkness and look into the face of some little fellow,—he is sitting, his eyes staring at the teacher, frowning from close attention, and for the tenth time brushing away the arm of his companion, which is pressing down on his shoulder. You tickle his neck,—he does not even smile; he only bends his head, as though to drive away a fly, and again abandons himself to the mysterious and poetical story, how the veil of the church was rent and it grew dark upon earth, —and he has a mingled sensation of dread and joy.

Now the teacher is through with his story, and all rise from their seats, and, crowding around their teacher, try to outcry each other in their attempt to tell what they have retained. There is a terrible hubub,—the teacher barely can follow them all. Those who are forbidden to tell anything, the teacher being sure that they know it all, are not satisfied: they approach the other teacher; and if he is not there, they importune a companion, a stranger, even the keeper of the fires, or walk from corner to corner by twos and by threes, begging everybody to listen to them. It is rare for one to tell at a time. They themselves divide up in groups, those of equal strength keeping together, and begin to tell, encouraging and correcting each other, and waiting for their turns. "Come, let us take it together," says one to another, but the one who is addressed knows that he can't keep up with him, and so he sends him to another. As soon as they have had their say and have quieted down, lights are brought, and a different mood comes over the boys.

In the evenings in general, and at the next lessons in particular, the hubbub is not so great, and the docility and the confidence in the teacher are greater. The pupils seem to evince an abhorrence for mathematics and analysis, and a liking for singing, reading, and especially for stories.

"What's the use in having mathematics all the time, and writing? Better tell us something, about the earth, or even history, and we will listen," say all.

At about eight o'clock the eyes begin to get heavy; they begin to yawn; the candles burn more dimly,—they are not trimmed so often; the elder children hold themselves up, but the younger, the poorer students, fall asleep, leaning on the table, under the pleasant sounds of the teacher's voice.

At times, when the classes are uninteresting, and there have been many of them (we often have seven long hours a day), and the children are tired, or before the holidays, when the ovens at home are prepared for a hot bath, two or three boys will suddenly rush into the room during the second or third afternoon class-hour, and will hurriedly pick out their caps.

"What's up?"

"Going home."

"And studies? There is to be singing yet!"

"The boys say they are going home," says one, slipping away with his cap.

"Who says so?"

"The boys are gone!"

"How is that?" asks the perplexed teacher who has prepared his lesson. "Stay!"

But another boy runs into the room, with an excited and perplexed face.

"What are you staying here for?" he angrily attacks the one held back, who, in indecision, pushes the cotton batting back into his cap. "The boys are way down there, —I guess as far as the smithy."

"Have they gone?"

"They have."

And both run away, calling from behind the door: "Good-bye, Iván Ivánovich!"

Who are the boys that decided to go home, and how did they decide it? God knows. You will never find out who decided it. They did not take counsel, did not conspire, but simply, some boys wanted to go home, "The boys are going!"—and their feet rattle down-stairs, and one rolls down the steps in catlike form, and, leaping and tumbling in the snow, running a race with each other along the narrow path, the children bolt for home.

Such occurrences take place once or twice a week. It is aggravating and disagreeable for the teacher,—who will not admit that? But who will not admit, at the same time, that, on account of one such an occurrence, the five, six, and even seven lessons a day for each class, which are, of their own accord and with pleasure, attended by the pupils, receive a so much greater significance? Only by the recurrence of such cases could one gain the certainty that the instruction, though insufficient and one-sided, was not entirely bad and not detrimental.

If the question were put like this: Which would be better, that not one such occurrence should take place during the whole year, or that this should happen for more than half the lessons,—we should choose the latter. At least, I was always glad to see these things happen several times a month in the Yásnaya Polyána school. In spite of the frequently repeated statements to the boys that they may leave any time they wish, the influence of the teacher is so strong that, of late, I have been afraid that the discipline of the classes, programmes, and grades might, imperceptibly to them, so restrict their liberty that they would submit to the cunning of the nets of order set by us and that they would lose the possibility of choice and protest. Their continued willingness to come to school, in spite of the liberty granted them, does not, I think, by any means prove the especial qualities of the Yásnaya Polyána school,—I believe that the same would be repeated in the majority of schools, and that the desire to study is so strong in children that, in order to satisfy their desire, they will submit to many hard conditions and will forgive many defects. The possibility of such escapades is useful and necessary only as a means of securing the teacher against the most detrimental and coarsest errors and abuses.

In the evening we have singing, graded reading, talks, physical experiments, and writing of compositions. Of these, their favourite subjects are reading and experiments. During the reading the older children lie down on the large table in star-shaped form,—their heads together, their feet radiating out, and one reads, and all tell the contents to each other. The younger children locate themselves with their books by twos, and if the book is intelligible to them, they read it as we do, by getting close to the light and making themselves comfortable, and apparently they derive pleasure from it. Some, trying to unite two kinds of enjoyment, seat themselves opposite the burning stove, and warm themselves and read.

Not all are admitted to the class in experiments, only the oldest and best, and the more intelligent ones of the second class. This class has assumed, with us, a vespertine, most fantastic character, precisely fitting the mood produced by the reading of fairy-tales. Here the fairy-like element is materialized,—everything is personified by them: the pith-ball which is repelled by the sealing-wax, the deflecting magnetic needle, the iron filings scurrying over the sheet of paper underneath which the magnet is guided, present themselves to them as living objects. The most intelligent boys, who understand the cause of these phenomena, become excited and talk to the needle, the ball, the filings: "Come now! Hold on! Where are you going? Stop there! Ho there! Let her go!" and so forth.

Generally the classes end at between eight to nine o'clock, if the carpentry work does not keep the boys longer, and then the whole mass of them run shouting into the yard, from where they begin to scatter in groups in all the directions of the village, calling to each other from a distance. Sometimes they scheme to coast downhill into the village on a large sleigh standing outside the gate, by tying up the shafts: they crawl in and disappear with screaming in the snow-dust, leaving, here and there along the road, black spots of children tumbled out. Outside the school, in the open air, there establish themselves, despite all the liberty granted there, new relations between pupils and teachers, of greater liberty, greater simplicity, and greater confidence,—those very relations, which, to us, appear as the ideal of what the school is to strive after.

from An Empty Spoon

It's teachers like Stephanie Barns who, for all their proclaimed expertise, convinced me that a cultural gap is a far greater liability than a racial difference in dealing with our kids.

I was paired with her in Room 504. Although the school operates on three overlapping shifts to alleviate the population problem, there's a portion of the day when everyone's in the building and there just aren't enough classrooms. So the geniuses in the roster office scheduled two classes together in the barnlike 504. What they expected two teachers to do with eighty-five kids, I don't know. Showing movies is a fine idea once in a while, but when you're there five days a week and no movies have been ordered and there are no shades on those ten-foot windows anyway, you have to come up with another idea.

I knew enough, even as a beginner, to realize that once a discipline problem has been created, there's little hope of ever being anything but a policeman. But to avoid the problem from the outset involves incredibly tight structuring and planning. You've got a lot working against you. For one thing, you can't learn eighty-five names for a while, and the anonymity the kids have affords them a chance to make trouble without getting in trouble. You can't give out books, because there aren't more than forty copies of any one text in school. There musn't be any extensive writing, either. Room 504 has no desks—only chairs lined up on risers. To write, you need a book to lean on; and since most of the kids don't carry books, it's a lost cause.

I asked Stephanie if she'd teach the first week. I was at a loss as to where to begin with such a group, and I was very in awe of my partner, who'd intimidated me with her talk of creative dramatics, teaching Shakespeare, and the advantages of being black in dealing with the kids at North. She has incredible energy, and as she strode around in Those Clothes and talked of the myriad activities her classes were working on, I felt more than ever like a pimply-faced kid with a droopy lower lip. She was a lady, and an expert at her job; my dislike for her had to be nothing more than jealousy.

She agreed to teach, since she had stacks of some magazine with a play in it she'd been wanting to try. I was relieved; I didn't have to expose myself for a week, and I could pick up lots of pointers from her in the meantime.

The kids clattered in, seeing to it that they wasted a good fifteen minutes getting seated. Stephanie didn't say anything about the noise—I guessed she expected them to quiet down when she introduced the play. I was wrong. There was no introduction at all. She handed out the magazines, assigned parts randomly, and began to read the narrator's line. Wait a minute! You can't do that—a kid has to know what he's about—he has to have a reason to read; he has to be motivated to want to read. The noise level increased. Stephanie seemed oblivious. She continued to plow through her part, as kids tossed cigarettes to each other and joked about last night's party. Only the kids who'd been given roles were attentive—or were they scared? No one finds it easy to perform in front of a large group, and these actors hadn't even had a chance to read over their lines. Maybe they wouldn't know the words. Maybe they'd be laughed at. What was she saying, anyway?

It was a shocker of a week. No, it was only three days. By Wednesday, Stephanie told me she'd finished the play and it was my turn. I ventured a question about follow-up activities—discussions, quizzes, or any related project that would make the play meaningful, and involve the kids who hadn't yet done anything but make trouble. No, dramatizing it was sufficient. The play was finished. I was annoyed. That halting, expressionless reading was her conception of dramatization. The fact that three-quarters of the class had never opened the magazine didn't faze her.

She didn't even have any trouble looking me in the eye when, at lunch that day, she delivered a soliloquy on effective teaching.

I understood why the kids hated her. She'd never really spoken to them in three days. There was no attempt made to learn their names, or see to it that they did any work, or find out what they thought. She was a teacher of English —not of people. And her teaching was unquestionably lousy. The aura of superiority she created lasted about five minutes with the kids. Only suckers like me had failed to see through the veneer.

I couldn't wait to plan my lesson. I'd show her.

That night I wrote a list. Never trust a cop. All Jews are stingy. Negroes are inferior to whites. Teachers play favorites. Irishmen drink too much. Teen-age marriages don't last. Ten or fifteen juicy items. I mimeographed a sheet of open-ended sentences like, "The thing that makes me different from my friends is ———." That was designed as both an interest grabber (everyone likes to write about himself) and a sneaky way of getting the kids to discover that they describe themselves by their differences—not their similarities. I wrote out a bunch of questions and statements designed to make me look dumb, so the kids would do the teaching.

It wasn't hard to see to it that I was the first one in class —the kids had already decided there was no need to hurry, so they stopped off in the bathroom for a smoke or in the cafeteria for a sweet before they ambled to 504. I met them at the door with the mimeographed sheet and a big grin.

"Betcha can't do this in ten minutes," I said.

And because the sheet looked like fun and the challenge looked easy, they grabbed chairs and began to write. Newcomers arrived and were struck by the silence in the room. I didn't even have to be cute for them—they simply followed their classmates' example and got to work.

There was more than ten minutes' worth of statements on the paper, and I interrupted them before they'd had time to finish, just so they'd know I wasn't playing around. In the meantime, I'd plastered the blackboard with my list of stereotypes, and they were intrigued enough to keep quiet and listen. What did the papers they'd written about themselves have to do with the ruthless blasphemies on the board? What was this screwy lady up to anyway?

I began with a question. "Which of these statements are true and which are false?"

We went through the list. Then I asked about exceptions to the rule—had anyone ever met a nice cop? A fair teacher? What does this prove?

And take a look at those sheets you wrote. Did you describe yourself in terms of how you were *like* others, or how you're different from them? Oh, yeah. . . .

I hoped Stephanie Barns's brain was farther from her paper work than her flat little nose. It was killing not to be able to grab her by the shoulders and tell her how great I was.

By the end of the period, the kids had decided that if you can find one teen-age marriage that sticks or one sober Irishman, the stereotype falls apart. And where do people get off saying Negroes are inferior? They'd learned.

"What?" I asked, by way of summary.

"That you can't talk about all people like one," a girl said.

I was delighted.

"Except," she added. "Except Jews. Everyone knows all Jews are stingy."

The bell rang.

The ed courses I found so offensive were always stressing the mechanics of writing lesson plans. You've got to have an aim, which you print at the top of the page. Then your activities, designed to arrive at the aim at the lesson's end. It all sounded so pedantic—I was too cool to bother with what kind of stuff.

It took about a month of blundering before I gave in and wrote a real lesson plan. Funny, how the discipline of stating your ways and means on paper forces you to really teach. And if you've written it all out, you can step back and look at it before show time, to see exactly what's going on. That's where you can really save a lesson. There's got to be a balance between how much teacher talks, how much kids work alone, and how much interaction there is.

I'm a talker. It's so easy to rattle on, making terribly important points, and so easy to forget that kids will give you about ten minutes of that kind of self-indulgence before they shut you off. They've got to be involved. I could have told them in a second what a stereotype is and why it's used and what's wrong with it. But telling doesn't mean a damn thing, unless you're teaching kids who take notes and listen to lectures. They've got to discover their own truth, if it's to be a part of them.

But there are some points you just can't make. When I taught poetry, I talked about the sounds of words, and how some are hard, like hissing, and some are soft and round, like wallow.

"Look at a word like flower," I said. "It's not in the same class with buzz or whack, but it's full, like a blossom."

Dwaine Bulford sat in the back of the room looking devilish.

"Try hibiscus," he said.

Some kids are too smart for their own good.

Others are hard to convince for different reasons. They're a well-indoctrinated product of a superstitious culture that has an answer for everything. You can't fight mysticism. I learned that and much more from Christabelle Sands.

Kids very rarely laugh lovingly at someone. They are the cruelest kind of people. That's why I was amazed at their treatment of Chrissy. Everyone laughs at her—but they adore her.

Chrissy was a recent immigrant from a Georgia farm. She was one of nine children. Her dialect was almost unintelligible. She was built like *I'd* like to be. She was, in a very quiet way, the most delightful person I'd ever known. She rarely spoke, but when she got excited, something wild happened inside her, and torrents of ideas and opinions came raging out. That's when we'd laugh. She said bagogogy instead of biology, and imbication instead of education. I guess the kids liked her because she wasn't at all an oddball, she was very friendly, and she danced great. She just talked funny.

Her favorite subject was John Kennedy. She would have died for him willingly. When we discussed prejudice and stereotypes, Chrissy announced that she hated Catholics. Seizing an opportunity to make my lesson meaningful, I said, "But President Kennedy was a Catholic."

"He was not," she announced. "You cain burlieve evythin you read."

The kids laughed, but Chrissy *knew*. The subject was closed.

I learned a lot from her. Like if you want to make money, you sleep on an empty vanilla bottle. It makes you dream of someone who's dead. Then you call someone in the deceased's family on the phone. They give you three numbers. You bet on those numbers, and you always win. It's that simple.

My husband visited me at school one day, and the kids lost no time in engaging him in conversation. They're always amazed to discover that their teacher has an "other life." They seem to think we get locked up in closets at night and let out in the morning. They stared at him like mad, and asked questions furiously. At one point, he had occasion to answer Christabelle, and he addressed her by name. The next day, she began to talk about him.

"He's so nice," she said. "I can tell he don't beat you. And he's wise—he talks jest like Kennedy." A big breath. "And when he said my name, I liked to *die!*"

He'd said her name. He'd made her a person.

Because she couldn't stand the uncertainty surrounding the assassination, and because of Johnson's inability to relate to his public, Chrissy launched a hate campaign, based on the premise that Johnson killed Kennedy. Admittedly, the contrast between the two is a big comedown. Like most of us, Chrissy found the man's sparerib style offensive. She talked about Leecy Bird and Lacy Bird with teeth-grinding vengeance and spent lots of time discussing the wedding: "Who *else* spends all that money on a dress you never wear but once—and it were even ugly." And the presidential beagles: "Dem dogs eat better'n I do!"

After a heated discussion on Vietnam, Chrissy was prompted to write a letter to Johnson. It was the first letter she'd ever written, and she had a lot of trouble finding out where to buy a stamp. She waited three months for an answer. None came.

Sometime later in the term, I got a curt note: Christabelle Sands has been transferred to a speech class. Please drop her from your roll.

I was miserable. I'd miss her terribly, and I had the feeling that her speech was part of her charm and no one had any business tampering with charm.

She said a mushy farewell at our last class, and I asked her if our talks had helped her to form any new political opinions.

"Yes'm," she said. "I hates Johnson so much now, I won't even buy the wax!" . . .

Even when I work at it, I'm still a disappointment to myself. There's so much the kids should learn, and I used to get frantic trying to get it all in and make it stick. Sometimes I was sure I was the lousiest teacher in the world. I had just read another news article about a guy in New York who was superimaginative, and superdedicated, and who made his teaching a twenty-four-hour-a-day job. Which made me look bad. I raced the kids to the door on Friday afternoons—and other days, too. My lessons bored me stiff half the time. All winter, I prayed for a school-closing blizzard. The scariest part of my rotten attitude was that I was losing my sense of humor. On one awful Tuesday, I didn't laugh once. . . .

You've gotta get yourself together, is what the kids are always saying. I couldn't manage it, and that's why I botched up so much that first year, I was as self-centered as the teen-agers I was supposed to be helping. The outside things—mounds of clerical work, record keeping, lesson plans—had to be handled, and that left little time for inside things. I didn't really understand my position in the class. I did not understand a great deal of what I was doing or why I was doing it.

I was frantic about preparing for five classes a day, marking hundreds of papers a week, dealing with the records of forty home-room charges, and making the best of such demoralizing duties as hall patrol, which makes you a sort of rent-a-cop. Since I couldn't learn to challenge the ready reasons every kid had for roaming the corridors, and felt it was somehow better to accept their stories than accuse them of lying, I was a poor patroller. Making the best of things entailed hiding in the toilet, till the vice principal in charge of checking checked me out.

I didn't begin to know what to teach; my own need for organization and purpose hung me up as much as the school's limitations of books and supplies. In math or history, there's an inherent sequence to fall back on; in English there's the whole world. Challenging, yes—but far more frustrating to a newcomer who didn't know what a lesson plan was and couldn't work the mimeograph. There was no logical place to begin. The kids couldn't read, and I wasn't a reading teacher. They didn't speak my language, but I was damned if I'd presume to suggest that theirs was wrong. Hell—they communicated at least as successfully as I did, and that's what language is for, isn't it?

So what was I doing there? The first day of school taught me that I could not hope to have any fun with two hundred empty faces. Mischief would have been exciting; hostility challenging; but apathy was unendurable. I don't think I thought much about doing anything for the kids —I simply had to find some way of sparking my days. What happened inside the kids was a by-product.

The fashionable topic of teachers' meetings was "Let's Make Learning Fun"—which wasn't a bad idea. It's certainly preferable to making learning agony. I saw lots of inspired, missionary types playing with tape recorders and finger paints; they gloated because the kids were Relating and Socializing and Coming to Class. But the whole technique bothered me, somehow. I mean, you can't just play around when kids can't read a want ad in a newspaper. Making learning fun is a great premise, as long as learning is taking place. More often than not, it isn't.

The old-guard teachers throw up walls with their lectures and mickey-mouse assignments, and the kids turn them off. The experimentalists spend so much time Reaching the kids that little substance is ever conveyed. These dedicated souls understand the kids to death—and their classes play them to the hilt.

Teachers seem to assume that they play the starring role in the kids' lives. What rubbish that is. To many of the kids, school doesn't even exist, except as a place where you've got to go to stay out of trouble. Or to get warm. Or to pick up girls.

In my forty-five minutes a day with each class, I had the feeling I could accomplish more if I could provide something they couldn't get out on the street—skills and ideas. It was a meager philosophy to begin with, but it provided some modicum of direction for me. So I muddled along with the business of getting through each day's lesson, and pink forms, yellow forms, white forms, green forms, and the problems of manipulating two hundred kids, and the incredible job of sorting out my own ideas and putting them to work.

from *The Lives of Children*

There is no need to add to the criticism of our public schools. The critique is extensive and can hardly be improved on. The processes of learning and teaching, too, have been exhaustively studied. One thinks of the books of Paul Goodman, John Holt, Greene and Ryan, Nat Hentoff, James Herndon, Jonathan Kozol, Herbert Kohl; and of such researches as those of Bruner and Piaget; and of Joseph Featherstone's important *Report*. The question now is what to do. In the pages that follow, I would like to describe one unfamiliar approach to the problems which by now have become familiar. And since "the crisis of the schools" consists in reality of a great many crises in the lives of children, I shall try to make the children of the First Street School the real subject of this book. There were twenty-three black, white, and Puerto Rican in almost equal proportions, all from low-income families in New York's Lower East Side. About half were on welfare. About half, too, had come to us from the public schools with severe learning and behavior problems. . . .

Freedom is an abstract and terribly elusive word. I hope that a context of examples will make its meaning clear. The question is not really one of authority, though it is usually argued in that form. When adults give up authority, the freedom of children is not necessarily increased. Freedom is not motion in a vacuum, but motion in a continuum. If we want to know what freedom is, we must discover what the continuum is. "The principle," Dewey remarks, "is not what justifies an activity, for the principle is but another name for the continuity of the activity." We might say something similar of freedom: it is another name for the fullness and final shape of activities. We experience the activities, not the freedom. The mother of a child in a public school told me that he kept complaining, "They never let me *finish* anything!" We might say of the child that he lacked important freedoms, but his own expression is closer to the experience: activities important to him remained unfulfilled. Our concern for freedom is our concern for fulfillment—of activities we deem important and of persons we know are unique. To give freedom means to stand out of the way of the formative powers possessed by others.

Before telling more of the school, I must say that I was a partisan of libertarian values even before working there. I had read of the schools of A. S. Neill and Leo Tolstoy. I had worked in the past with severely disturbed children, and had come to respect the integrity of the organic processes of growth, which given the proper environment are the one source of change in individual lives. And so I was biased from the start and cannot claim the indifference of a neutral observer. Events at school did, however, time and again, confirm the beliefs I already held—which, I suppose, leaves me still a partisan, though convinced twice over. Yet if I can prove nothing at all in a scientific sense, there is still a power of persuasion in the events themselves, and I can certainly hope that our experience will arouse an experimental interest in other parents and teachers.

But there is something else that I would like to convey, too, and this is simply a sense of the lives of those who were involved—the jumble of persons and real events which did in fact constitute our school. The closer one comes to the facts of life, the less exemplary they seem, but the more human and the richer. Something of our time in history and our place in the world belongs to Vicente screaming in the hallway, and José opening the blade of a ten-inch knife—even more than to Vicente's subsequent learning to cooperate and José to read. So, too, with other apparently small details: the fantasy life and savagery of the older boys, the serenity and rationality of the younger ones, teachers' moments of doubt and defeat. Learning, in its essentials, is not a distinct and separate process. It is a function of growth. We took it quite seriously in this light, and found ourselves getting more and more involved in individual lives. It seems likely to me that the actual features of this involvement may prove useful to other people. At the same time, I would like to try to account for the fact that almost all of our children improved markedly, and some few spectacularly. We were obviously doing something right, and I would like to hazard a few guesses at what it might have been. All instruction was individual, and that was obviously a factor. The improvement I am speaking of, however, was not simply a matter of learning, but of radical changes in character. Where Vicente had been withdrawn and destructive, he became an eager participant in group activities and ceased destroying everything he touched. Both Eléna and Maxine had been thieves and were incredibly rebellious. After several months they could be trusted and had become imaginative and responsible contributors at school meetings. Such changes as these are not accomplished by instruction. They proceed from broad environmental causes. Here again, details which may seem irrelevant to the business of a school will give the reader an idea of what these causes may have been. A better way of saying this is that the business of a school is not, or should not be, mere instruction, but the life of the child.

This is especially important under such conditions as we experience today. Life in our country is chaotic and corrosive, and the time of childhood for many millions is difficult and harsh. It will not be an easy matter to bring our berserk technocracy under control, but we *can* control the environment of the schools. It is a relatively small environment and has always been structured by deliberation. If, as parents, we were to take as our concern not the instruction of our children, but the lives of our children, we would find that our schools could be used in a powerfully regenerative way. Against all that is shoddy and violent and treacherous and emotionally impoverished in American life, we might propose conventions which were rational and straightforward, rich both in feeling and thought, and which treated individuals with a respect we do little more at present than proclaim from our public rostrums. We might cease thinking of school as a place and learn to believe that it is basically relationships: between children and adults, adults and adults, children and other children. The four walls and the principal's office would cease to loom so hugely as the essential ingredients.

It is worth mentioning here that, with two exceptions, the parents of the children at First Street were not libertarians. They thought that they believed in compulsion, and rewards and punishments, and formal discipline, and report cards, and homework, and elaborate school facilities. They looked rather askance at our noisy classrooms and informal relations. If they persisted in sending us their children, it was not because they agreed with our methods, but because they were desperate. As the months went by, however, and the children who had been truants now attended eagerly, and those who had been failing now began to learn, the parents drew their own conclusions. By the end of the first year there was a high morale among them, and great devotion to the school.

We had no administrators. We were small and didn't need them. The parents found that, after all, they approved of this. They themselves could judge the competence of the teachers, and so could their children—by the specific act of learning. The parents' past experience of administrators had been uniformly upsetting—and the proof, of course, was in the pudding: the children were happier and *were* learning. As for the children, they never missed them.

We did not give report cards. We knew each child, knew his capacities and his problems, and the vagaries of his growth. This knowledge could not be recorded on little cards. The parents found—again—that they approved of this. It diminished the blind anxieties of life, for grades had never meant much to them anyway except some dim sense of *problem,* or some dim reassurance that things were all right. When they wanted to know how their children were doing, they simply asked the teachers.

We didn't give tests, at least not of the competitive kind. It was important to be aware of what the children knew, but more important to be aware of *how* each child knew what he knew. We could learn nothing about Maxine by testing Eléna. And so there was no comparative testing at all. The children never missed those invidious comparisons, and the teachers were spared the absurdity of ranking dozens of personalities on one uniform scale.

Our housing was modest. The children came to school in play-torn clothes. Their families were poor. A torn dress, torn pants, frequent cleanings—there were expenses they could not afford. Yet how can children play without getting dirty? Our uncleanliness standard was just right. It looked awful and suited everyone.

We treated the children with consideration and justice. I don't mean that we never got angry and never yelled at them (nor they at us). I mean that we took seriously the pride of life that belongs to the young—even to the very young. We did not coerce them in violation of their proper independence. Parents and children both found that they approved very much of this.

Now I would like to describe the school, or more correctly, the children and teachers. I shall try to bring out in detail three important things:

1) That the proper concern of a primary school is not education in a narrow sense, and still less preparation for later life, but the present lives of the children—a point made repeatedly by John Dewey, and very poorly understood by many of his followers.

2) That when the conventional routines of a school are abolished (the military discipline, the schedules, the punishments and rewards, the standardization), what arises is neither a vacuum nor chaos, but rather a new order, based first on relationships between adults and children, and children and their peers, but based ultimately on such truths of the human condition as these: that the mind does not function separately from the emotions, but thought partakes of feeling and feeling of thought; that there is no such thing as knowledge *per se,* knowledge

in a vacuum, but rather all knowledge is possessed and must be expressed by individuals; that the human voices preserved in books belong to the real features of the world, and that children are so powerfully attracted to this world that the very motion of their curiosity comes through to us as a form of love; that an active moral life cannot be evolved except where people are free to express their feelings and act upon the insights of conscience.

3) That running a primary school—*provided it be small*—is an extremely simple thing. It goes without saying that the teachers must be competent (which does not necessarily mean passing courses in a teacher's college). Given this *sine qua non,* there is nothing mysterious. The present quagmire of public education is entirely the result of unworkable centralization and the lust for control that permeates every bureaucratic institution.

In saying this, I do not mean that the work in a free school is easy. On the contrary, teachers find it taxing. But they find it rewarding, too—quite unlike the endless round of frustrations experienced by those at work in the present system. . . .

But how does a teacher, deprived of the familiar disciplinary routines, maintain order in his classroom? The answer is, he does not. Nor should he. What we call order, in this context, does not deserve that name at all; it is not a coherent relationship of parts to a whole, but a simple suppression of vital differences. Nor does the removal of the suppression lead to chaos, but to cyclical alternations of individual and group interests, of which the former are noisy (though rarely irrational), and the latter quiet. Not that real crises will ever occur, or important refusals on the part of the children; but for the most familiar kinds of unruliness, the observation holds. The principle of true order lies in the persons themselves.

The usual complaints of teachers are that the children talk among themselves and pay no attention to the teacher; that they interfere with the attention given by others; that they nag at the teacher and sabotage his efforts; that they fight over some object, a pencil, a book, a candy bar. In crowded classrooms, things of this sort, countered by efforts to stifle them, are endlessly disturbing. Even in smaller classrooms they prove to be difficult if the teacher is much given to formal discipline.

Here are some incidents that occurred at First Street.

Dolores, age nine, and Eléna, age ten, both Puerto Rican, begin talking to each other during the lesson in arithmetic, paying no attention to Susan, their teacher. To make matters worse, several of the children begin listening to them. Instead of calling the class to order, however, Susan also cocks an ear. Eléna is talking about her older sister, who is eighteen. Their mother had bought a voodoo charm, and the charm had been stolen. Dodie, a Negro girl of nine, enters the conversation, saying in a low voice, "Voodoo! It don't mean nuthin'!" "What kind of a charm?" says Susan. "A charm against *men!*" says Eléna. And now the whole class begins to discuss it. Rudella, a Negro girl of nine, says, in her broad, slow way, "Phooey! I bet she stole it herself. I know somebody I'd use that thing on." Susan agrees with Dodie that voodoo probably doesn't work, "though maybe it has a psychological effect." "Yeah," says Eléna, "it makes you afraid." The discussion lasts ten or twelve minutes, and then all return to arithmetic.

José used to burst into song, or jump up and do dance steps during our sessions in reading. This had nothing to do with exuberance; it was compulsive and frantic. But it was essential that he do it. The effort he was putting into his work aroused an intolerable anxiety. He needed to boil it off and feel the vigor of his body so as to reassure himself that he was "all there."

Eléna and Maxine are howling and screaming, and pushing and punching, the one with endlessly voluble Caribbean fury, the other with the wide-open, full-throttle voice of New York emergencies, cab drivers in a traffic jam, bargain-day shoppers at Kleins. Each claims possession of a piece of red corduroy cloth, a queen's gown in their theatrical game, now in its fourth day. Children and teachers alike are impressed by their ardor, and by the obvious question of justice, for the gown can hardly belong to both, though both are shouting, "It's mine!" "Where did it come from?" cries the teacher. Elêna repeats, "It's mine!" but Maxine, who now has tears in her eyes, yells, "My mother gave it to me!" "All right, we'll call Maxine's mother and find out." There is immediate silence, broken only by Maxine's voice, much lower (pointing her finger at Eléna): "You'll see, boy." Now fifteen children gather around the telephone, the conclusion of which conference is the teacher's announcement standing up: "It belongs to Maxine. Her mother gave it to her." Eléna hands it over, and Maxine limits her triumph to: "See! I told you, didn't I?" All the other faces have that grave, almost stoical child look of Important Issues Really Settled.

I would like to quote Rousseau again and again: ". . . do not save time, but lose it." If Susan had tried to save time by forbidding the interesting conversation about voodoo, she would first have had a stupid disciplinary problem on her hands, and second (if she succeeded in silencing the children) would have produced that smoldering, fretful resentment with which teachers are so familiar, a resentment that closes the ears and glazes the eyes. How much better it is to meander a bit—or a good bit—letting the free play of minds, adult and child, take its own very lively course! The advantages of this can hardly be overestimated. The children will feel closer to the adults, more secure, more assured of concern and individual care. Too, their own self-interest will lead them into positive relations with the natural authority of adults, and this is much to be desired, for natural authority is a far cry from authority that is merely arbitrary. Its attributes are obvious: adults are larger, are experienced, possess more words, have entered into prior agreements among themselves. When all this takes on a positive instead of a merely negative character, the children see the adults as protectors and as sources of certitude, approval, novelty, skills. In the fact that adults have entered into prior agreements, children intuit a seriousness and a web of relations in the life that surrounds them. If it is a bit mysterious, it is also impressive and somewhat attractive; they see it quite correctly as the way of the world, and they are not indifferent to its benefits and demands.

These two things, taken together—the natural authority of adults and the needs of children—are the great reservoir of the organic structuring that comes into being when arbitrary rules of order are dispensed with.

The child is always finding himself, moving toward himself, as it were, in the near distance. The adult is his ally, his model—and his obstacle (for there are natural conflicts, too, and they must be given their due)....

The really crucial things at First Street were these: that we eliminated—to the best of our ability—the obstacles which impede the natural growth of mind; that we based everything on reality of encounter between teacher and child; and that we did what we could (not enough, by far) to restore something of the continuum of experience within which every child must achieve his growth. It is not remarkable that under these circumstances the children came to life. They had been terribly bored, after all, by the experience of failure. For books *are* interesting; numbers are, and painting, and facts about the world.

Let me put this in more specific terms by saying a few words about José. At the same time, I would like to show that what are widely regarded as "learning problems" are very often simply problems of school administration.

José had failed in everything. After five years in the public schools, he could not read, could not do sums, and had no knowledge even of the most rudimentary history or geography. He was described to us as *having* "poor motivation," *lacking* "reading skills," and (again) *having* "a reading problem."

Now what are these *entities* he possessed and lacked? Is there any such thing as "a reading problem," or "motivation," or "reading skills"?

To say "reading problem" is to draw a little circle around José and specify its contents: syllables, spelling, grammar, etc.

Since we are talking about a real boy, we are talking about real books, too, and real teachers and real classrooms. And real boys, after all, do not read syllables but words; and words, even printed words, have the property of voice; and voices do not exist in a void, but in very clearly indicated social classes.

By what process did José and his schoolbook come together? Is this process part of his reading problem?

Who asks him to read the book? *Someone* asks him. In what sort of voice and for what purpose, and with what concern or lack of concern for the outcome?

And who wrote the book? For whom did they write it? Was it written for José? Can José actually partake of the life the book seems to offer?

And what of José's failure to read? We cannot stop at the fact that he draws a blank. How does he do it? What does he do? It is impossible, after all, for him to sit there *not listening*. He is sitting there doing something. Is he daydreaming? If so, of what? Aren't these particular daydreams part of José's reading problem? Did the teacher ask him what he was thinking of? Is his failure to ask part of José's reading problem?

Printed words are an extension of speech. To read is to move outward toward the world by means of speech. Reading is conversing. But what if this larger world is frightening and insulting? Should we, or should we not, include fear and insult in José's reading problem?

And is there a faculty in the mind devoted to the perception and recollection of *abc?* Or is there just one intelligence, modified by pleasure, pain, hope, etc. Obviously José has little skill in reading, but as I have just indicated, reading is no small matter of syllables and words. Then reading skills are no small matter either. They, too, include his typical relations with adults, with other children, and with himself; for he is fiercely divided within himself, and this conflict lies at the very heart of his reading problem.

José's reading problem is José. Or to put it another way, there is no such thing as a reading problem. José hates books, schools, and teachers, and among a hundred other insufficiencies—*all of a piece*—he cannot read. Is this a reading problem?

A reading problem, in short, is not a fact of life, but a fact of school administration. It does not describe José, but describes the action performed by the school, i.e., the action of ignoring everything about José except his response to printed letters.

Let us do the obvious thing for a change, and take a look at José. This little glimpse of his behavior is what a visitor might have seen during José's early months at the First Street School.

He is standing in the hallway talking to Vicente and Julio. I am sitting alone in the classroom, in one of the student's chairs. There is a piece of paper in front of me, and on it a sentence of five words. The words appear again below the sentence in three columns so that each word is repeated a number of times. Now since José came to us with a reading problem, let us see what relation we can find between these one dozen syllables and the extraordinary behavior he exhibits.

He had been talking animatedly in the hall. Now as he comes to join me, his face contracts spasmodically and the large gestures of his arms are reduced to almost nothing. There is no one near him, and he is absolutely free to refuse the lesson, yet he begins to squirm from side to side as if someone were leading him by the arm. He hitches up his pants, thrusts out his lower lip, and fixes his eyes on the floor. His forehead is lumpy and wrinkled like that of a man suffering physical pain. His eyes have glazed over. Suddenly he shakes himself, lifts his head, and squares his shoulders. But his eyes are still glassy. He yawns abruptly and throws himself into the chair beside me, sprawling on the tip of his spine. But now he turns to me and smiles his typical smile, an outrageous bluff, yet brave and attractive. "Okay, man—let's go." I point to the sentence and he rattles it off, for his memory is not bad and he recalls it clearly from the day before. When I ask him to read the same words in the columns below, however, he repeats the sentence angrily and jabs at the columns with his finger, for he had not read the sentence at all but had simply remembered it. He guffaws and blushes. Now he sits up alertly and crouches over the paper, scanning it for clues: smudges, random pencil marks, his own doodles from the day before. He throws me sagacious glances, trying to interpret the various expressions on my face. He is trying to reconstruct in his mind *the entire sequence* of yesterday's lesson, so that the written words will serve as clues to the spoken ones, and by repeating the spoken ones he will be able to seem to read. The intellectual energy—and the acumen—he puts into this enterprise would more than suffice for learning to read. It is worth mentioning here that whenever he comes upon the written word "I," he is thrown into confusion, though in conversation he experiences no such difficulty.

Now what are José's problems? One of them, certainly, is the fact that he cannot read. But this problem is obviously caused by other, more fundamental problems; indeed, his failure to read should not be described as a problem at all, but a symptom. We need only look at José to see what his problems are: shame, fear, resentment, rejection of others and of himself, anxiety, self-contempt, loneliness. None of these were caused by the difficulty of reading printed words—a fact all the more evident if I mention here that José, when he came to this country at the age of seven, had been able to read Spanish and had regularly read to his mother (who cannot read) the post cards they received from the literate father who had remained in Puerto Rico. For five years he had sat in the classrooms of the public schools literally growing stupider by the year. He had failed at everything (not just reading) and had been promoted from one grade to another in order to make room for the children who were more or less doomed to follow in his footsteps.

Obviously not all of José's problems originated in school. But given the intimacy and freedom of the environment at First Street, his school-induced behavior was easy to observe. He could not believe, for instance, that anything contained in books, or mentioned in classrooms, belonged by rights to himself, or even belonged to the world at large, as trees and lampposts belong quite simply to the world we all live in. He believed, on the contrary, that things dealt with in school belonged somehow to school, or were administered by some far-reaching bureaucratic arm. There had been no indication that he could share in them, but rather that he would be measured against them and be found wanting. Nor did he believe that he was entitled to personal consideration, but felt rather that if he wanted to speak, either to a classmate or to a teacher, or wanted to stand up and move his arms and legs, or even wanted to urinate, he must do it more or less in defiance of authority. During his first weeks at our school he was belligerent about the most innocuous things. Outside of school he had learned many games, as all children do, unaware that they are engaged in "the process of learning." Inside the school this ability deserted him. Nor had it ever occurred to him that one might deliberately go about the business of learning something, for he had never witnessed the whole forms of learning. What he had seen was reciting, copying, answering questions, taking tests—and these, alas, do not add up to learning. Nor could he see any connection between school and his life at home and in the streets. If he had heard our liberal educators confessing manfully, "We are not getting through to them," he would have winced with shame and anger at that little dichotomy "we/them," for he had been exposed to it in a hundred different forms.

One would not say that he had been schooled at all, but rather that for five years he had been indoctrinated in the contempt of persons, for contempt of persons had been the supreme fact demonstrated in the classrooms, and referred alike to teachers, parents, and children. For all practical purposes, José's inability to learn consisted precisely of his school-induced behavior.

It can be stated axiomatically that the schoolchild's chief expense of energy is self-defense against the environment. When this culminates in impairment of growth—and it almost always does—it is quite hopeless to reverse the trend by teaching phonics instead of Look-Say. The environment itself must be changed.

When I used to sit beside José and watch him struggling with printed words, I was always struck by the fact that he had such difficulty in even *seeing* them. I knew from medical reports that his eyes were all right. It was clear that his physical difficulties were the sign of a terrible conflict. On the one hand he did not *want* to see the words, did not want to focus his eyes on them, bend his head to them, and hold his head in place. On the other hand he wanted to learn to read again, and so he forced himself to perform these actions. But the conflict was visible. It was as if a barrier of smoked glass had been interposed between himself and the words: he moved his head here and there, squinted, widened his eyes, passed his hand across his forehead. The barrier, of course, consisted of the chronic emotions I have already mentioned: resentment, shame, self-contempt, etc. But how does one remove such a barrier? Obviously it cannot be done just in one little corner of a boy's life at school. It must be done throughout his life at school. Nor can these chronic emotions be removed as if they were cysts, tumors, or splinters. Resentment can only be made to yield by supporting the growth of trust and by multiplying incidents of satisfaction; shame, similarly, will not vanish except as self-respect takes its place. Nor will embarrassment go away simply by proving to the child that there is no need for embarrassment; it must be replaced by confidence and by a more generous regard for other persons. It need hardly be said that when these transformations take place, the child's ability to learn, like his ability to play and to relate positively to his peers and elders, will increase spectacularly. But what conditions in the life at school will support these so desirable changes? Obviously they cannot be taught. Nor will better methods of instruction lead to them, or better textbooks.

When, after ten minutes of a reading lesson, José said to me that he wanted to go to the gym, and I said "Okay," a little revolution began in his soul. His teacher respected his wishes! This meant, did it not, that the teacher took him seriously as a person? It became easier for José to take himself seriously as a person. And when he cursed, bullied, fought with classmates, and the teachers responded only with their own emotions, not ever with formal punishment, demerits, detention, etc., did it not mean that they were encountering him precisely as he was, and that in order to face them he did not first have to suppress everything but his good behavior? He could stand on his own two feet; they could stand on theirs. His anxiety diminished, and his resentment—and his confusion.

The gradual changes in José's temperament proceeded from the whole of our life at school, not from miniscule special programs designed expressly for José's academic problems. And not the least important feature of this life (it was quite possibly the most important) was the effect of the other children on him. I mean that when adults stand out of the way so children can develop among themselves the full riches of their natural relationships, their effect on one another is positively curative. Children's opportunities for doing this are appallingly rare. Their school life is dominated by adults, and after school there is no place to go. The streets, again, are dominated by adults, and sometimes by a juvenile violence which in itself is an expression of anxiety.

In writing these words I cannot help but compare the streets of our cities with my own environment as a child in the late-Depression small-town suburbs of Pittsburgh. There were woods all around us, and fields and vacant lots. And American parents had not yet grown so anxious about their children—or about themselves. When school let out, and on Saturdays and Sundays, our parents rarely knew where we were. I am speaking of the ages of eight, nine, and ten. We were roaming in little gangs, or playing in the woods, the alleys, the fields. Except at mealtimes we were not forced to accommodate ourselves to the wishes of adults. In the New York of today, and the world of today—with its anxieties, its plague of officials and officialdom, its rat race of careers, its curse of all-pervading politics, which seduces even intelligent minds into regarding abstractions as if they were concrete—the life of a child is difficult indeed.

Perhaps the single most important thing we offered the

children at First Street was hours and hours of *unsupervised* play. By unsupervised I mean that we teachers took no part at all, but stood to one side and held sweaters. We were not referees, or courts of last resort. Indeed, on several occasions with the older boys, I *averted* violence simply by stepping out of the gymnasium! We provided some measure of safety in the vent of injury, and we kept people out. It was a luxury these children had rarely experienced. . . .

It is so easy to underestimate the importance of conflict that I would like to stress for a moment that it is both inevitable and desirable—I mean desirable in a developmental sense, for it certainly hurts a teacher's ears and frays his nerves. I am referring, of course, to the noisy conflicts, the kinds that *do* arise and that only rarely have a parliamentary outcome. It boils down to this: that two strong motives exist side by side and are innately, not antagonistic, but incongruous. The one is that we adults are entitled to demand much of our children, and in fact lose immediacy as persons when we cease to do so. The other is that the children are entitled to demand that they be treated as individuals, since that is what they are. The rub is this: that we press our demands, inevitably, in a far more generalized way than is quite fitting for any particular child. And there is nothing in this process that is self-correcting. We must rely upon the children to correct us. They'll do it in their own interests, however, not in ours. In fact, they'll throw us off, perhaps with much yelling and jumping, like a man in a pair of shoes that pinch his feet. Let any teacher think back over the course of a month and ask himself how often this has occurred; and ask himself, too, if he would knowingly eliminate it, however much he might like to in the interests of his nerves. These mutual adjustments occur steadily in a broad, broad stream, and we notice everything about them —their noise, duration, obduracy, etc.—everything but the fact that their additive shape is beautifully rational and exceeds anything we might invent by the exercise of our wits.

I must admit that I have mentioned conflict just here because I have always been annoyed by the way some Summerhillians speak of love, of "giving love," or "creating an atmosphere of love." I have noticed, not infrequently, that the "love" of such enthusiasts is actually inhibited aggression. But this is by the way. The point itself is worth making: we cannot give love to children. If we do feel love, it will be for some particular child, or some few; and we will not give *it,* but give ourselves, because we are much more in the love than it is in us. What we *can* give to all children is attention, forbearance, patience, care, and above all justice. This last is certainly a form of love; it is—precisely—love in a form that *can* be given, given without distinction to all, since just this is the anatomy of justice: it is the self-conscious, thoroughly generalized human love of humankind. This can be seen negatively in the fact that where a child (past infancy) can survive, grow, and if not flourish, do well enough in an environment that is largely without love, his development in an environment that is largely without justice will be profoundly disturbed. The absence of justice demands a generalized suspicion of others and alters the sense of reality down to its very roots. The environments I have just referred to are not hypothetical but institutional. The former is an orphanage I had a chance to observe; the latter is Youth House. . . .

I am not exaggerating when I say that the play of children can be positively curative. Powerful factors are at work, and they combine into a dynamic that resembles that of the psychotherapeutic methods based on ego growth (though actually it is the other way around).

Children at play are intent upon pleasure and excitement, and in order to enjoy themselves they must relate to one another in terms of existing capabilitites. They arrive at a sense of these capacities in the most pragmatic way, making adjustments of all kinds, until finally they achieve what they desire, which is the greatest possible élan of play. This does not mean that they ignore one another's defects. On the contrary, they often seem harsh in their indifference to hurt feelings. If a crippled boy is playing in the game, no one pretends that he is not crippled, no one chooses him as a teammate, not until the very end, and then someone is sure to shout, "He can't run at all! If we gotta take him, you gotta give us Harry, too!" Yet if we look closer at this sort of thing, we see that the boys are not so much harsh as literal. The boy *is* crippled. He *can't* run. And in his own heart he knows that his feelings are not important to the boys, whereas the game *is* important. It is important to him, too, more important than his feelings. Furthermore, he can play only as a cripple . . . and if we wait to see what happens, it will be clear that this literalness, or harshness, is the only real acceptance the crippled boy can know. He joins in, and goes as fast as he can. The situation will change as the boys grow older. The expansiveness of play will give way to the rigors of competition, and the crippled boy will no longer have a chance.

But physical defects are not the only kinds of liabilities the children take note of and adjust to. They are acutely aware of temperament and traits of character. Vicente, as I have mentioned, was very babyish during his early weeks at First Street. He had to have his way, and threw tantrum fits when he could not get it. These traits were quite apparent during the dodge-ball games, and the other boys were annoyed. But they did not call off their game, or forbid Vicente to take part. Nor did they *only* criticize him. Nor did they play as if he were a "regular boy." They complained to him directly—"Quit stalling!" (when he spited them by freezing the ball)—and at the same time they slightly lowered the demands of the game, granting him many concessions. They did not, however, lower the game to *his* level, but only so close to it as to make him reach and exert himself. This combination of concession, pressure, criticism, and acceptance worked a powerful effect, as one might well imagine. Yet it was the ordinary dynamic of children at play—*at play without adults*. For if I had intervened, if it had been I who had yelled at Vicente instead of the other boys, there would have been no good effect, for I had not granted him concessions. Nor was I his rival. Nor would my criticism represent to him the same loss of pleasure, or the same hope of praise, as did that of the boys. Nor could Vicente's particular abilities mean much to me, as they came to mean much to his teammates. He was as agile as a squirrel, and though his teammates groaned when he threw badly (and he would turn and yell at them), they laughed with glee and approval when he put his hands in his pockets and dodged the hardest throws of their opponents. His face would light up when he heard their voices, and he would turn to them with a wide grin and an exultant shout. I watched this so often that I came to realize that what the boys were doing, quite instinctively, and out of necessity and self-interest, resembled, in its dynamics, the things I had done myself as a teacher and therapist (I was then in training) with the severely disturbed children at another school. For I had tried to relate to their strenths so as to add to them, and had dealt with symptoms only as actions, and had created precisely the demands that they could meet, given my own support and assistance. I had noticed, too, that even the disturbed children could help one another, though less frequently and in a far more limited way than normal children can.

When Stanley arrived at First Street, the boys' good effects on one another were much diminished. Yet even Stanley, from time to time, responded to the inducements and pressures of unsupervised play. One such occasion stands out in my mind and is worth describing, for it not only reveals the dynamics of play in a clear-cut way, but indicates that the nonintervention of the teacher is not a passive or nothing-at-all sort of thing, but exerts a particular kind of influence on the children.

The boys were playing dodge ball in the gym, Vicente, José, and Julio against Stanley and Willard. Stanley kept stepping over the center line when he threw the ball. The boys complained bitterly that he was cheating, but he threatened them and told them to shut up. All were afraid of him, but his cheating was really intolerable, and finally Julio yelled across the gym to where I was sitting on the floor, watching their game, as usual, from a distance.

"He keeps steppin' over the line!"

I reply only with a nod.

"Well, it's against the rules, man!"

Again I nod, indicating clearly that I know he is right.

Now José shouts, too, for they are all upset. "Well, tell him to quit it, man!"

I shake my head "no" and shrug. They understand that I'm saying, "It's your affair, not mine." They don't like this a bit. It increases their annoyance. Julio, who is the best player on the floor, and who is by far the angriest, makes a violent gesture with his arm and yells, "Shit, man, I quit!" and walks off the court. But now Stanley runs up to him with a cocked fist.

"You gonna quit, huh? Well, I'm gonna break your ass."

Julio cringes, but stands his ground and mutters, "I don't care, man."

Stanley is glaring at him, and Julio, somewhat mopingly, returns his stare. One can almost see the desires and apprehensions cross their faces. Both boys want to keep playing. The game was exciting; otherwise the argument would not have arisen. The rivalry was intense; otherwise the cheating would not have been so blatant, so much a deliberate insult. Stanley knows that he cannot force Julio to play. Even if his threats succeed, Julio will play half-heartedly, and Stanley, who is a good thrower, is especially dependent on Julio, who is a good dodger. Stanley sees his own pleasure in the game evaporating. He knows, too, that if he attacks Julio in earnest, the whole game will be destroyed, for the excitement of competition really does depend on prior agreements, and a fight would wipe these out. Too, Julio's teammates, though they are not fond of him, will certainly express their solidarity with a fellow Puerto Rican. All of these deliberations are more or less visible on Stanley's quite intelligent face. He had

been sticking out his chin and looking at Julio through
narrowed eyes. Now he grunts and punches Julio lightly
on the arm. Julio mutters, "Fuck you," and walks off the
court. He hesitates a moment, and then leaves the gym.
Vicente and José call to him, "Julio! Come on!" *"Mari-
cón!* Come back!" But he has disappeared, and so they
curse him and then yell, "Throw the ball, man! We can
beat you anyway!"—though they had been losing from
the beginning. Stanley throws, and the game goes on, but
it's woefully lacking in excitement. Willard has said nothing all this while. His silence, however, and his sullen face
make clear that his pleasure has been spoiled. Stanley
notices this at once and tries to talk the game into life,
raising a great hoopla and throwing as hard as he can.
His own face, however, is wooden. Vicente and José are
put out too quickly. The next round commences. Julio
appears in the doorway and watches. Vicente yells to him,
"Shit, man, come *on!*" but Julio shakes his head and
mumbles, "No man." Now Willard suddenly lifts his voice.
"Come on, Julio, he won't cheat no more." And Stanley,
who is holding the ball, yells, "That's right, chicken!
Come on, chicken!" and hurls the ball at Julio, who
catches it and hurls it back. Stanley catches it, and
screaming, "Come on, chicken! Come on, chicken!"
charges up to the line—not an inch over—and throws the
ball at Julio again. This time Julio dodges the ball, but he
dodges onto the field of play, and José immediately cups
his hands at his mouth and yells at Stanley, "Come on,
chicken, *quawk, quawk, quawk!*" and in a moment the
game is in full swing. The three Puerto Ricans, who are
masters of derision, flaunt themselves as targets, sticking
out their asses and waving their arms. They cup their
hands at their mouths and yell in unison, *"Quawk, quawk,
quawk, quawk!"* Stanley is grinning. He charges up to
the line—not stepping over—and shouts, "Buncha fuckin'
chicken over there!" and hurls the ball. Julio dodges the
ball, puts his hand at his groin and shouts, "Yeah, man,
you want a worm!" Once again the game is merry, obscene, and intense, though I should not say "once again,"

for the boys are in much better spirits than before. Most important, they leave the gym as one gang when the game is over, talking animatedly back and forth.

The effects of this game on Stanley and Julio hardly need comment. But what of my own refusal to intervene? What did it mean to the boys that their teacher wouldn't enforce the rules? Did it mean that he didn't care? Hardly, for they had come to know me through hundreds of other situations. They knew that I did care, and they knew very accurately (probably better than I) just where my caring ended. My refusal meant the most obvious thing. It meant not only that the game was theirs, but the rules of the game as well. And so I was not withholding myself, but was in fact putting myself in relation with something much larger than the game, something which the boys had again experienced in other contexts. This larger thing was their independent life in the world. My proper role vis-à-vis their independence was that of an observer and protector, and this was precisely the role I had taken. The effect of this was to locate all questions of ethics and conduct in the experience itself, that is, in the boys themselves, and not in some figure of authority. The further effect of this important shift in responsibility was that each boy was able to experience the *necessary* relationship between his own excitement and the code of conduct which joined him to others in a social group. Which is to say that their play —*because it was unsupervised*—acquired the moral pressures which are inherent in games, for at bottom this is precisely what morality is: the sense of the necessary relation between self and others, group conduct and individual fulfillment.

It is worth mentioning here that most of the games children play are not invented by themselves, though certainly they are embellished a great deal and often give way to less highly structured, purely creative play. The games are a form of lore, a tradition which in certain aspects reaches back into tribal origins. We tend to notice chiefly the physical aspects of games—the movements and skills, the excitement—and these are so important that we have no doubt of their great value to children. But the internal dynamics of the games—the strong and simple structures which bring rules, skills, individuals, groups, losses, rewards, energy output and rest into coherent wholes—these we often ignore, though it is just these that deserve to be called social artifacts. They have been arrived at in the most pragmatic way, often over the span of centuries, and the fact that they still exist is proof that we prize them highly. I point this out because we adults—teachers especially—watching children at their games, tend to think that because the children are new, we ourselves have a great deal to offer. We neglect to observe that we are competing with a durable and compelling tradition.

II. View from a Particular Stance

View from a Particular Stance

Theories or philosophies of education give a frame of reference to whatever goals or behaviors occur within a classroom. Although the study of these theories and testing and evaluation of their relative value is a vast subject in itself, I did attempt to select some of the most well-known with reference to what is happening in the 1970s. Three very important books, all written recently, are Jerome Bruner's *The Process of Education,* Ivan Illich's *Deschooling Society,* and Carl Rogers' *Freedom to Learn.* Chapters from these books were eliminated most reluctantly but I hope you can take the time to read them elsewhere.

A few obvious choices such as Maria Montessori, John Dewey, and Alfred North Whitehead were also left out. Their writings are so familiar to many and their basic ideas so incorporated into other selections included in this anthology that I have left them out as I did *Summerhill,* assuming that interested parties will go ahead and read on their own if they have not already done so.

Each of these selections has a particular way of looking at learning, roughly based on social values.

Finding a Place in Space

Gordon Ashby

YOU KNOW . . . THIS WHOLE BUSINESS OF ENVIRON-
MENTS AND LEARNING . . . AND PEOPLE . . . AND
THINGS . . . ALL HAS TO DO WITH . . .

FINDING A PLACE IN SPACE

FINDING A PLACE TO BE . . . YOUR PLACE
I'D LIKE TO READ YOU A LITTLE STORY ABOUT PLACES . . .
IT'S CALLED "THE TABLE"
HE HAD BEEN COMING TO THE TABLE NOW FOR TWELVE
YEARS,
TAKING HIS PLACE IN FRONT OF HIS KNIFE, FORK,
SPOON, PLATE AND CUP.
HE HAD BEEN DOING THIS, AS HE DISTINCTLY RE-
MEMBERS, SINCE THE AGE OF SIX.
THIS WAS HIS VIEW:
MOTHER TO THE RIGHT,
BROTHER TO THE LEFT,
ANOTHER BROTHER TO THE RIGHT OF MOTHER, AND
FATHER AT THE HEAD OF THE TABLE.
THE VIEW IN FRONT OF HIM WAS ALWAYS THE SAME,
SILENCE HAD PERMEATED THIS TABLE ARRANGEMENT
FOR TEN OF THE TWELVE YEARS.
ONE DAY HE DECIDED TO REARRANGE THE PLACING OF
THE DISHES AND GLASSES.
AND EVEN THE CHAIRS.
FOR SOME TIME IT WAS STARTLING AND EVEN DISCON-
CERTING,
BUT IT SOON LED TO CONVERSATION AND DISCUSSION.
HE CHANGED THE PLACES FURTHER IN THE MONTHS
WHICH FOLLOWED, AND EVENTUALLY EVERYONE PAR-
TICIPATED IN THE REARRANGEMENTS.

FOR THERE WAS MUCH JOY AND EXCITEMENT IN FIND-
ING A NEW PLACE, IN SPACE.

IT SEEMS TO ME THAT THE JOB AHEAD AND THE THING
WHICH NEEDS DOING HAS TO DO WITH "PROVIDING
PLACES FOR THE LIVING THINGS OF THIS EARTH".

AND THERE ARE OLD POSSIBILITIES WHICH MUST BE
REINSTATED,
THERE ARE FUTURE POSSIBILITIES WHICH MUST BE
EXAMINED,
THERE ARE EXISTING POSSIBILITIES WHICH MUST BE
RETAINED,
AND THERE ARE OTHER POSSIBILITIES YET TO BE IMAG-
INED.

MANY RAISE THE QUESTION . . . "THAT'S FINE, BUT
HOW DO WE GET STARTED?"
AND TO ME . . . BY LOOKING AT THIS GROUP TONIGHT
WE ARE STARTED.

AND ONCE STARTED . . . THERE IS SOMETHING WE
MUST ALL KEEP IN MIND

"THERE ARE MANY WAYS OF DOING THINGS . . . BESIDES
YOUR OWN!"

AND THAT "CHANGE IS THE STUFF OF THE UNIVERSE."

WITH THIS IN MIND THEN . . . I WOULD LIKE TO
TOUCH ON SOME OF MY IDEAS ABOUT ENVIRONMENTS
. . . OR P L A C E S

AS I SAID EARLIER . . . PUTTING TOGETHER ENVIRON-
MENTS IS REALLY A WAY OF "SEEING" . . . A WAY
OF LOOKING AT A SITUATION . . . DETERMINING WHAT
MIGHT BE DONE AND ACTING ON YOUR FEELINGS
ABOUT IT.

FOR EXAMPLE: LET'S LOOK AT EXISTING PLACES

Existing Places:
LAUNDRIES LOOK LIKE LAUNDRIES

PRINT SHOPS LOOK LIKE PRINT SHOPS

FARMS LOOK LIKE FARMS

IF YOU SEE A SITUATION WHICH LOOKS LIKE WHAT IS GOING ON THERE, YOU KNOW IT IMMEDIATELY . . . IF IT DOES NOT REFLECT WHAT IS GOING ON THEN THERE IS A CHANCE THAT SOMETHING IS AMISS.

IT'S FAIRLY SURE THAT WHAT IS GOING ON THERE THEY WISH WASN'T.

HAVE YOU EVER GONE TO SOMEONE'S HOME WHERE THERE ARE THREE OR FOUR YOUNG CHILDREN . . . AND THE PLACE LOOKS LIKE A DENTIST'S OFFICE.

THE SCHOOL CERTAINLY HAS MUCH THIS SAME FEELING . . .

HOW IS IT POSSIBLE, THAT IN A PLACE WHICH IS ALLOWED TO TEACH, AND WHERE CHILDREN ARE ALLOWED TO LEARN, (WHICH MEANS TO MAKE MISTAKES, FAIL, INVENT, TAKE RISKS, ETC.) LOOKS LIKE A PLACE WHERE EVERYTHING IS RESOLVED.

HOW IS IT POSSIBLE, THAT THE 1ST GRADE CLASSROOM LOOKS JUST LIKE THE 9TH GRADE CLASSROOM, EXCEPT FOR THE GRAFFITI ON THE DESKS.

Non Existing Places:
DREAMS ARE NON-EXISTING PLACES

DREAMS LOOK LIKE DREAMS

ARE FANTASIES ONLY IN BOOKS

DREAM PLACES ARE NEW PLACES . . . PLACES WHICH ARE NOT TOTALLY THERE BUT ARE IN THE PROCESS OF BECOMING . . . DREAM PLACES REFLECT ALL THE THINGS WE WOULD LIKE TO DO BUT CAN'T . . . BECAUSE WE CAN'T FLY.

Changing Places: THE FOREST IS A PLACE
THE CITY IS A PLACE
THE OCEAN IS A PLACE
CHANGING PLACES MEANS MOVING SPACES . . . IT MEANS BEING HERE THEN BEING THERE . . . ALL WE NEED IS A RIDE!

Closed Places: CLOSED PLACES ARE SECRET PLACES
CLOSED PLACES ARE INSIDE SPACES
CLOSED PLACES DON'T OPEN
THERE IS A NEED FOR CLOSED PLACES . . . PLACES WHERE YOU CAN GET FAR AWAY . . . AND LET YOURSELF FEEL-OUT YOUR MIND AS WELL AS YOUR BODY . . . A PLACE WHERE, FOR A MOMENT YOU CAN GET A HOLD OF YOUR LIFE . . . AND KNOW ONE ELSE CAN KNOW HOW.

Open Places: OPEN PLACES ARE OPEN SPACES
OPEN SPACES LET OUT INSIDE PLACES
OPEN PLACES ARE NEVER CLOSED
CLOSED PLACES LET YOU GET HOLD OF YOURSELF, OPEN PLACES HELP YOU GET HOLD OF EVERYTHING ELSE . . . THERE IS A REAL NEED TO KEEP OPEN PLACES OPEN . . . FOR CLOSED SIGNS ARE CHEAP.

Hard Places: HARD PLACES ARE WORK PLACES
HARD PLACES TAKE OUR ENERGY
AND MAKE OUR BODIES PART OF OUR MIND
HARD PLACES PUT US IN CONTACT WITH OUR TIMES . . . THEY MAKE US AWARE OF THE FACT THAT MAINTAIN-ING OUR PLACES IN THESE SPACES IS NOT PAID FOR BY THE OTHER GUY . . . HARD PLACES MAKE US PAY OUR DUES.
FOR THERE IS NO SUCH THING AS A FREE LUNCH . . .

Soft Places: SOFT PLACES REMIND US OF HARD PLACES

SOFT PLACES GIVE US ENERGY
AND MAKE OUR BODIES PART OF
OUR WHOLE

SOFT PLACES ARE NECESSARY ALSO BECAUSE ANIMALS,
PARTICULARLY MAN, NEEDS TO HAVE A PLACE OUT OF
THE MAIN STREAM WHERE HE CAN FLOAT, WITHOUT
FEAR OF BEING DROWNED.

Output Places: OUTPUT PLACES LET US SHOUT TO
THE SKY, AND LET US HEAR
WHAT WE HAVE BEEN THINKING
OUTPUT PLACES ARE TO MAKE
CONTACT WITH OTHER MEMBERS
OF OUR FAMILY.

OUTPUT PLACES ARE PLACES WHERE WE CAN SEND OUR
MESSAGES, MAKE OUR SOUND, PAINT OUR PICTURES.
OUTPUT PLACES LET US EXPRESS WHAT IS GOING ON IN
OURSELVES.

Input Places: INPUT PLACES ARE PLACES TO
MEET AND GREET
INPUT PLACES ARE NECESSARY
FOR GUIDANCE FOR THEY TELL US
WHERE WE MIGHT BE GOING.

INPUT PLACES ARE THE PLACES WHERE WE FIND OUT
HOW WE ARE DOING. THEY GIVE US THE CHANCE TO GET
SUPPLIES FROM OTHERS WHO MAY HAVE TAKEN THE
TRIP BEFORE US . . . OR ARE ABLE TO SEE FARTHER THAN
WE BECAUSE THEY STAND ON THE SHOULDERS OF
GIANTS.

ALL THESE PLACES ARE NEEDED . . . IT IS NOT A QUES-
TION OF FINDING THE RIGHT ONE . . . AND REMEMBER
THAT IN ORDER TO HAVE PLACES THERE WILL BE VOIDS
. . . THAT THING IN BETWEEN THE PLACES . . . THERE
WILL ALWAYS BE VOIDS FOR THAT IS THE PLACE PRO-
VIDED BY THE GODS TO EXPAND INTO . . . TO GROW . . .
TO CREATE.

AND IT IS THE IDEA OF CONTINUOUS CREATION THAT SEEMS TO STICK IN THE CRAW OF A LOT OF FOLKS THESE DAYS . . . THEY SEEM TO FEEL THAT MIRACLES HAVE NO PLACE IN THE SCHEME OF THINGS . . . I WONDER HOW THEY EXPLAIN THE PRESENCE OF THOSE THINGS WHICH ALREADY EXIST IN THE UNIVERSE? NOW? . . . EITHER IT HAS ALWAYS BEEN HERE, OR . . . IT WAS CREATED OUT OF NOTHING AT SOME TIME . . . AND EITHER WAY . . . IT INVOLVES THE MIRACLE OF CREATION

IN CLOSING I WOULD LIKE TO SUGGEST A PROBLEM . . . AN ENVIRONMENT PROBLEM . . .

WE ALL WOULD LIKE A CREATIVE LEARNING ENVIRONMENT . . . THE PROBLEM THEN, TO ME, IS ONE OF ACCESS NOT OF FORM . . . THE PROBLEM IS:
"HOW DO WE GET EVERYONE IN TOUCH WITH EVERYONE ELSE?"

WHEW!!!!!!

from *Summerhill: For and Against*

INTRODUCTION

When *Summerhill: A Radical Approach to Child Rearing* was announced in 1960, not a single bookseller in the country was willing to place an advance order for even one copy of the book, for A. S. Neill was practically unknown in the United States. True, he had lectured here at the Rand School for Social Research in the early 1950's, but the handful who had heard him, however much impressed, were not sufficiently influential to establish a cult or a following of any dimension.

Now, some ten years later, Neill's book *Summerhill* is required reading in at least 600 university courses. And the number is constantly growing. During the calendar year of 1969, the sale of the book exceeded 200,000 copies, an increase of 100% over 1968. In fact, the interest in *Summerhill* has now become world-wide; there are now translations in French, German, Italian, Spanish, Portuguese, Japanese, Hebrew, Finnish, Norwegian, and Danish.

What accounts for the growing interest in this book ten years after publication? Most certainly, Neill's ideas have stirred up an enormous amount of controversy. His educational theories have, at one and the same time, been championed by some of the country's leading thinkers and utterly derided by scholars and specialists of equal eminence. It is quite possible that in some classes where *Summerhill* is used as a text, the book is primarily used to show how far off a man can be in his thinking. But no matter how you read Neill, *Summerhill* is a springboard that will engender heated discussion, whether the situs of the discussion be the classroom or the drawing room.

This polarity was evident from the start. When the book was first published, a postcard was placed in the fly-leaf to solicit the opinion of the reader. More than 25% of these cards were returned—an unusual response, as any mail-order man will testify. But even more striking was the intensity of the feelings which these cards revealed. Many of the writers plainly stated that *Summerhill* was "the greatest book I've ever read," and "the most important influence in my life." On the other hand, I remember one woman who returned her copy for a refund on the ground that her husband had told her that either she or the book must get out of the house.

Because of the enormous interest in Neill's basic concepts I invited a number of leading thinkers to discuss his principles pro and con. The essays which comprise this book were contributed by writers who have achieved recognition in a number of disciplines. No viewpoints were barred; no limits were imposed.

As expected, the opinions in this book vary widely. Max Rafferty, California State Superintendent of Public Instruction, regards the atmosphere of Summerhill as utterly iniquitous. He writes, "I would as soon enroll a child of mine in a brothel as in Summerhill." On the other hand, John Culkin, Jesuit priest, regards Summerhill as "a holy place."

SUMMERHILL: FOR AND AGAINST represents a fairly complete spectrum of present-day thinking about child training and education. If this book leads to a more thorough-going consideration of the problems, its goal will have been achieved.

HAROLD H. HART

MAX RAFFERTY

It's not really the headmaster's statement of principles which bothers me so much as it is his obvious hypocrisy. He wrote his book apparently to prove that the example set by Summerhill can and should be practiced by education in general. Yet he admits that he takes only the children of the well-to-do: "We have never been able to take the children of the very poor."

This, of course, makes Summerhill an exercise in aristocratic futility. In America, we educate everybody. True, we do it under certain difficulties, and the results, to say the least, are somewhat mixed. But we don't just teach the children of wealthy atheists, as Mr. Neill confesses he does. Neither are we able to limit luxuriously our enrollment to 70, and then to employ a staff of seven or more to instruct them. A pupil-teacher ratio of ten to one is a little rich for our Yankee blood. Our American ratio is more like 30 to one.

Just as an aside, almost *any* educational philosophy can be implemented with fair results if the school is able to supply one teacher for every ten pupils. With that kind of tutorial staffing and with above-average intellects to educate, Neill should be able to teach his kids to do everything except levitate.

In his book, he brags that Summerhill graduates succeed in later life. But how could they fail? With their background, their wealth, and their brains, they would probably have done well if they had been educated in the Himalayas, with yaks as instructors. The test of a school or of an educational philosophy is how well it educates *all* kinds of children—rich, poor, smart, stupid, black, white. When Summerhill starts doing this, I'll be glad to stop back for a second look.

Another detestably hypocritical posture is to be found in one of the beaming headmaster's more sordid little anecdotes:

"Some years ago, we had two pupils arrive at the same time: a boy of seventeen and a girl of sixteen. They fell in love with one another, and were always together. I met them one night and stopped them.

" 'I don't know what you two are doing,' I said, 'and morally I don't care, for it isn't a moral question at all. But economically I do care. If you, Kate, have a kid, my school will be ruined.' "

It doesn't matter one whit to Neill that the baby will be illegitimate. Like his bedraggled spiritual mentor, Rousseau, he would presumably clap the kid into an orphan asylum and forget about him. After all, what are the woes of one more miserable foundling compared to the joys of "let's-all-have-a-ball-and-to-hell-with-the-consequences"?

Nor does he worry about the chilling selfishness involved in premarital sex, the anguish guaranteed by sexual experimentation on the part of those least prepared to face the consequences, nor even the breakdown of our Western code of morality implicit in the spread of Neill's hedonism to the majority of the next generation.

No, he worries about none of these things. Morality be damned. Delinquency be hanged. Venereal disease? Pooh-pooh! The only thing which concerns him is whether his school will be ruined financially.

"Economically I do care . . ."

You'd better believe he does. Because his school is his livelihood. . . .

FRED HECHINGER

Summerhill is rightly opposed to fear as a pedagogical tool. But Neill admits that the search for approval is a strong human drive, and in the concern for lack of approval (even by Neill and the best, most saintly of his teachers) there is, of course, an element of fear.

The goal—and I think the Summerhill disciples might be persuaded to accept this revision of the absence-of-fear concept—ought to be to teach children to consider the consequences of their actions and inactions, and in the light of such considerations to curb their desires for instant gratification. What this calls for, however, is the abandonment of the search for immediate happiness in the hope of attaining greater happiness later—with lesser risks of creating unhappiness in others. Whether this can be expected of children, without more direct guidance and restraints than Summerhill admits (or without so much covert manipulation that it would make dishonest men and women of the faculty), seems to me highly questionable. Even if Neill, and an occasional genius like him, can bring it off, this seems to me the kind of success story that proves the exception rather than the rule.

There is a direct line from America's Progressive Education Movement of the 1920's to Summerhill. But in reality, there is nevertheless a fundamental difference. The old progressives believed fervently in what they thought of as life-adjustment education, and only the more radical among them also thought of the school as an instrument of social change or even revolution.

Neill clearly does not want to adjust children to the corruptions and sterile competition of a life that he sees around him. This is to his credit. Simply to train people to play the game, whatever it may be, and to aim for the jackpot under existing rules is surely a perversion of the educational process. It is not adjustment to life but to death-in-life, and I applaud Neill's refusal to have any part in such an enterprise.

But not to bring up children to understand, and cope with, the realities and the challenges of the competition "outside" is to offer them little more than an escape into their islands of happiness, impotent either to adjust to existing realities or to change them into better ones.

ASHLEY MONTAGU

At Summerhill Neill has, for the most part, had in his care children whose parents had failed them and who had become behavior problems. (For such children especially, Neill's methods could hardly be improved upon.) Children who have lost faith in others and in themselves, in most cases, have had that faith restored at Summerhill. Neill's is not a blind trust of the untrustworthy, but rather a measured realistic approach devoid of false expectations. Neill accepts children for what they are, without blaming them for not measuring up to what we have been told they ought to be.

Neill achieved his results through his perfect honesty with his children, and also through his ability to make children understand that the pose of unswerving rectitude that adults so often assume in the presence of the young is a sham. Adults only too often unreasonably expect children to be better than they are themselves. Neill points out that everyone errs; that one learns by trial and error, and that one should not make too much of the errors but should try to understand them, and not make a habit of them.

On occasion, Neill makes what seems to me a rather questionable statement as when he says that the child who wants to learn will do so no matter how he is taught. I find this statement to be more than doubtful, for surely it is well established through the experience of millions of children that a child's interest in any subject may be permanently destroyed by poor teaching. The manner in which that most elegant and beautiful of subjects, namely mathematics, has in the past been taught, and in many cases continues to be mistaught, constitutes a horrific example of the damage poor teachers have done to possible interest in the subject.

Contrary to Neill, I consider the *method* of teaching fundamental, for the method is the message. From this standpoint, what is most important is not *what* one teaches, but *how*. It is not the words so much as the music that conveys the message; and in this connection, the most important quality the good teacher has to offer his pupils is the gift of his own personality. This is, of course, where Neill himself has so eminently succeeded. He, however, seems to overlook the fact that the personality of the teacher is an essential part of the method.

In *Summerhill,* Neill himself forcefully remarks that "Learning in itself is not as important as personality and character."[1] That is a statement that cannot be sufficiently underscored. There was a time when schools made it a principle purpose of their being to cultivate character in their students. *Character* is a word that has virtually completely fallen into disuse, and a concept which has been replaced by the huckster term *personality*. Roughly, I sup-

---

[1] A. S. Neil, *Summerhill.* (New York: Hart Publishing Co., 1966, p. 6.)

pose, the distinction between *personality* and *character* could be made by saying that "personality" is what celebrities have, and "character" is what persons of integrity exhibit.

One of the most destructive traits of contemporary schools is what seems like a virtual dedication to the extinction of individuality and creativity in the child by treating him, among other things, as if he were a mere anonymous unit in an agglutinated mass of other similar anonymous units. The best thing that has happened for centuries on university campuses throughout the world is the current recognition of the attempt on the part of these so-called educational institutions to obliterate the individuality of their students, and the active revolt by contemporary students against continuation of that abuse. Students rightly claim an active role in determining how their educational institutions shall be conducted. It is interesting to note that Neill, from the very beginning, gave every student and every member of his staff an equal vote in determining the issues before the school at Summerhill's General School Meeting. . . .

Recently Emmanuel Bernstein reported his findings on 50 ex-Summerhillians.[2] His observations are extremely interesting. On the whole, he was favorably impressed. If there is a quality that could be called Summerhillian he found that it was tolerance, that is, accepting people as they are, without regard to race, religion, or any other label. An additional strong characteristic would be sincerity. Ten felt that the school had been highly beneficial to them; seven felt that it had been harmful. Most of them complained of the de-emphasis on academic subjects, and the lack of good teachers.

Perhaps the most interesting finding is that a short stay of several years at Summerhill seemed to be more beneficial than a long stay. All but one of the children who

[2]Emmanuel Bernstein, "What Does a Summerhill Old School Tie Look Like?" *Psychology Today*, October 1968, pp. 38-41, 70.

had been at Summerhill for a few years were enthusiastic about it and adjusted well to the regular schools which they afterwards attended. Bernstein reports:

> *When the positive remarks among the 50 former students were tabulated, five items were mentioned more than any others. Leading the list of benefits were a healthy attitude toward sex and relationships with the opposite sex; a natural confidence and ease with authority figures; and a natural development, in line with personal interests and abilities.*

A most important finding was that former Summerhillians were, without exception, raising their own children in a self-directed way. Their inter-relationship was warm, and the children appeared spontaneous and happy. Thus Summerhill had helped them become better parents, had helped them to become the kind of persons who understood their own children and were able to raise them in a wholesome way.

This dividend of the Summerhill experience constitutes an outstanding testimony to the essential health and soundness of Neill's approach to education. For the most important achievement of any human being is the making of another healthy human being. And that, quite clearly, Neill has succeeded in achieving for most of his students at Summerhill.

BRUNO BETTELHEIM

Here is a lesson for some of our permissive parents and schools. What Neill knew even then, and what everyone not shackled by his preconceived notions soon learns, is that to submit to coercion leaves both child and adult with nothing but hatred or contempt for each other. If we permit someone to coerce or intimidate us, we stop being of much use to that person. We cannot help them because they do not respect us; and furthermore, we can not help them because we dislike them, whether or not we admit that to ourselves.

Every one of Neill's specific reactions—as opposed to his stated philosophy—remains valid even for situations he could not possibly have considered because those situations did not exist at the time *Summerhill* was published. Neill's criteria apply because they stem from his deep respect for the person. This may be illustrated by what he says on the very first page of *Freedom—not License,* his follow-up on *Summerhill:* "I define license as interfering with another's freedom. For example, in my school a child is free to go to lessons or stay away from lessons because that is his own affair, but he is not free to play a trumpet when others want to study or sleep." Maybe the passage hit me because student activists had just interrupted one of my classes believing, as do many of Neill's American followers, that they were fighting for their freedom, while in fact they were undermining all freedom by practicing license.

Would that our militant students, concerned as they are with their individual freedom, with being authentic and creating a better society, had learned what Neill, that great educator, considers the basic requirement for any better society: namely, respect for the individual. One must be convinced that one has no right to interrupt what others are doing, though one has every right to abstain from what is being done if that is his wish. . . .

In one sense, quite a few very liberal, well-educated, middle-class families, those most apt to believe they are raising their children in the philosophy of Summerhill, do sacrifice their children to the past. Not, as Neill suggests, by asking them to relive it, but by imposing on them the obligation to correct the errors of the past. Whether the child is burdened with reliving the past as it was, or burdened with reshaping the future, the child is being sacrificed to parental concerns. Too many parents fool themselves by assuming they believe in Neill's freedom, but do not grant their own child what Neill calls a child's most important privilege: the right to play in the present, that is, as I earlier quoted Neill, to play with guns at age ten. Instead, such parents ask their child to join at this age in their worries about the politics of the nation, and to do the work of the future.

Neill believes that to rear children well requires that "parents come to some sort of a compromise agreement; unhealthy parents either become violent [i.e., forcefully suppressive] or they spoil their children by allowing them to have all the social rights." And by forcefully suppressive, he includes the imposing of social or political convictions. Neill says, "A child cannot have real freedom when he hears his father's thunder against some political group." He recognizes that to give a child freedom is not easy, because "it means that we must refrain from teaching him religion, or politics, or class consciousness . . . I would never consciously influence children to become pacifists, or reformers, or anything else . . . Every opinion forced on a child is a sin against that child. A child is not a little adult, and a child cannot possibly see the adult's point of view."

This, I submit, is as true today as it was when Neill wrote it, and I wish that all liberal parents concerned with freedom would recognize how they deprive their children of freedom when they "thunder against" the inequities of our society, war, or the establishment. By thus raging against social inequities, justified as that may seem to the parent, they deprive their child of the most important thing of all: the right to form his own inner opinions, influenced not by the preachments of authority, but only by his own direct experience with life.

PAUL GOODMAN

Progressive education has been criticized as a middle-class gimmick. The black community, especially, resents being used for "experiments." Poor children, it is claimed, need to learn the conventional wisdom so they can compete for power in the established system. Black parents demand "equality education" and expect their children to wear ties.

In my opinion, this criticism is wrongheaded. The scholastic evidence, shows that the more experimental the high school, the more successfully its graduates compete in conventional colleges.

Black communities should run their own schools, and they should run them on the model of Summerhill. This has indeed been the case with the sporadic Freedom Schools which have been influenced, directly or indirectly, by Neill.

I don't agree with the theory of *Head Start* that disadvantaged children require special training to prepare them for learning. I find nothing wrong with the development of their intellectual faculties; they have learned to speak, and they can make practical syllogisms very nicely, if they need to. If they have not learned the patterns by which they can succeed in school, the plausible move is to change the school. But, as Elliott Shapiro has suggested, the trouble might be that these children have been pushed too early to take responsibility for themselves and for their little brothers and sisters as well. The trouble is that their real problems have been all too insoluble. It's not that these children can't reason; the fact is that pure reason is of no use to them in their coping with their all too real difficulties.

What these kids need is freedom from pressure to perform. And, of course, they need better food, more quiet, and a less impoverished environment to grow up in— AT THEIR OWN PACE. These things are what the First Street School on the Lower East Side in New York, which was somewhat modeled on Summerhill, tried to provide.

Nevertheless, we must say that progressive education has been almost a total failure. The societies that have emerged after fulfilling their programs, were not what the visionaries had hoped for. French or American democracy was not what Rousseau had in mind. Dewey's social conceptions have ended up as technocracy, labor bureaucracy, and suburban conformity. The likelihood is that A. S. Neill's hope, too, will be badly realized. It is not hard to envisage a society in the near future in which self-reliant and happy people will be attendants of a technological infrastructure over which they have no control whatever, and whose purposes do not seem to them to be any of their business. Indeed, Neill describes with near satisfaction such success-stories among his own graduates. Alternately, it is conceivable that an affluent society will support its hippies like Indians on a reservation.

How to prevent these outcomes? Perhaps Neill protects his community a few years too long, both from the oppressive mechanistic world and from adolescent solitude—it is hard to be alone in Summerhill. Moreover, it seems to me that there is something inauthentic in Neill's latitudinarian lack of standards. For example, Beethoven and Rock 'n Roll are considered equivalent (though Neill himself prefers Beethoven). We are not only free organisms but parts of a mankind that historically has made strides with great inspirations and through terrible conflicts. We cannot slough off that accumulation of cultures, however burdensome, without becoming trivial.

The Abundance of Environmental Educators

Mark Terry

from *Teaching for Survival*

I

There is no shortage of environmental educators now, and there never has been. Only as there is a shortage of teachers in general is there a shortage of environmental educators. Throughout the history of this country, our students have been receiving about as much environmental education as one could expect. There could be no better evidence for this than the magnificent ecological crisis that has just jarred the nation into rhetorical alarm. We have taught ourselves the magic principles of a wonderful environment, we have applied those principles with an unmatched faith in their accuracy, and we have commended them to our own future generations and to the peoples of the world. Lately, we have discovered our principles belong only to our imaginations and not to the environment. Perhaps an example from my own education will show how easily and successfully environmental lessons are taught in classrooms every day.

I attended an elementary school just outside Seattle, Washington, during the early fifties. In those days I was convinced the way to train for space flight was writing and illustrating my own science fiction. I wrote stories and drew rockets at a furious rate, aiming them all at the desks of my early teachers. Somehow those good people managed to read them all and return them with glowing words of encouragement, knowing full well this meant

longer stories and more rockets. Their stamina in facing
these reams of pulp fiction and even more their success in
teaching me the values of imagination and expression
command my respect. But these same good teachers were
also successfully teaching me environmental lessons that
have endured for years.

Innocently, through their own ignorance and misinformation, my teachers taught me that paper would always
be in infinite supply. Never was I asked to conserve and
reuse my discarded mistakes, or to use both sides for a
finished story. Never did I have to tolerate a lack of paper.
The magic stacks of newsprint were never allowed to disappear from the shelves of the classrooms. The provision
of this seemingly unlimited supply was the most effective of
the lessons about paper, but supporting information filled
in the environmental picture and left me little room for
doubt.

We were taught that our state of Washington produced
paper at a rate exceeded only by our friendly rival to the
south, Oregon. And if each state produced so much and
even competed to produce more than the other, it was
clear our classroom would never have to worry about its
supply. We knew paper was produced in pulp mills, because we occasionally were plagued by the funny smoke
from the mills in Everett or Tacoma. And we were told
the paper came from trees.

I could see it came from trees when I looked closely at
our newsprint. In the magnificent picture space at the top
of each sheet there were little flecks and fibers that looked
like wood, and the teacher said they were. But knowing
that paper was produced by men in nearby towns, I came
to the easiest conclusion: trees gave us paper as cows gave
us milk, and we produced paper as we produced milk.
Vaguely, I knew the trees were cut, but that seemed the
least important part of the process.

So I and all my classmates learned these three lessons:
(1) There will always be paper. (2) Paper comes from
trees. (3) Men produce paper. In these lessons lies an
environmental education upon which a nation has been

built. Never were we asked to consider any of the contradictions and paradoxes implied in the three "truths." Indeed, their solid simplicity has helped educators teach them with ease to the present day. Were it not for lessons learned from the environment itself I am sure I would be passing on the misinformation myself.

I learned something nearer the truth about paper and trees from a bit of environment near the mouth of the Columbia River known as Long Island. A town once tried to claim the island for man but is now only a collection of skeleton pilings. I owe my introduction to the island to a teacher, but he was wiser than most. He merely showed us how to canoe to the island and how to make its acquaintance. He knew the larger lessons would be taught best by the island itself.

Long Island forms part of a large wildlife refuge in a hundred-square-mile shallow bay on the Washington coast. Geologically it is a stray from the Willapa Hills, part of the Coast Range that extends from Washington into California. It was cut off from its brothers by the waters rising since the last glaciation.

The north-facing basalt cliffs, camouflaged in mosses and ferns, darkened by shadows from great overhanging trees, and obstructed by the fallen trunks that could not hold, were in no way made for man. I have never seen or heard a dinosaur on the island, but scrambling for footholds along the base of the northern wall I am never sure that they are not eyeing me from above. In the interior of the island, the wetness, the size of the ferns, and the number of insects date the island to the coal-forming forests of the Carboniferous. But to any reader of Tolkien, the island can be nothing other than the home of the Ents, the trees towering in their wisdom.

Long Island was logged once, and most of the forest is second growth. Some of the virgin cedars, however, were too large for the early loggers and were left. There is nothing to prepare one for their size. Through the younger firs and cedars one of these elders appears first as an illusion, perhaps a stand of lesser trunks that has not yet come into focus. When the reality of the single trunk is finally undeniable, one simply stops. There is no casually passing by such age and power.

Overtowering the young forest, several of the virgin cedars had drawn lightning and been hollowed and blackened inside, their outer bark untouched by the flames. If I were to tell how the lightning left them eyes and upraised arms, looking out over the island and the bay, you would not believe me. Yet they have such heads, they do oversee the bay, and who am I to say they do not move slowly like the Ents?

Some of these gutted cedars have become the spacious quarters of local bears. Living in such elegance the bears are clearly feudal lords of the island's animals, while innumerable raccoons are condemned to a thieves' existence prowling the tideflats.

Signs of the first loggers offended us in the form of roads turned to swamps and the impossible undergrowth that follows sloppy logging. But the new forest, under the tutelage of the great cedars, appeared to have a stronghold, and we thought the island had been legislated into safety. I was impressed by the wisdom of my fellow men, who had instituted a wild life refuge and outlawed all but bow-and-arrow hunting, and had not rushed to provide easy access across the bay. I tried to imagine what my children's children might find when the forest was that much older, and I resolved to leave instructions for them to return.

I did not have to worry long how to leave such instructions. Soon after the island and I became acquainted, I began to see how paper and lumber are produced: the second growth is disappearing from the south end, new logging roads are following the red surveyor's flags across the island. My children's children are not likely to find anything approaching the Long Island I have known; perhaps they will find instead the efficient, calculated growth of a tree farm.

I have seen, now, how paper comes from trees: a living forest is killed; the soil it held loses its natural fertility and erodes; streams once clear are filled with sediment;

the animals and plants dependent on the forest are forced into neighboring forests, if there are neighboring forests; and in a short season of logging, the members of the forest community are shown the folly of their existence. And, of course, never can the trees be allowed to grow to the irrelevant and useless size of the virgin cedars.

In this manner was my newsprint produced, in this manner it came from trees. And only if the soil is artificially maintained and forest communities are never allowed to mature, never allowed to support the animals they could, never allowed to reach the size they could; only under these conditions of environmental strife is there anything like an infinite supply. I still have trouble comprehending this environmental cost of newsprint, but I have learned, at least, that it is anything but cheap.

II

My elementary and secondary schools taught me many environmental lessons in equally innocent and effective ways. It would be neither useful nor original for me to condemn the education I received. But a beginning list of the erroneous environmental principles I learned, as well as a scheme for analyzing the educational encouragement of exploitive, insensitive environmental attitudes, may help demonstrate the nature of our problem: to change the environmental content of education, not to begin environmental education.

Environmental lessons I have learned:

Any amount of garbage is all right, just don't litter.

Population growth is good, bigger families are more fun and more people mean more friends.

The Asians won't starve, as long as I eat everything on my plate and we harvest the sea.

Water won't be polluted, as long as we pay "them" to build sewers.

Man has always had problems, and he'll always be able to solve them through science and industry.

Wildlife is a precious, but unnecessary, resource.

Hydroelectric dams bring nothing but good: power, irrigation, recreation.

Standard of living is based on annual income and purchasing power.

Driving to school is approved if I am licensed, permitted by my parents, and safe.

The history of man is the history of his growing mastery over nature.

And there are others I could list, as well as plenty of which I am not yet aware. Even the few listed, however, describe an environment not to be found on this good Earth.

Admittedly, more than teachers taught me about my environment. Madison Avenue is undoubtedly our most eloquent and successful educator. But the support and reinforcement the above ideas received in school was by no means insignificant. Presented without a prescribed curriculum, environmental philosophy was taught by every teacher, the school was a living laboratory, and the lack of texts on the subject only made it easier to learn. The reason for this ease of learning about the environment leads to a crucial lesson in itself.

There is no escape from environmental education, because environment *is* desks, blackboards, classmates, bulletin boards, teachers, office records, lights, windows, PA systems, grades. Each of these things is as much a part of Earth's household as any other. As each teacher approaches and interacts with every aspect of his school each day he is providing his students with a model environmental attitude. My lesson about the infinitude and cheapness of paper succeeded with hardly a word spoken: the teachers merely made sure we never ran out and never discouraged us from using as much as we wanted.

Since environment itself is unavoidable, negligence,

lack of action, as even lack of comment implies that certain environmental decisions have been made. Perhaps the only other concept as sticky as "environment" is "humanity." How can we fail to project an attitude toward man by every one of our student-observed actions during the day? And perhaps we have been as dangerously inaccurate in our description of man as of environment. I believe, in fact, that the two concepts are seen as separate from one another only to the detriment and confusion of an understanding of both.

Schools may not be able to be the most forceful environmental educators; they will be hard put to command more attention than television, radio, and printed advertising. But schools need not, indeed they must not remain silent collaborators in the miseducation of the public. Both as model environments themselves, and as actual institutions making significant demands on the world environment, schools can become the focal point of a revolution in environmental understanding. They run the risk of becoming the generators of yet more environmental rhetoric. They do not run the risk of being the ultimate solution: having been asked to solve, or at least accommodate all the problems of society, schools should not even rhetorically be asked to be the solution to environmental degradation. To bring the environmental education they provide into accordance with our best environmental understanding is goal enough for schools.

A brief catalog of the most fundamental problems of environmental misunderstanding follows to complete this chapter. It is included to amplify our notion of the problem at hand and to demonstrate the dangers of teaching as usual when we are beginning to know much better.

III

It is imperative for every teacher and administrator to examine his own environmental prejudices and misinformation. Since the subtlest of everyday actions communicates about the environment as it affects the environment, a teacher cannot really know what he is teaching until he analyzes his own beliefs and habits. If we cannot discover the misconceptions we live by, then no amount of curriculum reform is going to alter the most significant content of our teaching, our actions in the school.

I have tried to catalog some general learning outcomes that provide bases for environmental misunderstanding. Achieving these outcomes is quite like falling off a log and can be done every day in the best of classrooms. We must examine our own teaching behaviors to determine how we are contributing to each learning category. Having this picture of our own teaching behavior-learning outcomes in mind, a beginning study of basic ecology, even an investigation into the nature of environment such as is provided in the next chapter, can be the means to alter environmental education to fit the environment.

AWARENESS

Our senses were made for the environment, there is nothing else of which they can be aware. So the problem of environmental awareness is the general problem of sensory awareness. And if anyone wonders whether or not awareness is a problem, let him visit Los Angeles, or if he lives there, let him leave.

Lack of awareness is the only explanation I can find for the Angelinos who can persist in assuring me that the smog is really not so bad on a day when I cannot help but see, smell, taste, and feel just how bad it really is. Granted they do sense the smog, but their major adaptation to it has been a lessening of sense awareness: their senses continually providing them with unpleasant reports, they have learned to ignore the information. And they have taken the imaginary environment of the media as a better, for it is surely more pleasant, indication of the way things really are: the smog alert sign says "MODERATE," the billboards all show blue sky, the travel ads are inviting people to come for the climate, and the newspaper, telling how things really are, can still be read.

A sad parallel exists in the life of most schoolrooms. Other than for the ability to read, no premium is given to acuteness of the senses. What counts is the written and spoken word. No special training is given to develop sight, hearing, smell, taste, touch. These senses are considered largely irrelevant when they do not contribute to verbal communication. And the traditional classroom is usually dull enough to inhibit much sense exploration. Since the senses provide such irrelevant information, students learn to ignore them.

The imaginary environment of the textbook, blackboard, bulletin board, overhead projector, and ditto sheet often presents all the important stimuli. Contact with real objects is at a minimum. This projected media environment is *the* center of attention in such classrooms, and success is predicated upon familiarity with it. Verbal communication is the key. The senses provide, at best, unreliable help not approved by the curriculum directors.

Through such typical practices, sensory capabilities are given no help and enough discouragement for anyone. The environment quite easily becomes the printed page, the earphone, the TV screen, the movie. They all describe the real world, which we lose the ability to sense for ourselves. (Unsettling as it is, I am afraid that lack of awareness and reliance on verbal media lie at the heart of the "success" of the Earth Day "revolution.")

As long as environmental problems can be kept in the media, there will be concern and the beginnings of action. But as the focus of the media shifts, the concern and action will shift, even though the original problems are as close at hand as ever. The Angelinos may continue to go along with their smog, if it is no longer sensed through the headlines.

Insofar as any teacher fails on any day to provide an environment in which all the senses are needed, so he contributes to lack of awareness and makes toleration of environmental problems an ideal. It may sound ridiculous to ask a high-school English teacher to ensure daily that sight, touch, smell, taste, and hearing are valuable and necessary components of his classes. I suspect it sounds ridiculous only because we are already so far strayed from the awareness we once had, so adapted to rely on verbal communication. We are supposedly the most intelligent of animals, but our adaptability has taken a strange turn when we can watch the death of Los Angeles's forests from smog at a mile elevation, yet continue to live at the bottom of that deadly basin.

It is perhaps of interest to note that the Los Angeles schoolchildren, who have been feeling the smog in their lungs for years, had to be ordered to keep from poisoning themselves by exercise. Lack of awareness (of their own burning eyes and of pains in their chests) had allowed them to continue playing in the deadly gases.

CONCERN

Given that we and our students can become aware of environmental phenomena, what next? The ultimate problem is achieving constructive involvement in solutions to environmental problems, which will be discussed under the heading "Competence." Besides failure of competence and failure of awareness, however, I believe we educate for yet another kind of failure. I have called it concern, but the name is not important. An example from my own education may help explain.

I attended public schools near Lake Washington, a large fresh-water lake surrounded by the metropolitan growth of Seattle. This lake nearly died the premature death of Lake Erie through eutrophication, first from raw, then from treated sewage. The symptoms were the typical algae growths and an annual decline in clarity of the water.

Concerned citizens launched an effective campaign and enlisted the help of limnologists at the University of Washington. The lake was dramatically saved and is clearer now than in the early fifties. No large lake with similar problems has been treated so effectively anywhere else in the world.

I saw the sewers go in, saw the lake at its worst, felt

my parents' concern, was aware that somebody was taking care of it. This all occurred during my elementary and secondary education in local public schools. Yet it never was a matter of concern in any of my classrooms. We were not encouraged to bring the situation up, our teachers acknowledged that the lake was being saved, and we all basked calmly in the assurance that something was being done.

The lesson most easily learned in those days was that pollution is not a matter of interest except ever so briefly in a Health class. If it was not worth the classroom's time, then it could not be important for success in school: it did not pay to be interested or concerned in school, even if we were aware of the problems outside. Even sensitive students can be taught to lack concern.

The environmental bandwagon now complicates matters by fostering concern without awareness: concern, in other words, focused only on the media-textbook verbalized environmental problems. Teachers boarding the bandwagon to keep their classes current run the risk of building aimless concern, even distress, in the absence of any contact with the environmental problems right under their noses.

But granting success with both awareness and concern, the difficult task of responsible involvement remains.

COMPETENCE

By competence I mean a combination of responsibility and relevance, of commitment and feeling adequate to the task. If one is aware and concerned, it is still easiest to do nothing. Some form of lack of competence is the usual excuse for inaction.

Taking a hypothetical excursion from my Lake Washington story, consider what might have happened if the schools were alive with interest and concern over the condition and treatment of the lake. I would guess that talk of solutions would begin and end with sewers: once we paid "them" to install sewers, the problem would be solved. Never would we have been asked to consider either the content or the volume of our daily generation of waste. The notion that we each were responsible for the problem, and that we each could put some limits on ourselves to help solve it would never be discussed. Nor would the heresy "Perhaps there are too many of us living around the lake" pass anyone's lips. Having paid for our sewers, we would have made sacrifice enough.

Every pollution/population problem can be directly traced to the individual: to me, to you. We have no right to feel incompetent and to distance ourselves from the problems our own demands create. Our institutional framework clouds the direct relationships that are there, but we must see through those clouds, literally, to save our lives.

Most teachers either possess the common Humanity or the Educational Psychology credits to know that students cannot be left hanging with impossible and frustrating dilemmas. Waiting, perhaps, but left hanging without hope, no. The traditional solutions to such situations are either to avoid them entirely or to end the discussion with *"They* are working on it and will find a way." Of the two, I prefer the former. At least it puts the class squarely in the field of lack of interest. The latter approach is evasive, unworthy of students' respect, often a complete lie, and promises reward for incompetence.

To educate for competence, I cannot conceive of a better way than for the teacher to be able to point to the example of his own involvement. Indeed, if the teacher is in no way involved in active solutions to environmental problems, he is a great part of the problem. More will be said of this under "Hypocrisy."

Teachers who bring snatches of their own lives into their classrooms always run risks. Those who never bring such fragments of themselves into their classrooms should not be teaching in the first place. In the case of the environment's ills, everyone is asking to see how it's done, how to clean it up. The teacher has got to begin learning himself and showing his students how. Unless such lessons of competence are learned, we will forever be ensnared in the trap that holds us now: the power company is only meeting the demands of its customers, the customers are only awaiting the company's best advice, the government is only awaiting the words of both company and customer, and all are confident that the others will soon have the solution.

Most of the remainder of this book will be given over to suggesting ways of teaching for awareness, interest, and competence. There remain two other categories of miseducation, however, which will be dealt with briefly below.

SUBSTANTIVE MISINFORMATION

Return to the list on pages 7–8 for a sample of the sort of environmental misinformation that is taught. It is clear that misinformation is passed on by the misinformed, which is why the first task of any teacher committed to sound environmental education is to tend to his own education. The following story from my own brief teaching experience illustrates the complexity of the web of misinformation that is daily describing the environment.

For use in biology classes, our school had obtained a series of movies of superior quality. I was particularly impressed by one on insects. The close-up photography was impeccable, color was startlingly good, editing was smooth, the announcer was plainly a human being, even the score was less obnoxious than usual. But the lessons it taught were something else again.

Produced for schools by a major petrochemical company, the film's text told us the following: insects number more than any other class of animals (true); insects are highly evolved, very successful organisms (fine); outside of the silkworm and honeybee, very few other insects are of any use to man (false); in fact, being more numerous than any other group, insects are simply man's greatest competitors for the world's food (because of whose population growth?); the most successful form of war man can wage against his "rivals" is chemical "control" on a world-wide scale (true, only in the sense that the most successful form of war itself is a nuclear holocaust). And with cutting reminiscent of the best Hollywood suspense movies, we are shown the international headquarters of the UN's war on disease and malnutrition, the company scientist in his lab, the maps of target areas, the loading of the planes, and the magnificent trails of insecticides streaming over the forests.

In order to get good close-ups of insects, it is not necessary to put up with this onslaught of disastrously misguided propaganda. The film can be shown without the sound track. Or it can be treated, with sound, as a museum piece, similar to a documentation of the arguments opposing Copernicus. One might as well be teaching that the Earth is, after all, flat, if the film is to be used simply as it comes.

The need for teachers to return to their own education and to become sensitive to the environmental implications of their own methods and of the materials they use: this need can never be emphasized enough. In terms of the environment, a misinformed teacher is a dangerous teacher. One would not want to learn first aid from one who had never studied it, but who read about it occasionally in the papers.

HYPOCRISY

In the wake of the environmental revolution, curriculum guidelines are being changed, textbooks written, teaching aids prepared, all to teach the environment. New courses are being offered, old ones are covering environmental units and reading environmental chapters. Constructive as these changes may be, they are potentially disastrous if made in isolation from the school's own environment.

Teachers offering environmental courses without subjecting their own environmental attitudes to criticism are educating for hypocrisy. Small-scale examples of this were to be found in schools throughout the country on Earth

Day: a lecture on resource depletion was delivered by the teacher who drives the biggest gas-eating luxury car on the market; an assembly cautioned students about the dangers of polluting natural cycles with poisonous chemicals, while outside the weeds on the athletic field were being sprayed again; a display case was filled with heart-rending pictures of our vanishing wildlands, while the oldest oak on the school grounds was cut to clear ground for the new parking lot; first-graders were taken on a litter-collecting walk, while they were still encouraged to bring their lunches wrapped in two square feet of additional paper each day.

In the self-assurance that accompanies establishing credit or time for environmental study, the danger of overlooking the real environmental problems of the school is great. If students become academic experts on ecology, yet cannot see their own ecological roles and cannot judge their own lives by the ecological principles they have learned, environmental education will not have contributed to environmental quality.

IV

"But if we tell them not to use this and not to buy that, if we tell them to limit their families, if we impose restrictions on materials in classrooms, won't we be indoctrinating rather than teaching? We can't do that!"

The teaching of environmental principles that oppose notions of property and freedom which we have held for centuries is bound to be met with the charge of indoctrination. I believe this charge can be met best with the countercharge: We *have been* indoctrinating according to one environmental view throughout the history of American education. Was it not a very successful indoctrination that taught me the "truths" listed on pages 7–8?

But the reform of environmental education should not be taken as an excuse for new indoctrination. Indoctrination should not be the method, for three reasons. In the first place, the few principles that form a sound picture of the real environment are no more controversial than Newton's laws of motion. They simply need to be taken seriously. And secondly, the science of ecology is not yet so well established that detailed, specific environmental information can be provided in most cases. For a yet more important reason indoctrination must be avoided. There is never justification for teaching students only one belief. The art of asking good questions and the science of answering them—these must be the aims of any education. Bringing our antique environmental assumptions into question, and beginning to develop the science that can provide better assumptions, these must be the aims of environmental education. Far from limiting a student's viewpoint, an awakening of environmental criticism in the classroom serves to sharpen the focus of his free inquiry into all knowledge.

It is incumbent upon all educators to face the environmental implications of their present teaching and to judge whether they have constituted an indoctrination. To open their students' inquiry into the environment, it is then incumbent upon all educators to rethink their own environmental preconceptions. It is hoped the next chapter will provide a framework from which such rethinking can be structured.

Versatility and Innovation

John Gardner

from *Self Renewal*

Versatility

EDUCATING FOR RENEWAL

We are beginning to understand how to educate for renewal but we must deepen that understanding. If we indoctrinate the young person in an elaborate set of fixed beliefs, we are ensuring his early obsolescence. The alternative is to develop skills, attitudes, habits of mind and the kinds of knowledge and understanding that will be the instruments of continuous change and growth on the part of the young person. Then we will have fashioned *a system that provides for its own continuous renewal.*

This suggests a standard in terms of which we may judge the effectiveness of all education—and so judged, much education today is monumentally ineffective. All too often we are giving our young people cut flowers when we should be teaching them to grow their own plants. We are stuffing their heads with the products of earlier innovation rather than teaching them to innovate. We think of the mind as a storehouse to be filled when we should be thinking of it as an instrument to be used.

Of course, our schools cannot be wholly preoccupied with educating for innovation; they are concerned with continuity as well as change. There are continuities in the human condition, continuities in our own tradition and lessons to be learned from the past. When young people learn what and who they are it helps them to think about what they wish to become—as individuals and as a peo-

117

ple. At the higher levels of education they must be given the opportunity to examine critically the shared purposes of their society—a major element in continuity—and to subject these purposes to the reappraisal that gives them vitality and relevance. In every area in which creative thought or action may occur, the individual builds on the heritage of earlier work. It is true that excessive preoccupation with that heritage may diminish his creativity. And it is true that his mode of building on his heritage may be to rebel from it. Still it is his starting point.

But the educational system has always been *relatively* successful in dealing with continuity. The pressing need today is to educate for an accelerating rate of change. Some observers have feared that the need would lead the schools into frantic pursuit of the latest fads, but it has had the opposite effect. Change is so swift that the "latest thing" today may be old-fashioned by the time young people enter adulthood. So they must be taught in such a way that they can learn for themselves the new things of tomorrow. And that leads us back to fundamentals.

We are moving away from teaching things that readily become outmoded, and toward things that will have the greatest long-term effect on the young person's capacity to understand and perform. Increasing emphasis is being given to instruction in methods of analysis and modes of attack on problems. In many subjects this means more attention to basic principles, less to applications of immediate "practical" use. In all subjects it means teaching habits of mind that will be useful in new situations—curiosity, open-mindedness, objectivity, respect for evidence and the capacity to think critically.

GENERALISTS AND SPECIALISTS

Education for renewal is to a considerable degree education for versatility. And that fact brings us face-to-face with a well-worn controversy: should we be training specialists or generalists? Though many educators respond with vehement confidence, the question poses extremely complex issues.

Specialization is a universal feature of biological functioning, observable in the cell structure of any complex organism, in insect societies and in human social organization. In human societies, division of labor is older than recorded history and has flourished wherever urban civilization has existed.

Specialization involves selective emphasis on certain functions and the dropping of other functions. The human organism is capable of an unimaginably broad range of behavioral variations. Out of this vast range, any individual can develop only a small fraction of the total. All learning is specialization in the sense that it involves reinforcement of some responses rather than others. Nothing illustrates the process better than language learning. The infant has the capacity to understand and to produce a vast variety of speech sounds. Out of this variety he will come to recognize and to utter chiefly those sounds present in his own language—a fraction of the total—and will, as an adult, have considerable difficulty in recognizing and uttering sounds not in his own language. Thus we are all specialists despite ourselves. And so it has always been.

In short, specialization is biologically, socially and intellectually necessary. The highest reaches of education will always involve learning one thing in great depth. The great artist or scientist often achieves the heights of performance through intensive cultivation of a narrow sector of his potentialities.

Clearly, then, we cannot do away with specialization, nor would we wish to. But in the modern world it has extended far beyond anything we knew in the past. And, unfortunately, there are many tasks that can be effectively performed only by men and women who have retained some capacity to function as generalists—leadership and management, certain kinds of innovation, communication and teaching and many of the responsibilities of childrearing and of citizenship. Furthermore, the extremely specialized man may lose the adaptability so essential in a changing world. He may be unable to reorient himself when technological changes make his speciality obsolete.

Note that it is not a question of doing away with the specialist. It is a question of retaining some capacity to function as a generalist, and the capacity to shift to new specialties as circumstances require.

All social hierarchies involve a kind of specialization, and this too results in losses as well as gains. Subordinates who are deprived of the opportunity to make certain kinds of decisions may lose the capacity to make those decisions. An ironic consequence of such hierarchial specialization is that the individual higher in the scale may lose more in functional capacity than those below him. No one is more helpless than the boss without his accustomed aides. A slave-owning class may experience a deterioration in capacity that is damaging to its own survival. This process has interesting parallels in insect societies. Among certain slaveholding formicine ants, many normal capacities (nest making, care of young, even the capacity to feed themselves) have literally disappeared, leaving only a hypertrophied "military" or slave-making competence.

In human societies there is no reason whatever why the specialist should not retain the capacity to function as a generalist. Whether he actually does so depends partly on his motivation, partly on the manner in which he was educated and partly on the nature of the organization or society in which his abilities mature.

Frontier societies and organizations in early stages of development tend to be simple, fluid and uncompartmentalized, and this puts great pressure on the individual to be functionally generalized. Thus we most commonly encounter the "universal man" in young and relatively unstructured societies or early in an "era." (Recall the versatility of our Founding Fathers.)

In later stages, societies and organizations develop a complex division of labor, high specialization and a great deal of compartmentalization—all of which press the individual to specialize. Every student of organization can comment on the possible hazards of such compartmentalization. To the extent that it diminishes the versatility of the individual it lessens the capacity of the organization to renew itself. If individuals are rigidly specialized and unprepared for change, the human cost of change will be high and the society will resist it stubbornly. But if they are flexible and capable of learning new ways, the human cost of readjustment will be low and there will be little resistance to it. In short, in a world of change the versatile individual is a priceless asset.

The farsighted administrator can and does take action to prevent excessive compartmentalization. He reorganizes to break down calcified organizational lines. He shifts personnel (perhaps even establishes a system of rotation) to eliminate unnecessary specialization and to broaden perspectives. He redefines jobs to break them out of rigid categories.

A free society cannot be rearranged in any such summary fashion, and in the long run perhaps the most effective means of achieving comparable results is through the educational system. Education can lay a broad and firm base for a lifetime of learning and growth. The individual who begins with such a broad base will always have some capacity to function as a generalist, no matter how deeply he chooses to specialize. Education at its best will develop the individual's inner resources to the point where he can learn (and will *want* to learn) on his own. It will equip him to cope with unforeseen challenges and to survive as a versatile individual in an unpredictable world. Individuals so educated will keep the society itself flexible, adaptive and innovative.

Innovation

SOMETHING NEW UNDER THE SUN

Lyman Bryson said, ". . . the purpose of a democratic society is to make great persons. . . . A democratic way of doing anything is a way that best keeps and develops the intrinsic powers of men."

The institutional arrangements of an open society are not themselves the means of renewal. Their virtue is that they nourish free men. And such men are, at their best, inexhaustible sources of renewal. We may learn something about the renewal of societies if we look at the kind of men who contribute most to that outcome—the innovators. But first we must examine the process of innovation.

Some writers have emphasized that innovative activity starts with a problem to be solved. That is usually true. But man is an inquisitive, exploring kind of creature, who cannot keep his restless mind inactive even when there is no problem to be solved. He cannot help poking at things, turning ideas over in his mind, trying new combinations, groping for new insights. Surely, from the beginning, many of the most significant advances have come from just such exploring by gifted minds. Everyone who has spent any time with scientists knows that the answer to the question "Why did you try that particular thing?" is not infrequently "I was just curious to see what would happen."

Innovation is sometimes dramatized as a powerfully disruptive force that shatters the *status quo*. And so it sometimes is. But undue emphasis on its disruptive character can be misleading. Historically, the *status quo* in human societies, primitive or civilized, has been threatened not by innovation but by ancient and familiar crises —failure of food supply, disease, the hostility of neighboring societies, competition from superior technologies, inner decay. In such cases effective innovation may increase the chances of survival of a threatened system. (Ironically, this fact that the innovator may come in the role of savior does not necessarily make him any more acceptable to those who love the *status quo*. Like children, they may fear the doctor more than the disease.)

Just as societies come to a point of crisis at which they must move on to new solutions or perish, so particular fields of activity reach such a point. Just as a population may exhaust its food supply, so artists may exhaust the potentialities of a particular art form and scholars may exhaust the possibilities of a given line of inquiry.

The image of innovation as the shatterer of a serene *status quo* is particularly inappropriate in the modern world. Today, in the tumultuous sweep of technological and social change, one would be hard put to find any placid *status quo*. The solutions of today will be out of date tomorrow. The system that is in equilibrium today will be thrown off balance tomorrow. Innovation is continuously needed to cope with such altered circumstances.

Today even the most potent innovator is unlikely to be effective unless his work coincides with a crisis or series of crises which puts people in a mood to accept innovation. The Paul Revere story is a very inadequate guide to action in a complex modern society. It was all too wonderfully simple. He saw danger, he sounded the alarm, and people really did wake up. In a big, busy society the modern Paul Revere is not even heard in the hubbub of voices. When he sounds the alarm no one answers. If he persists, people put him down as a controversial character. Then some day an incident occurs that confirms his warnings. The citizen who had refused to listen to the warnings now rushes to the window, puts his head out, nightcap and all, and cries, "Why doesn't somebody tell me these things?"

At that point the citizen is ready to support some new solutions, and wise innovators will take advantage of that fact. A man working on a new air-traffic control technique said recently, "I haven't perfected it yet, but it wouldn't be accepted today anyway because people aren't worried enough. Within the next two years there will be another spectacular air disaster that will focus the public mind on this problem. That will be my deadline and my opportunity."

The reader will assume, of course, that he is not the night-capped citizen mentioned above. It is an unsafe assumption. How many of us can really recognize in the vast clutter of modern life the seedlings of new ideas and new ways that will shape the future? The new thing rarely comes on with a flourish of trumpets. The historic innovation looks exciting in the history books, but if one could question those who lived at the time, the typical response would be neither "I opposed it" nor "I welcomed it," but "I didn't know it was happening."

The capacity of public somnolence to retard change illuminates the role of the critic. In the early years of this century Abraham Flexner touched off a revolution in medical education by placing before the public a brilliant exposé of existing medical schools. Critics who call attention to an area that requires renewal are very much a part of the innovative process. (Of course, all critics are not heralds of the new. Some are elegant connoisseurs of that which has arrived, and when they approve of something it is likely to be long past its creative period. Like Hermes conducting the souls of the dead to Hades, they usher ideas and art forms into the mausoleums of "the accepted.")

One of the most serious obstacles to clear thinking about renewal is the excessively narrow conception of the innovator that is commonly held. It focuses on technology and on the men who invent specific new devices: Alexander Graham Bell and the telephone; Marconi and wireless; Edison and the phonograph; the Wright Brothers and the airplane. Starting from this narrow view, we would not find it easy to accept Jakob Fugger, the Renaissance merchant prince, as an innovator, yet he deserves the label. Claudio Monteverdi was functioning as an innovator when he modified and synthesized a number of musical traditions to create Italian opera. Several of our Founding Fathers were impressive innovators in statecraft. Dorothea Dix was an immensely effective innovator in social welfare.

We tend to think of innovators as those who contribute to a new way of doing things. But many far-reaching changes have been touched off by those who contributed to a new way of thinking about things. Thus did Planck, Einstein and Rutherford end the Newtonian era and usher in modern physics. Thus did Socrates, Zeno of Citium, St. Augustine, Copernicus and Darwin alter the course of intellectual history. One cannot reflect on such names without recognizing how striking is the diversity in content and style of innovation.

It would be a mistake to distinguish too sharply between those who contribute a new way of doing and those who contribute a new way of thinking. Many do both. As Hippocrates taught his contemporaries a new way to practice medicine, he taught them a new way of thinking about medicine, a way that lifted it out of the context of magic and superstition. As Louis Sullivan introduced a new way of building, he introduced a new way of thinking about building.

But we shall never fully comprehend the process of renewal if we limit our attention to the most spectacular historical figures. Many of the major changes in history have come about through successive small innovations, most of them anonymous. Our dramatic sense (or our superficiality) leads us to seek out "the man who started it all" and to heap on his shoulders the whole credit for a prolonged, diffuse and infinitely complex process.

It is essential that we outgrow this immature conception. Some of our most difficult problems today are such as to defy correction by any single dramatic solution. They will yield, if at all, only to a whole series of innovations. An example may be found in the renewal of our metropolitan areas. To bring these sprawling giants back under the rational control of the people who live in them will require a prolonged burst of political, economic and social innovation.

Robert Rosenthal and Lenore Jacobson

from *Pygmalion in the Classroom*

Summary and Implications

The central idea of our book has been that one person's expectation for another's behavior could come to serve as a self-fulfilling prophecy. This is not a new idea, and anecdotes and theories can be found that support its tenability. Much of the experimental evidence for the operation of interpersonal self-fulfilling prophecies comes from a research program in which prophecies or expectancies were experimentally generated in psychological experimenters in order to learn whether these prophecies would become self-fulfilling.

The general plan of past studies has been to establish two groups of "data collectors" and give to the experimenters of each group a different hypothesis as to the data their research subjects would give them. In many such experiments, though not in all, experimenters obtained data from their subjects in accordance with the expectancy they held regarding their subjects' responses. Quite naturally, some of the experiments involved expectations held by the experimenters of the intellectual performance of their subjects.

In addition to those experiments in which the subjects were humans, there were studies in which the subjects were animals. When experimenters were led to believe that their animal subjects were genetically inferior, these animals performed more poorly. When experimenters were led to believe that their animal subjects were more favorably endowed genetically, their animals' performance was superior. In reality, of course, there were no genetic differences between the animals that had been alleged to be dull or bright.

If animal subjects believed to be brighter by their trainers actually became brighter because of their trainers' beliefs, then it might also be true that school children believed by their teachers to be brighter would become brighter because of their teachers' beliefs. Oak School became the laboratory in which an experimental test of that proposition was carried out.

Oak School is a public elementary school in a lower-class community of a medium-size city. The school has a minority group of Mexican children who comprise about one-sixth of the school's population. Every year about 200 of its 650 children leave Oak School, and every year about 200 new children are enrolled.

Oak School follows an ability-tracking plan whereby each of the six grades is divided into one fast, one medium, and one slow classroom. Reading ability is the primary basis for assignment to track. The Mexican children are heavily over-represented in the slow track.

On theoretical grounds it would have been desirable to learn whether teachers' favorable or unfavorable expectations could result in a corresponding increase or decrease in pupils' intellectual competence. On ethical grounds, however, it was decided to test only the proposition that favorable expectations by teachers could lead to an increase in intellectual competence.

All of the children of Oak School were pretested with a standard nonverbal test of intelligence. This test was represented to the teachers as one would predict intellectual "blooming" or "spurting." The IQ test employed yielded three IQ scores: total IQ, verbal IQ, and reasoning IQ. The "verbal" items required the child to match pictured items with verbal descriptions given by the teacher. The reasoning items required the child to indicate which of five designs differed from the remaining four. Total IQ was based on the sum of verbal and reasoning items.

At the very beginning of the school year following the schoolwide pretesting, each of the eighteen teachers of grades one through six was given the names of those children in her classroom who, in the academic year ahead, would show dramatic intellectual growth. These predictions were allegedly made on the basis of these special children's scores on the test of academic blooming. About 20 percent of Oak School's children were alleged to be potential spurters. For each classroom the names of the special children had actually been chosen by means of a table of random numbers. The difference between the special children and the ordinary children, then, was only in the mind of the teacher.

All the children of Oak School were retested with the same IQ test after one semester, after a full academic year, and after two full academic years. For the first two retests, children were in the classroom of the teacher who had been given favorable expectations for the intellectual growth of some of her pupils. For the final retesting all children had been promoted to the classes of teachers who had not been given any special expectations for the intellectual growth of any of the children. That follow-up testing had been included so that we could learn whether any expectancy advantages that might be found would be dependent on a continuing contact with the teacher who held the especially favorable expectation.

For the children of the experimental group and for the children of the control group, gains in IQ from pretest to retest were computed. Expectancy advantage was defined by the degree to which IQ gains by the "special" children exceeded gains by the control-group children. After the first year of the experiment a significant expectancy advantage was found, and it was especially great among children of the first and second grades. The advantage of having been expected to bloom was evident for these younger children in total IQ, verbal IQ, and reasoning IQ. The control-group children of these grades gained well in IQ, 19 percent of them gaining twenty or more total IQ points. The "special" children, however, showed 47 percent of their number gaining twenty or more total IQ points.

During the subsequent follow-up year the younger children of the first two years lost their expectancy advantage. The children of the upper grades, however, showed an increasing expectancy advantage during the follow-up year.

The younger children who seemed easier to influence may have required more continued contact with their influencer in order to maintain their behavior change. The older children, who were harder to influence initially, may have been better able to maintain their behavior change autonomously once it had occurred.

Differences between boys and girls in the extent to which they were helped by favorable expectations were not dramatic when gains in total IQ were considered. After one year, and after two years as well, boys who were expected to bloom intellectually bloomed more in verbal IQ; girls who were expected to bloom intellectually bloomed more in reasoning IQ. Favorable teacher expectations seemed to help each sex more in that sphere of intellectual functioning in which they had excelled on the pretest. At Oak School boys normally show the higher verbal IQ while girls show the higher reasoning IQ.

It will be recalled that Oak School was organized into a fast, a medium, and a slow track system. We had thought that favorable expectations on the part of teachers would be of greatest benefit to the children of the slow track. That was not the case. After one year, it was the children of the medium track who showed the greatest expectancy advantage, though children of the other tracks were close behind. After two years, however, the children of the medium track very clearly showed the greatest benefits from having had favorable expectations held of their intellectual performance. It seems surprising that it should be the more average child of a lower-class school who stands to benefit more from his teacher's improved expectation.

After the first year of the experiment and also after the second year, the Mexican children showed greater expectancy advantages than did the non-Mexican children, though the difference was not significant statistically. One interesting minority-group effect did reach significance, however, even with just a small sample size. For each of the Mexican children, magnitude of expectancy advantage was computed by subtracting from his or her gain in IQ from pretest to retest, the IQ gain made by the children of the control group in his or her classroom. These magnitudes of expectancy advantage were then correlated with the "Mexican-ness" of the children's faces. After one year, and after two years, those boys who looked more Mexican benefited more from their teachers' positive prophecies. Teachers' pre-experimental expectancies for these boys' intellectual performance were probably lowest of all. Their turning up on a list of probable bloomers must have surprised their teachers. Interest may have followed surprise and, in some way, increased watching for signs of increased brightness may have led to increased brightness.

In addition to the comparison of the "special" and the ordinary children on their gains in IQ it was possible to compare their gains after the first year of the experiment on school achievement as defined by report-card grades. Only for the school subject of reading was there a significant difference in gains in report-card grades. The children expected to bloom intellectually were judged by their teachers to show greater advances in their reading ability. Just as in the case of IQ gains, it was the younger children who showed the greater expectancy advantage in reading scores. The more a given grade level had benefited in over-all IQ gains, the more that same grade level benefited in reading scores.

It was the children of the medium track who showed the greatest expectancy advantage in terms of reading ability just as they had been the children to benefit most in terms of IQ from their teachers' favorable expectations.

Report-card reading grades were assigned by teachers, and teachers' judgments of reading performance may have been affected by their expectations. It is possible, therefore, that there was no real benefit to the earmarked children of having been expected to bloom. The effect could very well have been in the mind of the teacher rather than in the reading performance of the child. Some evidence was available to suggest that such halo effects did not occur. For a number of grade levels, objective achievement tests had been administered. Greater expectancy advantages were found when the assessment was by these objective tests than when it was by the more subjective evaluation made by the teacher. If anything, teachers' grading seemed to show a negative halo effect. It seemed that the special children were graded more severely by the teachers than were the ordinary children. It is even possible that it is just this sort of standard-setting behavior that is responsible in part for the effects of favorable expectations.

The fear has often been expressed that the disadvantaged child is further disadvantaged by his teacher's setting standards that are inappropriately low (Hillson and Myers, 1963; Rivlin, undated). Wilson (1963) has presented compelling evidence that teachers do, in fact, hold up lower standards of achievement for children of more deprived areas. It is a possibility to be further investigated that when a teacher's expectation for a pupil's intellectual performance is raised, she may set higher standards for him to meet (that is, grade him tougher). There may be here the makings of a benign cycle. Teachers may not only get more when they expect more; they may also come to expect more when they get more.

All teachers had been asked to rate each of their pupils on variables related to intellectual curiosity, personal and social adjustment, and need for social approval. In general, children who had been expected to bloom intellectually were rated as more intellectually curious, as happier, and, especially in the lower grades, as less in need of social approval. Just as had been the case with IQ and reading ability, it was the younger children who showed the greater expectancy advantage in terms of their teachers' perceptions of their classroom behavior. Once again, children of the medium track were most advantaged by having been expected to bloom, this time in terms of their perceived greater intellectual curiosity and lessened need for social approval.

When we consider expectancy advantages in terms of perceived intellectual curiosity, we find that the Mexican children did not share in the advantages of having been expected to bloom. Teachers did not see the Mexican children as more intellectually curious when they had been expected to bloom. There was even a slight tendency, stronger for Mexican boys, to see the special Mexican children as less curious intellectually. That seems surprising, particularly since the Mexican children showed the greatest expectancy advantages in IQ, in reading scores, and for Mexican boys, in over-all school achievement. It seemed almost as though, for these minority-group children, intellectual competence may have been easier for teachers to bring about than to believe.

Children's gains in IQ during the basic year of the experiment were correlated with teachers' perceptions of their classroom behavior. This was done separately for the upper- and lower-track children of the experimental and control groups. The more the upper-track children of the experimental group gained in IQ, the more favorably they were rated by their teachers. The more the lower-track children of the control group gained in IQ, the more unfavorably they were viewed by their teachers. No special expectation had been created about these children, and their slow-track status made it unlikely in their teachers' eyes that they would behave in an intellectually competent manner. The more intellectually competent these children became, the more negatively they were viewed by their teachers. Future research should address itself to the possibility that there may be hazards to "unwarranted," unpredicted intellectual growth. Teachers may require a certain amount of preparation to be able to accept the unexpected classroom behavior of the intellectually upwardly mobile child.

There are a number of alternative "theories" available to account for our general findings. One such class of theories, the "accident" theories, maintain that artifacts are responsible for the results obtained, that there is really nothing to explain. The problems of test unreliability and of pretest IQ differences were discussed and found wanting as explanations of our results. The possibility that teachers treated the special children differently only during the retesting process itself was considered. The patterning of results, the fact that a "blind" examiner obtained even more dramatic expectancy effects than did the teachers, teachers' poor recall of the names of their "special" children, and the fact that the results did not disappear one year after the children left the teachers who had been given the expectations, all weaken the plausibility of that argument. Most important to the tenability of the hypothesis that teachers' expectations can significantly affect their pupils' performance are the preliminary results of three replications all of which show significant effects of teacher expectations. These replications also suggest, however, that the effects of teacher expectations may be quite complicated and affected both as to magnitude and direction by a variety of pupil characteristics and by situational variables in the life of the child.[1]

It might reasonably be thought that the improved intellectual competence of the special children was bought at the expense of the ordinary children. Perhaps teachers gave more time to those who were expected to bloom. But teachers appeared to give slightly less time to their special children. Furthermore, those classrooms in which the special children showed the greatest gains in IQ were also the classrooms in which the ordinary children gained the most IQ. The robbing-Peter theory would predict

---

[1] As this book went to press we learned of an additional experiment showing the effects on pupil performance of teacher expectation (Beez, 1967). This time the pupils were sixty preschoolers from a summer Headstart program. Each child was taught the meaning of a series of symbols by one teacher. Half the sixty teachers had been led to expect good symbol learning and half had been led to expect poor symbol learning. Most (77 percent) of the children alleged to have better intellectual prospects learned five or more symbols but only 13 percent of the children alleged to have poorer intellectual prospects learned five or more symbols ($p < 2$ in one million). In this study the children's actual performance was assessed by an experimenter who did not know what the child's teacher had been told about the child's intellectual prospects. Teachers who had been given favorable expectations about their pupil tried to teach more symbols to their pupil than did the teachers given unfavorable expectations about their pupil. The difference in teaching effort was dramatic. Eight or more symbols were taught by 87 percent of the teachers expecting better performance, but only 13 percent of the teachers expecting poorer performance tried to teach that many symbols to their pupil ($p < 1$ in one million). Surprisingly, however, even when these differences in teaching benefit were controlled, the children expected to be superior showed superior performance ($p < .005$, one-tail), though the magnitude of the effect was diminished by nearly half. We are very grateful to W. Victor Beez for making his data available to us.

that ordinary children gain less IQ where special children gain more IQ.

On the basis of other experiments on interpersonal self-fulfilling prophecies, we can only speculate as to how teachers brought about intellectual competence simply by expecting it. Teachers may have treated their children in a more pleasant, friendly, and encouraging fashion when they expected greater intellectual gains of them. Such behavior has been shown to improve intellectual performance, probably by its favorable effect on pupil motivation.

Teachers probably watched their special children more closely, and this greater attentiveness may have led to more rapid reinforcement of correct responses with a consequent increase in pupils' learning. Teachers may also have become more reflective in their evaluation of the special children's intellectual performance. Such an increase in teachers' reflectiveness may have led to an increase in their special pupils' reflectiveness, and such a change in cognitive style would be helpful to the performance of the nonverbal skills required by the IQ test employed.

To summarize our speculations, we may say that by what she said, by how and when she said it, by her facial expressions, postures, and perhaps by her touch, the teacher may have communicated to the children of the experimental group that she expected improved intellectual performance. Such communications together with possible changes in teaching techniques may have helped the child learn by changing his self concept, his expectations of his own behavior, and his motivation, as well as his cognitive style and skills.

It is self-evident that further research is needed to narrow down the range of possible mechanisms whereby a teacher's expectations become translated into a pupil's intellectual growth. It would be valuable, for example, to have sound films of teachers interacting with their pupils. We might then look for differences in the way teachers interact with those children from whom they expect intellectual growth compared to those from whom they expect less. On the basis of films of psychological experimenters interacting with subjects from whom different responses are expected, we know that even in such highly standardized situations, unintentional communications can be incredibly subtle and complex (Rosenthal, 1966). Much more subtle and much more complex may be the communications between children and their teachers, teachers not constrained by the demands of the experimental laboratory to treat everyone equally to the extent that it is possible to do so.

The implications of the research described herein are of several kinds. There are methodological implications for the conduct of educational research, and these were discussed in the last chapter. There are implications for the further investigation of unintentional influence processes especially when these processes result in interpersonally self-fulfilling prophecies, and some of these have been discussed. Finally, there are some possible implications for the educational enterprise, and some of these will be suggested briefly.

Over time, our educational policy question has changed from "who ought to be educated?" to "who is capable of being educated?" The ethical question has been traded in for the scientific question. For those children whose educability is in doubt there is a label. They are the educationally, or culturally, or socioeconomically, deprived children and, as things stand now, they appear not to be able to learn as do those who are more advantaged. The advantaged and the disadvantaged differ in parental income, in parental values, in scores on various tests of achievement and ability, and often in skin color and other phenotypic expressions of genetic heritage. Quite inseparable from these differences between the advantaged and the disadvantaged are the differences in their teachers' expectations for what they can achieve in school. There are no experiments to show that a change in pupils' skin color will lead to improved intellectual performance. There is, however, the experiment described in this book to show that change in teacher expectation can lead to improved intellectual performance.

Nothing was done directly for the disadvantaged child at Oak School. There was no crash program to improve his reading ability, no special lesson plan, no extra time for tutoring, no trips to museums or art galleries. There was only the belief that the children bore watching, that they had intellectual competencies that would in due course be revealed. What was done in our program of educational change was done directly for the teacher, only indirectly for her pupils. Perhaps, then, it is the teacher to whom we should direct more of our research attention. If we could learn how she is able to effect dramatic improvement in her pupils' competence without formal changes in her teaching methods, then we could teach other teachers to do the same. If further research shows that it is possible to select teachers whose untrained interactional style does for most of her pupils what our teachers did for the special children, it may be possible to combine sophisticated teacher selection and placement with teacher training to optimize the learning of all pupils.

As teacher-training institutions begin to teach the possibility that teachers' expectations of their pupils' performance may serve as self-fulfilling prophecies, there may be a new expectancy created. The new expectancy may be that children can learn more than had been believed possible, an expectation held by many educational theorists, though for quite different reasons (for example, Bruner, 1960). The new expectancy, at the very least, will make it more difficult when they encounter the educationally disadvantaged for teachers to think, "Well, after all, what can you expect?" The man on the street may be permitted his opinions and prophecies of the unkempt children loitering in a dreary schoolyard. The teacher in the schoolroom may need to learn that those same prophecies within her may be fulfilled; she is no casual passer-by. Perhaps Pygmalion in the classroom is more her role.

SHAW'S SUMMARY

... You see, really and truly, apart from
the things anyone can pick up (the dressing
and the proper way of speaking, and so
on), the difference between a lady and
flower girl is not how she behaves, but how
she's treated. I shall always be a flower girl
to Professor Higgins, because he always
treats me as a flower girl, and always will;
but I know I can be a lady to you, because
you always treat me as a lady, and always
will.

G. B. SHAW, *Pygmalion*

Musical Thinking

Hans Furth

from *Piaget for Teachers*

Dear Teacher:

Let me close this "practical" part of our letters on a more joyful note, then, by introducing the happy sound of violins and cellos under the direction of a music teacher who is one of many who intuitively put into practice what we are attempting to analyze here in a more explicit fashion. Asked about his method of introducing violin music to grade-school children in an environment where string instruments are not yet known, he began by saying, "No textbook or method is successful and valuable unless it offers a basis for motivation. Our method takes into account that children generally desire to participate in music-making as part of a group. The task of the group is made obvious and simple. From the beginning musical notation and terms are introduced as part of a game. The children do not view these things as something extraneous and special, apart from playing the instrument."

The teacher continued by pointing out that in the very first lessons the children play music together, starting with simple rhythmic patterns and musical interactions between various groups of players. The young student, as part of the group, applies the correct rhythm because if he did not, he would find himself outside the group. Moreover, the young player's imagination is encouraged by his being asked to construct and write down patterns consisting first of rhythmic notes and rests and later of simple melodies. These musical phrases are then played by the composer together with the entire group. He thus becomes aware of his active part in the shaping of the group's musical experience. Without his specific voice there would be something missing in the collaborative music that is being constructed. This makes each child conscious of the importance of his contribution.

When I hear a teacher express himself in such words and then observe how well this method is suited to the growing personality of the young child, I am greatly encouraged in my present attempt to make clear to teachers what does and what does not encourage the budding intelligence of these young children. The remarkable thing, of course, is that we do not usually connect musical skill with intellectual development. And, as you can guess, this music program, though regarded highly in the school district, was still considered an extracurricular activity, something of a luxury next to the traditional disciplines of an elementary school.

You said to me once before that the concept of intelligence which I propose is really quite close to what other people call "creativity." Although creativity is usually related to specific personality characteristics rather than primarily to intelligence, I would not hesitate to equate intelligence and creativity, because in Piaget's view intelligence is identical with development, with a going beyond present structures and an active transformation of present situational data. I have consistently suggested that our traditional view of intelligence is too limited in scope and impoverished by its failure to integrate intrinsic motivation. The purpose of the elementary grades should be to provide a setting in which intelligence, understood in Piaget's broad sense, is encouraged and rewarded. My reason for mentioning what this music teacher is doing—apart from my own love of music—is to show you how the opportunity can be given to children to express facets of their personalities that go along with their developing intelligence in the medium of music. To play in rhythm, to control intonation and intensity of tone, to construct musical phrases over time, and to symbolize all these things in musical notation, as well as to interact with others and submit one's activity to the group task—all this is part and parcel of human intelligence. It is for this reason that the music teacher can justifiably rely on intrinsic motivation. His goal is musical thinking, with the accent on thinking. He is not concerned with turning every child into a professional violinist or musician. This would require, besides an ordinary structure of developed intelligence, special talents, interests, and environmental opportunities.

There is no doubt in my mind that other forms of creative art are just as suitable and wholesome for the young child. A school system that focuses on thinking will not neglect any of the ordinary media in which men express their intelligence constructively.

We realize that the use of "leisure" time is becoming a serious national problem. On this account alone schools can be expected to provide a foundation for activities that do not produce income or scholastic degrees but are as close to expressing what is best in human life as is science or social cooperation. Let me outline for you how the music teacher encouraged musical thinking and why this kind of activity is appropriate for the young child and contributes to his intellectual development.

The first lesson proceeded as follows. Twelve children from grades three and four came into the room, eight children carrying violins, four carrying cellos. The children sat down and listened as the teacher and another musician played some lively short pieces. "Would you like to play like this?" the teacher asked. He then promised the eager children that before this lesson was over, they would play music together.

The children then grouped the chairs so that each pair of children faced a music stand. They were shown how to hold the instrument with the left hand. (The bow is not used during the initial lessons.) They exercised as a group, lifting the instrument, putting it down, and holding it in playing position. The teacher showed them how to pluck the open A string and explained that in music one note follows the other, as do the beats of the heart or the steps of walking feet. And then the music started. The teacher took the instrument and plucked the A in the strict rhythm of four beats. He urged the children to follow him. Together they played four bars of four beats. The music notation was directly in front of the performing children; the five lines, the key, the bars, the notes. Everything was real, as in real music-making.

The children were now ready for an important step. The teacher crossed out the first note in each bar for the violins and in its place put the wavy line of a rest, whereas for the cellos he left the first note, but crossed out the following three notes to be replaced by three rests. Now the first beat was plucked by the four cellists and the remaining beats belonged to the eight violinists. This sequence continued for four bars. When the children were playing confidently, the teacher started improvising a melody over the rhythmic plucking of the children. Is there any child who would not be delighted with this musical performance? Perhaps I should ask the other rhetorical question. Is there any child at this age level who would be incapable of making music?

In the second lesson children were asked to write down different rhythms where the plucked notes were divided between the cellos (C) and the violins (V). Here are some of the rhythms which the children made up: CVCV, CVVC, VVCC. The teacher then introduced the piano and forte signs as well as crescendo ($<$) and decrescendo ($>$). With the help of these signs, the four- or eight-bar musical phrases were played with different dynamic characters—soft to loud, or soft-crescendo-loud-decrescendo-soft.

In subsequent lessons a second open string, D, was employed and the children's imagination produced many interesting phrases, such as the following:

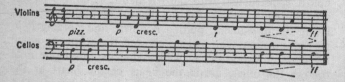

This particular phrase started very softly and gradually became louder, ending with a thunderous D.

Eventually all four open strings were introduced, and the children realized that the cello and the violin each had one string peculiar to the instrument. So far each rhythmic beat was played either by both or by one of the instruments. Now, for the first time, general rests were introduced; that is, all players were quiet and silently rested for a specific number of beats. The first general rests were for a whole bar. After this came quarter-note rests with rhythms like 1-2-rest-4 or 1-2-3-rest.

Music classes met only twice a week. At the beginning of the fourth week, all children had developed a good sense of rhythm. At this time the teacher showed them how to beat rhythm and conduct the ensemble in playing together. Until now they had always played four beats to a bar (4/4). Now they learned three, two, and even five beats. In addition, eighth notes were added to the already familiar quarter notes. While the cellos plucked a string in quarter notes, the violins plucked in eighth notes. Then the roles were reversed and eventually more difficult combinations were attempted. In all this playing the performance was constantly controlled by written signs. The child matched a musical notation (a symbol) with a concrete sound (reality), not unlike the symbol thinking we discussed in Letter 8.

After that the use of the bow was introduced. The handling of the bow was explained to the children as a function of the position of the instrument. With the bow it became possible to play whole, half, and three-quarter notes, and the appropriate symbols were accordingly introduced. After two lessons in which the children bowed on open strings, they began to use the fingers of the left hand to produce new tones. The teacher explained that the fingers worked like stoppers or hammers. To help with intonation, a piece of tape was put a whole tone above the open string to indicate the position of the first finger.

The teacher told me that from then onward the little musicians started playing songs and pieces, covering the entire range of notes in the first position. They were constantly in demand to perform for others, particularly parents and school administrators. This need to "justify the program and show results" interfered somewhat with the immediate goal of making music. Rehearsals for the concerts limited the possibilities for letting the children experiment with original melodies or combinations. The teacher also suggested that three meetings a week should be the minimum, because the children did not take their instruments home to practice. However, success of this string program was evident, as could be seen by its popularity among the children and its obvious accomplishments.

After being in the program for two years, the children were secure in the basic skills of being musicians. This meant intelligent control of behavior with the musical instrument according to the visually written and aurally interpreted requirement of the task, together with constant attention to the needs of the group. Such a task is in itself rewarding and supportive of the child's healthy development. If there were any aesthetic considerations, they were not a direct aim and were never the topic of lengthy discussion. The children were good sight readers and played as part of the group. They learned to correct an occasional mistake by listening to others and coming in at the appropriate place without interrupting the ensemble. They were familiar with more than one instrument and more than one key. When some children later transferred to playing the viola or the bass, they were remarkably quick at getting used to the alto clef or to different strings.

Asked about special talent, the teacher was not sure that any of the two hundred children he worked with had any outstanding predisposition. He thought it unlikely that any of them would become professional violinists. But what kind of education would aim primarily at the exceptional? We teach mathematics and history without expecting our children to become mathematicians or historians. Likewise, the children in this Virginia town played music because they were ordinary human beings. The teacher was sure that *any* children from any other environment would enjoy such a program and benefit from participating in it. Moreover, he had no doubt that the lives of these rural children had been permanently enriched even if they did not continue actively with music in subsequent school years.

As I listened to the string orchestra and observed the enthusiasm of the children and the audience, I too realized that for the children these were not trivial, secondary activities. Active participation in a constructive group task is the kind of food the human child needs in his growth toward maturity. Here the school encourages an active attitude toward enjoyment of music on which the child can draw in future years. For many adults, musical enjoyment is merely a passive experience of sound configurations which make an emotionally soothing background to an uninteresting activity. Such is the static, figurative knowing we described in previous letters. In contrast, the music teacher here knew how to engage operative knowing toward music and in addition provided an example of what good teaching is all about.

Sincerely yours,
Hans Furth
(for Piaget)

III. Specific Techniques

Specific Techniques

These selections were made on the basis of their relevance to modern classrooms, their clarity, and their possibility to serve as reasonable models for those who would like to try the techniques. Parents may be especially interested in them if they are either busy supporting an already flexible school system or trying to make some dents on inflexible ones. Here are some specific dent-makers.

Daniel Fader and Elton McNeil

from *Hooked on Books: Program and Proof*

ONE FOR THE STREET

This is a hard story to tell right. In fact, it's a hard story to tell at all:

The principal and I had been to lunch. As we stepped out of our air-conditioned car into 90 degrees of September heat, he said he'd only be a minute and walked across the narrow street into the shade of a very small, two-story, flat-roofed house. My vision was blurred by the reflected heat, but I could see a pretty young girl in the window. They talked, she smiled and showed him something that I couldn't see, and then he came back across the street.

"Pretty little thing," I said. "How come she's not in school?"

"She's working," he said, shortly, and I let it go. But it wasn't gone for good, because when we got back to his office he turned to me and asked, "Did you see what she showed me?"

"No," I said. "You were in the way."

"It was one of our paperbacks. Judith Scott's *The Art of Being a Girl.*"

"Well?" I said, when he didn't say any more. There was a point to what he had told me, but I didn't know what it was.

"Like I said, she's working today." When he saw that I didn't know the language, he told me straight. She was thirteen years old and she worked two days a week as a prostitute to help support herself and her family. The other three days she came to school. It was something, he said, to see how the students treated her. Especially the boys. The girls, so far as he could tell, treated her like any other girl. But not the boys. They *never* fooled with her

149

and they cooled any new stud who pawed her ground. They were good to her, he said, and that was the only way to put it. They were considerate. They knew how it was with her and they didn't try to make it worse.

That's all there is to the story, but I can't get it up and it won't go down. It's not that I haven't known thirteen-year-old prostitutes before. I just never knew one who read *The Art of Being a Girl* while waiting for business, and I never knew any junior high school boys who knew enough to be kind to her. But it's more than that.

Maybe it's the pap we feed them. Maybe it's the peeled and overripe bananas we feed them in the schools, when they've got the teeth to bite through tough fiber and scaly skins. How can we offer them Dick and Jane and the castrated classics when fourteen-year-old Dick protects the peace of thirteen-year-old Jane on Mondays, Wednesdays and Fridays, and purchases a piece of the same Jane on Tuesdays and Thursdays? How can we get them to believe that we're for real when we spend our hours from eight to three eluding them in a ground fog of words, and they spend their time from three to eight plus Saturdays, Sundays and holidays bumping and scraping against HOW IT IS? We can't. We're not for real; they know it, and they've put us down.

Who are the unreachables? Who are the unteachables? Do they have any reality other than in the blind eyes of the beholder? Is their existence a function of our failures as teachers rather than their failures as students? How does a boy make it all the way down to the bottom tenth grade class in a large high school in a very large city when, with emphasis in his voice and excitement in his face, he can tell one of his classmates, "I don't care if you seen the movie. You *got* to read the book!" Does the I.Q. of the average child in a Harlem public school *deteriorate* 4 points between the third and sixth grades because the child can't learn or because we can't learn him?

The child *is*. We've never managed to find out *who* or *what* he is because we've been so fatally distracted by who *we* are and what *we* want him to be.

The stories begin to run together. Have you heard about the sizable town (with a college) not very far from Ann Arbor, Michigan, where no child in the public schools uses or may possess paperbound books in any classroom "because they are shoddy and they contain literature that is shoddy"; or the large high school library in the Detroit area where *Inherit the Wind* was removed from the shelves by the librarian "because it has the word 'damn' in it"? Or the high school in the Chicago area where the principal ordered the librarian to remove *all* the paperbacks because he had received a phone call from *one* irate parent whose child had told him that "James Bond and all that trash" was actually available in the school library?

You hadn't heard, you say? Where have you been? Where have we all been? Where were we when the intelligent, upper-middle-class boy got so traumatized in his California public schools that he had to be put into a very special reading class staffed by psychologists from the University of California at Los Angeles? Summoned by the teacher from his seat in a rear row, he began to walk directly toward the front of the room; suddenly he stopped, backed up a few steps, turned about and walked around the periphery of the room to reach his teacher. What had stopped him? An open book lying on a desk halfway toward the front of the room. Who knows what horrors it symbolized for him, after ten years of scarifying failure in the public schools?

Has anybody told you about all the desperate children, no longer children but unable to become adults, who inhabit the Job Corps camps? What do they want? A job, a trade, a way to buy a decent piece of the world they never made. We'll give them the currency of a vocation, we say, and they'll be able to buy that place in society. But how do you teach a boy to become a man who drives big rigs or repairs cars and trucks or cooks in a restaurant kitchen, if the boy can't read? You can't hold a job as first or twenty-first cook if you can't read the recipes. Put paperback books in their Job Corps classrooms; the immediate and overwhelming favorite becomes *30 Days to a More Powerful Vocabulary*. They know where they hurt the worst.

If this book appears to be speaking only of children in penal institutions and children in the poorer public schools, then its appearance is deceiving. For the kind of poverty that identifies the child who is the true subject of this book is a poverty of experience—a poverty which can afflict lives lived at $100,000 a year just as readily as it curses the $1,000 a year existence. The poorest man in the world is the man limited to his own experience, the man who does not read. This book is about every child who may become such a man.

Preface To The Program

Hogman was sweating and so was I. The morning was hot, and we had hundreds of paperbound books to unload from the rear of my Volkswagen sedan. Why hadn't we boxed them before putting them into the car? Why my car? Why me at all—a teacher of English literature, a lover not a mover of books? We talked as we waited for some cartons.

"That a mighty tiny sheen," he said.

"Mighty tiny," I said, looking at the pile of books filling up the rear.

"Them's tiny books," he said, asking me to talk.

"We get any of yours?" I asked. The principal of the school and I had spent two hours in Cottage Unit A searching the boys' rooms for books. Those we had found were now sprawled in the back of the car. Hogman had come with us from the cottage, where he had helped to collect the books and load them into the car.

"Had all them James Bondys, but I done read 'em a couple times."

"We get anything you weren't done with?"

"I reckon."

"What?"

"The chuck what makes hisself into a splib."

"*Black Like Me?*"

"That the one."

I reached back and shuffled through the pile until I found one of the many reclaimed copies of Griffin's book. "Here. Bring it back when you're done."

He ducked his chin and half turned his big body away from me. Then he took the book and slipped it into his back pocket. We were both sweating through our shirts, but he didn't have to be back in Ann Arbor to give a two o'clock lecture. I was thinking about that lecture when Hogman turned toward me, a broad smile on his face, and said kind of low and chuckly, "Like reading, man. You know—it ain't so bad."

You know, it ain't. The program for teaching English in the public schools, outlined in this book, is based upon the idea that reading ain't so bad and it's time more people learned how good it is. Since everybody agrees that people never learn better than when they're children, this book describes a school program suitable in some measure to all children in all American school systems from kindergarten through twelfth grade. Though suitable to all, this program is particularly concerned with the student whom educators have identified as "general," meaning all too often that the school system has few specific programs to satisfy his educational needs. This is the same student who can sometimes be identified as disadvantaged and can more often be characterized as impoverished. He is disadvantaged if he is poor, but he may be impoverished and be rich. He is impoverished if he does not read with pleasure, because if he does not read with pleasure then he is unlikely to read at all.

Big Bill, Superduck, Hogman, Lester—all were students in the W. J. Maxey Boys' Training School at Whitmore Lake, Michigan, a few miles north of Ann Arbor. Their routes to the school were as varied as the faces of poverty; but if their pasts were various, their futures were alike: they would return to Maxey or to another penal institution, whether state or federal, juvenile or adult. They spoke of Jacktown (Jackson, Michigan, State Penitentiary) like an old and reliable acquaintance. They were boys, they were old men, they were tough, they couldn't fight their way out of a Girl Scout meeting. Sometime during the first weeks of my work at the school I said to one of the physical education teachers, "You must get some pretty fair athletes out here." I'll never forget his answer:

"These boys ain't good at nothing. If they was, they wouldn't be here."

I watched them fight. He was right—they didn't have anything but hate going for them. Awkward right-handed leads from flat-footed stances; long, looping punches that landed, when they landed at all, on shoulders and tops of heads. More than one teacher and cottage supervisor told me that he'd just as soon let them fight because they seldom hurt each other. Basketball, football, softball—sadball. They were society's losers. The hate they had as their sometime ally was as likely to be directed against themselves as against others. "Man, what's the use?" The words were engraved on their lips.

On this hot September morning, Leon Holman (principal of the Maxey School) and I, Daniel Fader (Assistant Professor of English at the University of Michigan), were holding a shakedown. Criminals' cells and delinquents' rooms have, in the history of penal institutions, been shaken down for everything from money and drugs, to knives, guns, files and blunt instruments, but this may have been the first time they were shaken down for books. The wingman went ahead of us, unlocking the doors; Hogman followed, pushing the cart. We knew we'd find books, but we never thought it would be like this. Books were everywhere: on their shelves, on their desks, their beds, their washstands. Their teachers said they were reading; the books they carried with them, stuffed in their pockets, said they were reading; the number of books missing from the library said they were reading . . . but here, suddenly, was evidence we couldn't question. It was a perversely happy two hours for both of us, faced as we were with the stolen evidence of our program's success.

That program, as it has been developed and tested, is described in our book, *Hooked on Books*.

THE PROGRAM

"English in every classroom" is an approach to learning based on the dual concepts of SATURATION and DIFFUSION. The first of these key concepts, SATURATION, proposes to so surround the student with newspapers, magazines and paperbound books that he comes to perceive them as pleasurable means to necessary ends. The advantages inherent in selecting such materials for classroom use are very great. First, and most important, all newspapers, most magazines and the great majority of paperbound books are written in the knowledge that commercial disaster is the reward for creating paragraphs that people *should* read. With the choice a clear one between market success and business failure, publishers, editors and writers know that survival depends on producing words that people *will* read. This program advances the radical notion that students are people and should be treated accordingly.

A second and perhaps equally important advantage in saturating the student's school environment with newspapers, magazines and paperbound books is their relationship to the world outside the school building. No one believes that we are training children from any social level to be performers in school; everyone believes that students come to the schools to learn skills they will need when they leave school, no matter at what level they leave. And yet, instead of importing materials from that world for teaching the literacy that world requires, we ignore such materials as unworthy of the better world we teachers are dedicated to creating. This program yields to none in its desire to help make a better world. It is equally strong, however, in its desire to educate students to deal with the world as it is. No literature better represents that world than the various periodicals and softbound books which supply the basic materials for the SATURATION program.

The third advantage of these materials is closely related to the second. Not only do newspapers, magazines and paperbound books *enable* the student to deal with the world as it is, but they *invite* him to do so. All educators are only too familiar with the school-text syndrome, that disease whose symptoms are uneducated students and unread materials. School texts often go unread just because they are school texts and apparently have very little to do with the nonschool world. One certain way to break the syndrome is to remove the proximate causes—in this case traditional school texts—and substitute newspapers, magazines and paperbound books.

A warning to those who follow the foregoing advice: You'll have at least three unhappy types on your hands when you remove traditional school texts and substitute paperbound materials. Least important will be the parents who want to see their children with traditional texts because paperbound books (or magazines or newspapers) "don't look right." "They were never used in *my* day in school!" Yes, you may reply, and look what we turned out.

Most important of the unhappy types will be the teachers who won't change "and nobody's going to make me." Whether they act from the pressure of invincible ignorance or forty (or four) years of lesson plans, they will prove to be immovable and should be fired. But since removal is the prerogative of employers whose staff members take responsibility for their products—a description in no way applicable to the business of education—such teachers must be ignored. In my experience, they are very much in the minority and the harm they do can be greatly mitigated by their colleagues.

Last among those who will be predictably unhappy at the change in texts will be certain students. These are the ones who have built up a careful and relatively complete system of defenses against the varied apparatus of the school world. We see the worst of them in Maxey and in a few of the big-city public schools where parts of the program have been installed. They are immediately recognizable by their anger, which is very funny in a bizarre way. They are angry because they have been given paperbound books, magazines and newspapers instead of the customary texts. "Where are the *real* textbooks?" they ask. What they are really asking is—"Where are the recognizable symbols of a world we know how to resist? Make us comfortable with the old texts, and we'll be able to fight back because we'll recognize the enemy."

The fourth and final asset of softbound materials reflects a new sort of hope. Though it's not exactly what I had in mind when I first advocated replacing classic school texts with paperbound material, it is an asset which can hardly be overlooked. Its spokesman is a former English teacher who, in the best tradition of a peculiar profession, has been rewarded for excellence in teaching by being removed from the classroom to the position of administrator. He speaks here in the reduced voice of a principal:

"If you couldn't say anything else for newspapers and magazines for teaching our kind of student, you'd have to say that they get a mighty important message across to him. Maybe the most important. No matter how bad he feels about his world, he has only to read a newspaper or magazine to know that somebody else has got it worse."

SATURATION applies in principle not only to the selection and distribution of periodicals and softbound texts throughout the curriculum, but to the explosion of writing in the student's school environment. This explosion is based upon the practice of DIFFUSION, the second of the two key concepts in the design of *English in Every Classroom* and the concept implied in its name. Whereas SATURATION refers to the materials used in every classroom to induce the child to enter the doorway of literacy, DIFFUSION refers to the responsibility of every teacher in every classroom to make the house of literacy attractive. In discharging this responsibility, every teacher becomes an intermediary between the student and functional literacy. In order that the student may come to view writing as a means to all ends, all ends which he pursues in a scholastic context must insist upon writing as the means through which they can be approached. In short, every teacher becomes a teacher of English, and English is taught in every classroom. . . .

Implementation of the practice of shared responsibility for the student's training in English has proved not only relatively easy in the Maxey Boys' Training School and the Garnet-Patterson Junior High School, but also unexpectedly pleasant for the faculties involved. When I first met with the full faculties of the Maxey and Garnet-Patterson schools for three-day training seminars in August of 1964 and 1965, respectively, I was uncomfortably aware on both occasions of how cold a welcome my program might receive. For it proposes an approach to the teaching of reading and writing which challenges two of the dearest and most ancient misconceptions of the profession. These are the myths, customarily paired for strength, of the teacher as individualist and the classroom as castle. Together they have done more harm to the profession of teaching than any other combination of ideas or events. The myth of the teacher as individualist serves as an example; because of it and the mental set it represents, meaningful cooperation among teachers is essentially nonexistent. Each teacher is so concerned with perpetuating the values and conditions of his own preparation, so concerned with protecting his feudal rights as a free man, that he effectively isolates himself from his peers. Teachers have *no* peer group in the functional sense of that term. They may attend professional classes, taking courses during the academic year and during the summer, but they tend to be speakers and auditors of monologues rather than participants in dialogues. *They do not profit from each other* because they are the true inheritors of the modern theory of compartmentalized education, a theory which declares each man sufficient unto his subject and each subject sufficient unto itself. General practitioners are as little respected and as meagerly rewarded in teaching as they are in medicine.

The inevitable corollary to the idea of teacher as individualist is the theory of classroom as castle. Without the second, the first could hardly be as destructive as it is. Part of our feudal inheritance is the notion that a man's home is his castle. Sanctified by law and custom, this theory has become a practice imitated in the schools. Like most imitations, the shape of the thing has undergone subtle change. Whereas in the home a man has the freedom *to* order his life and raise his family, in the classroom this tradition has been interpreted as freedom *from*. Rather than exercising freedom *to* experiment and freedom *to* criticize (both self and colleagues), teachers distinguish themselves by a process of in-gathering which frees them *from* all criticism to a degree foreign to any other profession. I would be the last to deny that public criticism—often reflecting only ignorance and prejudice—has given teachers one very good reason for insulating themselves from further shocks. But the insulation has become a burden rather than a protection. Teachers now suffer most from their inability to hear each other. . . .

Educators simply cannot afford the luxury of ignoring the products and the knowledge of the commercial world. The very idea of an inviolate "school world" is worse than indefensible; it is damaging in the extreme to the very concept it seeks to perpetuate and protect.

Fundamental to the malaise from which conventional school libraries suffer is the universal assumption that students will use them because they are there. Were this assumption applied to other human activities, ranging from toilet-training to the use of tools, only catastrophe would result. Regarding the library as something less than an irresistible attraction to students is a useful first step in revitalizing it. Implicit in this approach is an objective review of its lending procedures. Instead of placing the responsibility for first (and, too often, last) acquaintance upon the student and/or the teacher, the responsibility should be put where it rightfully belongs—upon the books themselves. *Give* each child a paperbound book or two to begin his school year. Let him understand that he may have any other paperbound book in the library by the simple expedient of trading a book he has for a book he wants. Then *schedule* him twice each week for the opportunity of book borrowing, and if our experience at the Maxey and Garnet-Patterson schools has been any guide —stand back and enjoy the sight of children reading.

Selecting the Books

Just what selection procedures create the best paperback library? The youngest boy at B.T.S. is twelve, the oldest eighteen; the average boy reads as well as a fourth-grader, and most are in junior high before they come to the Maxey School. Almost all have lived materially disadvantaged lives; almost all have come from culturally impoverished worlds. At the age of twelve they know more about physical man—from sex of some kinds to violence of all kinds—than any child should and most adults ever will. At the age of eighteen they know less about the world outside the neighborhoods in which they have lived (all alike; moving often is easier than paying the rent) than middle-class children half their age. Everybody knows *about* them. But who *knows* them? And who knows what kind of books they might read?

Haunted by the specter of our own ignorance, we took refuge in a copy of the 1964 *Paperbound Books in Print*. We tore the title list into six equal sections, one section for each English teacher. In his section, each teacher placed a check beside each book he thought the boys would like to read, and two checks beside each book he thought the boys would like to read and he would like to teach. Then he exchanged sections with another teacher and, using crosses instead of checks, did the same with the second section he received. Next, each teacher found a section he hadn't yet read and no third reader had marked; this section he marked with small circles in the same way. Finally, each teacher took the last section in his possession, made a list of the books with three kinds of marks beside them, and a list of the ones that had at least one of those marks twice. When the last step had been performed, we had our library list. In addition, we had a list of books the teachers would like to have in class-size sets for teaching purposes.

Now for appeal to the final authority—the boys. First we had to arrange for the books to be obtained with the privilege of returning them. We knew that our list was intelligent, democratic, inclusive, unique. What we didn't know was whether it contained books the boys would read. If we spent the little money we had on books that would go unread, we might just as well have stocked our school library with all the hardbound books that nobody ever reads anyway and saved ourselves a good deal of trouble. Out of our need came the best experience we were to have at the Maxey School. We discovered the wise charity of Ivan Ludington Sr. and his Ludington News Company of Detroit.

The letter I wrote him was something less than a masterpiece. Only college presidents and skid-row bums are really good at begging. But the answer I got would have made a president proud and a bum delirious. Two days after I mailed the letter the phone in my office rang. Ivan Ludington speaking—what did I need and where did I need it? He would be glad to come to Ann Arbor to make arrangements. No, I would come to Detroit. Somehow that seemed to be the least I could do. It was. It was also the most I could do. Since then, Mr. Ludington has been supplying the school for almost three years with all the paperbound books and magazines we request—absolutely free of any charge. Thus far the numbers are upwards of 10,000 paperbacks and 25,000 magazines. Combine these figures with the equally remarkable generosity of that excellent paper, *The Detroit News* (one hundred copies a day, seven days a week), and the principle of saturation is vividly illustrated. But more about the Ludington story later.

Those of us who participated in selecting the original 1,200 titles for the Maxey paperback library will never again have to be reminded of how little we know about the students we teach. None of us will forget the untouched 700 titles that decorated our gleaming drugstore spinners while the boys read and reread the 500 they liked.

My private prediction for our list was that some 200 books might go unread, largely because they seemed to me to be either too difficult or too passive for a sixteen-year-old boy with a ninety I.Q. who reads at a fourth-grade level. But I had no doubt whatever that the remaining thousand were books the boys would read if we could display them attractively within an effective language program. I could hardly have been more mistaken. Not only was I one hundred percent wrong in my estimate of the number of successful books on our list, but seventy-five of the books I had thought would be ignored proved to be popular with the boys. The 500 winners of the book Derby are included in the Reading List (pp. 148-173) of *Hooked on Books*. . . .

One of the most common and most serious flaws in programs for poor readers is the relationship between the teacher and the material he uses to engage his students in the reading process. If the instructor does not take pleasure in the texts he uses, what then is the likelihood of pleasurable response from the pupil? The answer is not only obvious in the abstract, but all too obvious as well in schools I have visited, where texts were apparently chosen with neither the individual teacher nor the poor reader in mind. With these observations as a guide, I have refrained from prescribing specific classroom materials and have limited my specific suggestions to matters of type, format and style. I do not believe that desirable results will be obtained unless English teachers are offered a freedom of selection which allows them to consider both the students' needs and their own inclinations.

This recommendation also speaks of "creation" by the English teacher of his own reading materials. Stories, plays and essays written by the teacher who knows what his students' vocabularies really are, rather than what they should be; who knows particular facts rather than patent generalizations about their background, environment and aspirations; who knows, in short, his students as individuals rather than types—such reading materials can be of unequaled value in involving students in the process of reading and writing. In response to the objection that few people, even teachers of writing, are effective creative writers, the answer must be made that anyone who can tell a child a bedtime story, or recount a narrative he has read in a newspaper, book or magazine, can create stories, plays and essays appropriate as teaching devices. Any teacher who has not written such materials before is likely to be very pleasantly surprised at the ease with which he can create them and the readiness with which they are accepted by his students. . . .

The newspaper is in many ways an ideal text for the English class; its format, style and content all qualify it as an excellent vehicle for teaching reading and writing with special attention to the social point of view. The sense of informality and immediacy which the very presence of the newspaper conveys a sense so useful yet so difficult to achieve in many other kinds of literature, is also communicated in many magazines and softbound, pocket-size books. Each of these three types of literature provides readily available materials designed to engage the interest of the most reluctant reader; each therefore commends itself for considerable and continuing use in the English class. . . .

Cartoon books are an indispensable part of our library because they provide a temporary haven and refuge for students who doubt their ability to read. We have observed that many boys at Maxey, a community in which books have value and confer status, try to give themselves the protective coloration of being readers by picking up a cartoon book. More often than not, they're first hooked on the antics of Peanuts and Dennis the Menace and then hooked on the pleasures of reading. Is reading *Dennis the Menace* cartoons *really* reading? It is if you think it is. You may be looking mostly at pictures, but if Dennis and Charlie Brown can conspire to convince you that you're a reader *just like everyone else,* then you become a likely fish to swallow the bait of language when the line is attractively dangled. Experts may carp and the metaphor may flounder, but the child does neither. He reads. . . .

In addition to the two paperbound books from the library that each entering student is allowed to choose for his own, and the paperbound dictionary he is given to keep, he also receives from his English teacher at the beginning of the school year a spiral notebook. This is identified as his journal, an appropriate name for a notebook intended for daily use by every student. When he is given his journal, the student is told that quantity of production will be the only criterion for judging his writing. Content, style, grammar, rhetoric—all are insignificant compared to quantity. This journal, the student is told, has only one reason for existence: to provide you with a field upon which you can practice your writing. You will be required to write a minimum number of pages each week (two pages a week at Maxey and Garnet-Patterson), and you will be be asked each Thursday to turn in your journal to your English teacher who will return it on Friday. Your teacher will read your journal only if you invite him to read it. Under no circumstances, however, will your journal be corrected. It will be assessed for quantity, nothing else.

The use of the journal in the Garnet-Patterson Junior High School differs in one important way from its use at the Maxey School. Journals are given a cursory reading by the teachers in the public school. This is very different from the procedure of the training school, where the fact that the journal is never read by teachers, except by specific invitation, is one of its most attractive aspects from the boys' point of view. Journals can remain unread in the training school because a penal institution, no matter how progressive and enlightened, is still a closed system designed to remove offenders from society. Each member of the training school staff teaches and counsels there precisely because he understands that vituperation and obscenity are methods by which disturbed children may free themselves from some of the frustration and fear that shackle them to illiteracy. In the public schools, however, this problem must be handled very differently because of the public nature of all the students' school language, spoken or written. The simple expedient of telling the students that their notebooks will be glanced at each week, though neither read carefully nor corrected, largely solves the problem of preventing the use of publicly unacceptable words and ideas.

The quantitative view of writing has as a necessary corollary the permissive handling of journal entries by the teacher. Whether written inside or outside of class, whether legible or barely intelligible, whether a sentence, a paragraph or a page—each entry is another building block in the structure of the student's literacy. If the teacher can bring himself to regard the journal in this way, he will be equally satisfied with prose that is original and prose that is copied from a newspaper, a magazine or a book. And both he and his students will be more than satisfied with work which is evaluated by no one. If this permissiveness in the nature of the entry is closely coupled with an unvarying weekly check on the amount of production, then the formula for success in much of human enterprise—a little license with accompanying obligation—can make the journal an exceptionally useful teaching tool.

Teachers in the program have found that varying the pace of the journal's use by varying its place has been an especially successful teaching strategem. One teacher alternates weekly periods of using the journal in the classroom for brief writing assignments with having his students write outside of class. He has observed that he gets a good deal of personal writing outside of class, but that the diarist recedes into the background when the students are called upon to write in their journals in class. Furthermore, he has found that he gets surprisingly creative production when he reserves the last ten minutes of the hour rather than the first ten for journal writing.

In the early stages of the program at the Maxey School, a disappointingly small number of boys wrote more than the required minimum of two pages in their journals. We had half expected that the journal would be used by many as a kind of private stamping ground where they could work over their enemies, work out their fears, and work at the habit of writing. We were wrong; now, three years later, we know why. The journal became all we had expected it to be, and more, but instead of taking its anticipated and immediate place as a cause of change in student attitudes, it became a result of that change. As language took on real value, as speed with a dictionary and ability to write for the school newspaper and literary magazine became means for achieving peer esteem, the average weekly production in the journal increased slowly but surely. A page a day, once highly remarkable, became more usual, and five pages a day became the average output of one young man, who confided to his teacher that he'd written that much in the first fifteen days just to see if the school would really give him another notebook when he filled the first one. It would and did; he filled eight notebooks before he left the school.

Among the many creative uses found for the journal, one of the most interesting is the "good listening" device employed by one of the English teachers. The more she spoke with her students, the more she had come to believe that though they appeared to understand what she was saying—and, when asked, would claim that they did —they did not in fact usually understand her spoken directions. With this realization came the inspiration to employ the journal as a dictation workbook in which "listening good" became a challenging pursuit. A few days of this practice every two weeks has become a popular pastime with her students as they concentrate upon reproducing exactly what she is saying. She believes that the interest in her exact words which this exercise fosters carries over into closer attention to her words when interpretation rather than mere transcription is the requirement. . . .

Of the five other sets of papers received in every two-week period by instructors in subjects other than English, one set per week is read and commented upon for content by the class instructor, one set every two weeks is passed on by him to the students' English teacher who corrects grammar and rhetoric, and one set per week is filed *unread* in the students' folders. This treatment of one set of papers each week in every classroom recognizes and encourages the idea that the practice of writing may be distinguished from its performance. It offers the student opportunity to condition himself for performance by allowing him time to exercise his writing muscles. Filing one set of papers each week without either reading or correcting them serves as a constant reminder to English teacher and subject teacher alike of the real purpose of these continuing exercises—to develop the student's prose-writing muscles to the point where he can use them without fear of aches and strains. Until that point is reached, practice will be far more beneficial to the student than correction.

The idea of unread papers has long been rejected in American education on the basis that "children must have some tangible evidence that their efforts are appreciated or they won't work." Translation of this unchallengeable truth into the notion that everything a student writes may be read, or otherwise he won't write, is a tribute to the human capacity for the illogical. And whoever thought that "appreciation" and "reward" could be equated with papers covered by red-pencil corrections?

The unsurprising fact is that a child can be taught to practice writing, both in the classroom (brief papers) and outside of it (the journal), just as he can be taught to practice a musical instrument or an individual sport. Just as in music and sports, the key to practice in writing is expectation. Our experience at both the Garnet-Patterson and Maxey schools has been that even the worst students take some pleasure in the idea of uncorrected writing when they have been conditioned to expect and value their freedom to practice. . . .

A discussion of the journal would not be complete without the story of Lester. Lester came to the penal school by the surest of several possible routes; he got himself born a Negro. Having managed that, he proceeded to increase his chances greatly by growing up in his mother's care in Detroit's Negro ghetto. Get born a Negro, get raised by your mother on Detroit's East Side, and you've done about all you can to make it to a training school. The rest is a matter of luck.

Lester had the luck, all of it bad. If you're a white boy from a rural area, just drag race your car, badmouth the sheriff, and WHAM! B.T.S. But if you're a Negro or white boy from Detroit, you've got to go some to make the scene at Maxey. Lester went some. When he arrived at the school, he was sixteen years old and a habitual criminal. He had to be, to get one of the places reserved for Wayne County boys.

During his stay in the reception center at Whitmore Lake, Lester underwent testing designed to produce a sufficient paper identity for juvenile penal authorities to classify and assign him to one of five available programs throughout the state. The sum of the testing was that Lester was passive, that he would like to be in a school program, and that he functioned on a fourth-grade level at the age of sixteen. With that identity, Lester came to Maxey.

Perhaps the experience he remembers most clearly from his first day in class at B.T.S. is the large spiral notebook he was given and the accompanying directions for its use. He remembers being told that he would be expected to write at least two pages a week in that notebook, and that under no circumstances would anyone correct what he wrote.

"Suppose I can't think of two pages worth?" Lester may have asked the question. Someone always does.

"Then copy from a newspaper or a magazine or a book."

"Copy? ! ! !" The boys are always shocked and incredulous. In school, COPY is the dirtiest four-letter word they know. Punch your teacher in the nose. Break the windows and destroy the books. What can happen to you? Suspension? Probation? But whatever you do, and by all that's damned and dumb, *don't copy!* Because for that you get thrown out. They'd rather scrawl almost any other four-letter word on the walls of the toilet or locker room. But COPY! That's a word right out of the darkness. And a teacher just said to——(It's hard to bring yourself even to say the word.)

But they *do* copy. They copy and they copy and they copy. Then they copy some more. The modern, no-holds-barred record for copying at B.T.S. is forty-five pages in the first week. Teachers are grateful, however, if they get two. One youngster, who had never read it before, was fascinated by *Time* magazine. For weeks he copied from the same well-worn issue. His teacher was delighted. Not only had he probably written more in that brief period than he had written before in his life, but his conversation was full of the things he was reading. During that period he passed from truculent reserve to something like happy participation in his English and social studies classes. (Our suggestion to the courts that, having copied an entire issue of *Time,* he had been punished sufficiently for his crimes, did not receive the attention it deserved.)

A few boys with remarkable stamina copy the bulk of their journal work throughout the entire academic year. Most get tired of copying, however, especially where no teacher renews its attraction by forbidding it. And so most go naturally to the next stage of journal usage— the diary. For almost all the boys this second stage is also the final stage of their journal development. Like the majority of his fellows, Lester filled his journal with the thoughts and happenings of his daily life. Unlike his peers, most of whom wrote little more than the prescribed two pages each week, Lester wrote and wrote and wrote. Fourth-grade attainment on a test validated upon white middle-class children by white middle-class adults would have meant nothing to him. He liked to write; he discovered he liked to write by writing.

What Lester wrote at first gave his teacher bad dreams. The truth is that most of the teachers at the Maxey School (and at other training schools where the *English in Every Classroom* program has been adopted) occasionally do read their students' journals. But no comment is ever made to the student, *no matter what he writes.* The journals are sometimes read, in spite of the teachers' original promise, because the information they contain can be so helpful to the psychologists and social workers who must deal with the child's welfare outside the classroom and, eventually, after he leaves the school. Precisely because a boy's increasingly erratic conduct had sent his English teacher to his journal, in an attempt to understand his behavior, we have had the experience at B.T.S. of being able to anticipate and to treat the causes rather than the symptoms of a boy's "going high."

Lester filled his pages with the sickness of an adolescent tortured by every confusion and every desire—magnified unbearably by intelligence and incarceration. One obscene word repeated six to eight times on each line for seven full pages is an index to the depth from which Lester viewed the world above him. He was striking out with the only weapon he had. With patience and understanding, the only weapons *she* had, his English teacher waited. And waited and waited and waited. Neither she nor any of us could have said exactly what it was she waited for. But we all knew that Lester had to get that sickness up and out before anything good could come from him.

Then, before class on a Thursday morning (the journals are collected each Thursday and returned the next day, after having been checked for quantity), Lester brought his journal to his teacher and told her to read it. She reports that her knees got weak and she felt suddenly queasy as she tried to guess what he had spilled onto the page. "Lester," she began, "I don't think that I . . . uh . . . well, that I should. . . ." She had intended to say that she would read it later or that evening or next year . . . but she knew he meant *now* and she had to read it *now*. She remembers the sensation of narrowing her eyes against the shock as she opened the notebook.

It was a poem. A nice, inconsequential piece of verse carefully divided into four stanzas of four lines each and painstakingly rhymed on alternate lines. Some sixth sense reserved for teachers in a bad spot told her not to ask him why he wanted her to read a poem she recognized as having been copied from a daily newspaper. Instead, she praised it. And she praised poetry. And she praised the writing of poetry. Her praise included the people who write poetry, because they find it helps them to say what they mean. She was fishing, and he was watching her like a hawk waiting for the right catch before he swooped. She was running out of words and ideas when he suddenly reached inside his shirt and drew out a sheaf of papers covered with his own handwriting.

It was poetry. Some of it. Some was just doggerel verse. And some was nothing at all. But Lester had been trying to write poetry for months, not quite knowing how, not knowing whether or to whom to show it, failing often, giving way to emotions he couldn't control and couldn't express, and, occasionally, succeeding. His teacher praised it as much as she dared. Now that he had come out into the open, she had to be careful to give him no cause, including effusiveness, to return to heavy cover.

Lester brought in new poems before every English class. The poem copied from the newspaper, his own sheaf of poems finally revealed, the teacher who didn't snigger or patronize—all had combined to break the wall Lester had been building for all his sixteen years. The breach became a spillway down which Lester poured.

"Miss Farnell, can I publish my poems?"

Put yourself behind the teacher's desk. What do you reply? But Lester didn't mean that he wanted to publish a book. He only wanted to make a mimeographed booklet —a sheaf of papers prefaced by a title and his name—for distribution within the school itself. Certainly a booklet like that should be easy enough to make, even in a training school? Yes, and easy to distribute. But impossible to recall, once distributed.

Lester was in the midst of the most significant change-process of his life. The changes were so radical that they hardly seemed real. A relatively few months of accomplishment—perhaps the first unqualified success of his life —had begun a process powerful enough to change a passive, effeminate, obnoxious boy into an aggressive, masculine, obnoxious boy. But the process was reversible. And the fearful vision that haunted his teacher was the reception those poems might receive in the school.

For what is a poet in a training school? He walks with a certain lightness of foot, you can hear him swish as he passes, and, baby, in a training school that is VERY BAD. So bad that we would have given a great deal to spare Lester the experience. He had been promised an answer to his request on the following day. Our collective decision to publish the poems was based, finally, on the simplest of reasons—none of us had the strength to say no. But our "yes" was weak and worried. The poems were mimeographed and distributed throughout the school. We held our breath.

Of all our private predictions, varying from hot disaster to cold indifference, none dared to be as hopeful as reality. None of us, barricaded within the assumptions of our middle-class worlds, foresaw the eminence that poetry would bring to Lester at B.T.S. And we were even less capable of foreseeing the value that Lester's writing would give to poetry at B.T.S. One type of book we had omitted completely from our original paperback library was the poetry anthology and the book of poems by a single author. If we were collectively certain of anything, it was that these boys had never willingly read poetry in their lives and were unlikely to begin at B.T.S. We think somewhat less now of collective certainty. Lester's poems were published. Lester was lionized. And we were overwhelmed by the discovery of thirty-five poets in the Maxey School population.

Lester published two further collections before he completed his stay at Maxey. With each publication, the group's view of Lester and poetry (and Lester's view of himself) changed profoundly. Lester saw something in himself to value, and his peers saw something in poetry. Lester is long gone from Maxey, but the librarian is still having trouble meeting the demand for books of poetry.

What began as an improbable story ends as an impossible fantasy. As Lester underwent the dramatic change from a passive to an aggressive human being, from a local laugh to a local leader, his aspirations changed as well. To him, the world of the W. J. Maxey Boys' Training School at Whitmore Lake became even smaller than it was. Lester wanted to copyright his extensive production of poetry. Acting upon the advice of his English teacher, Lester wrote to Congressman Weston Vivian, Democrat, then representing Michigan's Second District, of which Whitmore Lake is a part. Lester sent along his poems with a letter inquiring about copyright. Mr. Vivian's response was predictable—if you still believe in the Age of Miracles. All this remarkable Congressman did was to read one of Lester's poems into the *Congressional Record,* get Vice President Humphrey's autograph on a copy of that edition of the *Record,* fly to Detroit, motor to Whitmore Lake, and present the autographed copy to Lester at an assembly of the entire school. No one will ever be able to assess accurately what Mr. Vivian's visit did directly for Lester's ego, vicariously for those of his fellow students, and incidentally for the causes of poetry and literacy at Maxey. The results of that visit are still being tallied.

Because improbability is boundless, Lester's story has a sequel. After his release from B.T.S., Lester called his teacher regularly to report on his activities. A few months after his release I walked into the school library one afternoon to find her staring vacantly past the spinners full of paperbound books.

"Lester called this morning." I could barely hear the words.

"What's wrong?" Nobody makes it, I thought. Even Lester.

"He says he just got a five hundred dollar check from a publisher for his poems."

It was true. Improbable. Impossible. Nevertheless true.

Another B.T.S. alumnus who keeps in touch with his former teachers came to visit the school sometime after Lester's telephone call. He was able to verify the story with the best kind of evidence—he had *seen* the check. It was no surprise to him, he said. "When that cat come from Washing Town," he told us, "everybody *know* Lester going to be *the man.*"

Ten Minutes a Day

Herbert Kohl

from *The Open Classroom*

People who have been students in authoritarian class-rooms cannot expect themselves to develop their own open classrooms easily. I started out as an authoritarian teacher. It was the only way I knew to teach; the way I had been taught. It took several years before I was able to function in a freer environment. Indeed, the students were much more ready for freedom than their teacher was. Perhaps it was better to start tentatively than to pretend that a change had come over me suddenly, and to try to turn everything upside down in the classroom. My beliefs in a free, non-authoritarian classroom always ran ahead of my personal ability to teach in one.

There are several ways to experiment in the classroom. It depends upon who the teacher is. One ought not to try something basically incompatible with one's personal-ity. It is likely to cause frustration and hostility, and to make further experimentation seem more dangerous than it really is. A crucial thing to realize is that changing the nature of life in the classroom is no less difficult than changing one's own personality, and every bit as danger-ous and time-consuming. It is also as rewarding.

The starting point of change is discontent. If you are perfectly content with an authoritarian style of teaching and pleased with your pupil's lives in the classroom there, an attempt to change will be pointless. Some of the best authoritarian teachers, often charming and brilliant people who succeed in persuading young people to perform what the school demands and to like it at the same time, may find change irrelevant.

If, on the other hand, the authoritarian mode is distressing—if being an unquestioned authority is too difficult and unpleasant a role to sustain, if the boredom of your pupils or the irrelevance of what they are learning distresses you, then perhaps other approaches should be tried. Before doing so you should try to think as honestly as you can about your teaching experience and try to articulate to yourself or a friend what it is that makes you want to change. It also may be of use to remember yourself as a pupil in school—to think back to your early experiences of frustration, joy, anxiety, learning, boredom in the classroom. I found that my memories of school helped me to avoid doing hateful things to my pupils that my teachers had done to me. This isn't to say that you will be able to make a list of all that's troubling you. But it is a good way to begin perceiving the classroom as a place where strong and interesting experiences take place, rather than one where the objective performances of students are measured.

One way to begin a change is to devote ten minutes a day to doing something different. There is never any problem of finding ten minutes to play with, since what the pupils "must cover" is usually padded in order to fill up time. During that ten minutes present the class with a number of things they can choose to do. Present them with options you feel may interest them. Allow them the option of sitting and doing nothing if they choose. Moreover, make it clear that nothing done during that period will be graded, and nothing need be shown or explained to the teacher. That ten minutes is to be their time and is to be respected as such. Step out of the way and observe the things your pupils choose to do.

Step out of the way, but don't disappear. Make it clear that you won't tell people what to do or how to do it, but that you will be available to help in any way you can, or just to talk. For ten minutes cease to be a teacher and be an adult with young people, a resource available if needed, and possibly a friend, but not a director, a judge, or an executioner. Also try to make it possible for the ten minutes to grow to fifteen, twenty, so long as it makes sense to you and your pupils. It is not unlikely that those ten minutes may become the most important part of the day, and after a while may even become the school day.

Some specific hints on the use of the ten minutes:

—in English class it is possible to read, write (set three or four themes and leave it open for students to develop other ones), talk, act.

—in mathematics the students can set problems, solve problems, build computers, compute, design buildings (or other structures or things), talk about money, set problems for each other and the teacher.

—in social studies it is possible to talk about history; about newspapers, events, people; write about them; compose or listen to poems, play songs about them; talk or invite people in to talk about what's happening.

—in all classes students can do nothing, gossip, write, start a newspaper, a newsletter, listen to music, dance, talk about or play games, bring in things that may interest the teacher or other students and talk about them, write about them . . . .

Think about what is happening during those ten minutes and learn to be led by the students. If certain things are particularly interesting to one group, find out about those things, learn as much as you can, and, seeing their interest, present them with ways of getting more deeply into what they care about. If, for example, a group of students is interested in animals and their relationship to people, you can refer them to fables, to Konrad Lorenz, to experimental psychology, to whatever you can discover yourself. And if you don't know about such matters find someone who does, and invite him to class to meet your pupils.[1] Then—and this is crucial—step out of the way

---

[1] It is always a good idea to bring as many non-teachers into your classroom as possible. Painters, writers, businessmen, journalists all have valuable experience to offer young people that teachers don't have. So do people who have no specific vocations to talk about.

again. Do not insist that because you have uncovered all these new options for your students that they *must* pursue them. Maintain your own freedom from the authoritarian mode and help your students maintain their freedom, however modest it may be. Learn, though it is difficult, to allow your students to say, "No," to what you want them to learn no matter how much stake you have in it. This means that one must understand one's own stake in making young people learn what one wants them to learn and not take it overseriously. Teachers must develop a sense of what they look like to young people and understand how pointless and even funny it can seem to young people to see adults losing their cool over someone's refusal to take the division of fractions or the imagery in Act I of Macbeth seriously. . . .

TROUBLES WITH STUDENTS

Students are no more used to making choices and functioning in a free environment than their teachers are. We have all been taught to obey and be dependent, and breaking the habit of dependency is difficult. Consequently when one tries to develop an open classroom the students themselves will often be bewildered and frustrated at first. They will even at times insist that the teacher tell them what to do.

Last year I taught a special class in education at the University of California, Berkeley. The class was to be free and open, and the students could pursue whatever they wanted to. For the first three meetings members of the class sat around and bitched because I refused to tell them what to do. They wanted to know what I wanted them to do and since I had nothing in mind for them they were angry. I even got a sense that they felt rejected because they weren't directed. It took over a month for people to begin to look about and examine their school careers, sort out what they wanted to learn about and what they needed to forget. As it turned out, some students wanted to write poetry, others to study the high school curriculum, and most of the students wanted to find out about each other. We all realized that they had been at college for three or four years, sat in innumerable classes looking at their professors and never knew the people who sat next to them.

I considered my role in that class was to bring in things to share with the students and to be available to help them. I brought books and articles and poems to class, and left them there. Sometimes we talked about them though often we didn't. However, my bringing what I cared about to the class made it easier for them to bring things that were important to them.

One has to be patient with freedom and have as rich an environment as possible available for students so there will be things they can choose to do. One cannot ask pupils to be free or make choices in a vacuum. There is no limit to what can be brought to class to enrich the environment. A partial list would include:

—second-hand books
—old magazines
—scraps of wood, metal, and cloth discarded by factories
—old billboard posters
—parts of broken machines—cars, TVs, radios, toasters, etc.
—tape recorders and tape
—old toys
—old clothes to be used to create a classroom costume closet
—a sewing machine and needles and thread
—discarded advertising materials such as signs, posters, booklets, sales tags, handbills
—comfortable old furniture or rugs
—light fixtures, flashlights, wire, bulbs, batteries
—typewriters
—posters and buttons of all sorts

Children will use materials brought into the classroom and left around in the most unexpected ways. Recently a friend offered me a ton of balsa wood to use with my class and I readily accepted. He arrived a few days later with three ocean liner life rafts cut up in sections. Some were six feet long, others nine and twelve feet. Many of the pieces were rounded at the ends. He dumped the whole pile in the back yard and showed me that beneath the canvas, the life rafts were indeed made out of balsa wood and glue in about equal proportions. The balsa wood was not retrievable and in despair I just let the rafts lie in the back yard for several months. One day several of my students decided to paint the sections and bring them into our room. After a few days all of our chairs were replaced by the life rafts. They made wonderful room dividers, seats, and tables. Also, when piled on top of each other they made a cozy little house or boat for the kids to play in. Every day the rafts were used in different ways. The students saw in those forms possibilities I had never imagined.

Being free enough to let the kids explore such possibilities is not easy. As Zelda Wirtschafter, a teacher with a good deal of experience in work with open classrooms, has put it:

> Helping teachers to understand that there is nothing sacrosanct about the standard curriculum outlines—and that providing children with the opportunity and resources to explore their own questions is far more important and valid a learning experience than "covering" a paper sequence of topics—is to my mind the overriding problem of the day. My experience has been that once teachers free themselves of the feeling that they "are not teaching their kids anything," and learn to perceive as real learning the activities and questions and conversations which develop spontaneously in their classrooms, they become much more confident and relaxed and many of the former problems of control simply disappear.

ON SELECTING A SCHOOL FOR YOUR TRAINING

If you can, pick a school of education that is small and inconspicuous. Avoid large conservative institutions like Teachers College, Columbia, and the University of California, Berkeley. The big places are likely to be more conventional than the smaller ones and are likely to give less conventional, freer teachers a much more difficult time. The greater the reputation an institution has to defend, the more resistant it is to change. Schools of education that consider themselves little more than "credential factories" are more likely to let one through than schools with a "philosophy." This may seem an excessively cynical view, yet it has been my experience that very little of interest is happening in *any* school of education and therefore if one wants credentials one might as well get it in the easiest and least painful way.

What Can You Learn . . . ?

Richard Saul Wurman, editor

from *Yellow Pages of Learning Resources*

EDITOR'S NOTE

This booklet is only a handshake with a city. We hope that it will serve as a welcome mat to the endless possibilities for learning all around you. We hope it will reduce your anxieties about using your community as the schoolhouse it really is, and we hope, in turn, you will add greatly to our brief listings. . . .

INTRODUCTION

What is the *Yellow Pages of Learning Resources?*

The city is education—and the architecture of education rarely has much to do with the building of schools. The city is a schoolhouse, and its ground floor is both bulletin board and library. The graffiti of the city are its window displays announcing events; they should reveal its people to themselves, tell about what they're doing and why and where they're doing it. Everything we do—if described, made clear, and made observable—is education: the "Show and Tell," the city itself.

This book is concerned with the potential of the city as a place for learning.

Education has been thought of as taking place mainly within the confines of the classroom, and school buildings have been regarded as the citadels of knowledge. However, the most extensive facility imaginable for learning is our urban environment. It is a classroom without walls, an open university for people of all ages offering a boundless curriculum with unlimited expertise. If we can make our urban environment comprehensible and observable, we will have created classrooms with endless windows on the world.

What is the *Yellow Pages of Learning Resources?*

This book is an invitation to discover the city as a learning resource.

The purpose of the *Yellow Pages* is to turn people on to learning in the city and to assist them in taking advantage of the wealth of available learning opportunities. There are three basic parts to this invitation. First, the *Yellow Pages* provides a selection of typical firsthand learning resources that can be found in almost any city. These examples and the others they suggest serve to make vivid the richness of learning potential readily at our disposal. The examples of typical learning resources included in the *Yellow Pages* are intended to indicate the depth and breadth of available learning possibilities. There are thousands of others that might have been considered had there been time and room enough. You will find those that most interest you. The key is to start realizing the learning potential in the people, places, and processes we encounter every day.

Second, the *Yellow Pages* outlines the avenues to follow in order to make these resources accessible. This is the "where" and "how" of converting people, places, and processes into sources of learning. The aim of this book is to encourage readers, through the examples provided, to extend their own entrepreneurial abilities to locate and utilize additional resources for learning. The extent of accessible learning resources is limited only by the reader's imagination and sensitivity to his environment.

We believe that schools are the places for education, and most of the time we know when we are being taught. As a result, most of us are apathetic when it comes to self-learning. We have television, light shows, teaching machines, cinerama, and a whole host of simulation techniques—a vast technology for making the artificial seem real. But in the glamor of our sophisticated informational and educational technologies we often fail to appreciate the reality in our everyday lives; we no longer place a premium on experiential learning. Reality is frequently too obvious, and we are rapidly becoming jaded. Too often we no longer look carefully, listen intently, or yield to our innate sense of wonder.

Yet the city is everywhere around us, and it is rife with invaluable learning resources. Even more than classrooms and teachers, the most valuable learning resources in the city are the people, places, and processes that we encounter every day. But in order to realize the vast learning potential of these resources, we must learn to learn from them.

We should learn to differentiate between products and performance. We must learn to use the city, to explore. We must learn not to overlook the obvious. We must learn to hear when we listen, to see when we look, to ask questions, and to realize that good questions are better than brilliant answers. We must learn to demand from our city that it fulfill its potential as a learning resource. Each of us should recognize his role as the developer of an invitation to learning.

We should be concerned about real experiences and encourage the development of new learning situations that are independent of traditional books and learning products, which focus on student experiences in classrooms and school buildings. We should be interested in the identification and the subsequent communication of the elements that make up the man-made environment. We should understand the need to develop the skills and abilities to communicate information about the environment both verbally and nonverbally. We should create in a student the confidence that will enable him to develop the criteria that might be used in the evaluation or creation of his own environments. And we should remember that we are all students. We should encourage a sense of ownership of the city and define the extent of the public environment. We should see the "environment issue," not simply as the causes and effects of air and water pollution, but in broader terms: the understanding of the total physical environment, both public and private.

This book is full of questions. These are provided in order to suggest how rich the learning resources can be and to cultivate the learning process by planting the seeds of inquiry. Questions, rather than answers, are the beginning of learning, but too often we find it difficult to pose good questions. . . .

What Can You Learn from a Butcher?

Fred has been a butcher for twelve years and says he could tell you "everything you want to know" about the trade. I met him in the small meat market near where I work. When I asked the first butcher I saw behind the counter if I could ask him a few questions, he directed me at once to Fred. Fred is the "meat man" and says the best training comes from actually handling the meat and from the meat itself. He thinks that butcher school is largely a waste of time ("You don't cut nothing in butcher school—guys out of there don't know pork from lamb") and that you learn the trade only when you start working. He himself received no school training ("You don't learn nothing about it from books") but started out in a chain store twelve years ago. He outlined for me the grades of beef, his specialty—prime, choice, good, commercial, utility, standard—and told me what each means. Grade, he explained, means how, where, and how much the cow was fed. Lamb, on the other hand, is all one grade. Pork, too, is usually one grade, but again it depends on how, where, and how much the pig was fed. Fred added that there is a shortage of meat cutters, even though a 40-hour a week apprentice makes $240 a week. A meat cutter (as Fred described it, "No slaughter. We get the meat once it's dead") specializes in meat, chicken, fish, or deli (lunch meat, cold cuts, potato salad—Fred didn't have much respect for this position). I got the impression that the meat man was the top man. Each step means different pay. Of the 1,000 butchers in this city, Fred said, about 900 are unionized and work in small markets like this one, wholesale or retail stores, hospitals, hotels, and in the big chain stores.

When I asked about meat and consumer protection, Fred explained that years ago powder, seasoning, and chemicals were sometimes added to the meat to help it retain its color and make it look fresh but that now strict governmental regulations prevent this.

As Fred and I talked (Fred in blood-spattered apron and white coat and me across the deli case from him leaning against the glass), Lou, the "chicken man," came over and, while Fred took care of a customer, told me about his specialty. After the chickens are eviscerated, that is, all cleaned with the liver, gizzard, heart, and neck in a plastic bag inside, he cuts them up into legs, breasts, and wings. He makes five-pound bags of legs and breasts, a special item of the store, and puts the rest out for sale separately. He told me they get their chickens from a packing house, which gets them from farmers. He, too, explained grade to me, this time of chicken. Chicken, he said, is usually either A or B grade; these include broiler (a two-pound chicken at two cents a pound), fryer (a three-pounder), capon (a "denatured" rooster, usually five to nine pounds and used as a roasting chicken), stewers (which, at the time we talked, were "too expensive" and the store was not carrying them), duck (which they get when the price is right), as well as cornish hens. Steak, he told me, keeps less than a week, while chicken can stay safely refrigerated for one week. He rotates the refrigerator case (that deli case I was leaning on) daily so that yesterday's chicken is sold first today. Prices for all the meat and fish, Lou said, come from a "market sheet," which comes to the boss in the mail—Lou didn't know from where.

Business was picking up so Lou had to go, but everyone I met there was happy to pause when he had the time and talk and tell about what he did. Next time I visit, I'm going to try to get on the other side of that deli case to see that Pennsylvania beef and those Iowa pork loins close up. As Fred said, "It's up to the individual what he learns."

What Can You Learn About Candy Making?

Mom used to hide the candy way up on the top of the bookcase, where I couldn't reach it. I remember thinking how neat it would be to be grown up and have tons of candy whenever I wanted. I figured that if I worked in a candy store, I could spend all day picking at chocolate covered cherries, gumdrops, and enormous, shiny lemon sticks.

Someone told me that in some candy stores the people don't just sell the candy, they make it as well. I imagined myself working in one of those stores someday, mixing up caramel and nuts, coconut and marshmallows, and creating all kinds of wild combinations. But it takes forever to grow up, and when you *really* love candy, it's awfully hard to wait. So I looked in the Yellow Pages. And under a listing of "Candy—Confectionery, Retail," I found a store that advertised homemade candy and that wasn't too far from my home.

Before I even reached the store, I could smell the cocoa. There were some people shopping in the store. After they left, the woman behind the counter asked me what I wanted, and I explained that I wanted to learn about candy making. She took me through a door into the back of the store where there was another woman stirring a huge pot on a stove. Mrs. Wimble—that was the stirrer—said she'd be happy to let me watch. She told me to guess what was in the pot. It was easy—nothing smells as pungent as peppermint. She used a big candy thermometer, which told her when the sugary mixture was just hot enough, and then she began to drip swirls of the peppermint onto a big slab of marble.

"Have one," she said. It was terrific. While she worked, Mrs. Wimble explained that many candy stores get their candy from factories, and that the name and address of the factory is printed on every box. So any time I wanted to see a really big operation, I should go to a factory, where candy is made by machines, instead of people.

When the peppermints were done, she picked up a huge basket of strawberries and sat down with them next to a pot of melted chocolate.

"Chocolate-dipped strawberries are very perishable," she said. "They must be eaten within a day or two." One by one, she dipped the berries in the chocolate and stuck them on toothpicks to dry. I'd never heard of putting strawberries and chocolate together. I wanted to make one myself, but Mrs. Wimble said she couldn't afford any mistakes. She suggested that I try my own candy making at home.

"Look up candy in a cookbook," she said. "Start with something easy, like fudge. Then work your way up." She gave me lots of hints on candy making. For example, you can't make good hard candies in a moist, hot atmosphere—they get sticky and sugary. She also told me to be sure the pot I used would hold four times as much as the ingredients, so that the syrup wouldn't boil over the top. Candies that call for butter, cream, milk, chocolate, or molasses are apt to burn if they're not stirred continuously the whole time they're cooking. Most of the ingredients I'd need would probably be in the kitchen already. The only investment I'd have to make would be for the candy thermometer, which the cookbook would tell me how to use.

Before I left, Mrs. Wimble gave me her peppermint drop recipe:

    2 cups of sugar
    ¼ cup of corn syrup
    ¼ cup of milk
    ¼ teaspoon cream of tartar

Cook and stir slowly until the candy thermometer reads 238 degrees. Cool slightly. Beat 'til creamy. Flavor with ½ teaspoon peppermint and add some food coloring if you want. Drop from a teaspoon onto waxed paper.

I was in such a hurry to get home and start, I almost forgot the bag of candy Mrs. Wimble gave me when she said good-bye.

WHAT CAN YOU LEARN FROM A CARPENTER?

In order to learn from a carpenter, your first task will be to find one. This can be done in several ways. You can (1) ask a friend if he or she knows a carpenter, (2) look for one at a construction site, (3) hang around a lumberyard, (4) look one up in the telephone book under "Carpenters," (5) call or visit a local carpenters' union, (6) visit a cabinet shop, or (7) listen for the sound of wood being sawed. Even if the carpenter you succeed in finding is not very talkative you can learn a lot by just watching. But chances are the carpenter you meet will willingly share his knowledge with you. I haven't met a carpenter yet who didn't enjoy talking about his trade.

A good strategy is to start by asking him where he learned his skills and how he decided to become a carpenter. Are there schools where carpenters learn their trade? Do carpenters take on and train apprentices? How does the carpenter's union operate? Next you can ask him to demonstrate how he uses his tools. If you can get the carpenter to describe what each of his tools is and how each works, you are off to a flying start. Make sure you get a chance to watch him work and use his tools—that's the best part.

Find out how he measures in different kinds of situations. Ask him to explain the concepts of "tolerance," "straight," "true," and "plumb" for you. See how he makes joints and how he turns corners with wood (therein lies a great deal of the art of carpentry), and ask him to tell you about the wood he's working with. What are its characteristics? Find out how he selects particular woods for particular jobs. How does he know which screw sizes and what nails are appropriate? Can he build without using nails or screws? See if he will let you try out his tools, but be prepared for a possible *no* answer. The carpenter's tools are his best friends, and an amateur can all but ruin an otherwise fine instrument by using it improperly. Part of the key to getting a difficult carpentry job done well is having the right tool for each job and knowing how to use it.

Some of the most interesting things to watch the carpenter doing include the following:

Making drawers
Hanging a door
Building stud walls
Finishing dry wall or sheetrock
Making cabinets
Building a roof
Laying a floor
Restoring old woodwork
Building a set of stairs
Installing a window frame and jamb

If after watching the carpenter, you should decide to try your hand at woodworking, start small and be prepared for mistakes and frustration. The carpenter will have probably made the job look a lot easier than it really is. And, although carpentry isn't difficult, there's a natural tendency for novices to underestimate the skill required to do it well. This could be a good place to augment experiential learning with some basic texts.

After learning from a carpenter you may want to extend your experience by watching other specialized woodworkers display their skills. For example, find a furniture maker or factory and learn how furniture is made. Perhaps you can locate an architectural model maker and watch scale models of buildings and urban designs being made. An industrial designer who makes scale models of prototype designs would also be fascinating. Or find an exhibit designer who builds museum displays or exhibits. If there are theaters nearby, you can stop in and see how carpentry skills are used to make theater sets. How many other places in the city can you find where carpentry skills are being applied in special ways?

A good carpenter can drive a 6d (penny) nail with three strokes: the first to start the nail, the second to drive it all but in, and the third to set it. Wow!

WHAT CAN YOU LEARN AT A CEMETERY?

"Death is nothing to us, since when we are, death has not come, and when death has come, we are not."
—Epicurus Diogenes Lairtius (born in 412 B.C.)

But when we are not, we leave our sign in a cemetery for others to see. Find a cemetery (look in the Yellow Pages, try next to a church, ask a clergyman, call City Hall, call a funeral home, read death notices in a newspaper) and walk around.

Watch the people who come there, and begin to think of all the people, in addition to the deceased and his friends and relatives, who may be involved for the death of each person buried in this one cemetery:

1. Undertaker
2. Clergyman
3. Tombstone engraver
4. Funeral director
5. Embalmer
6. Grave digger
7. Cemetery maintenance crew
8. Gardeners and security personnel
9. Florist
10. Caterer
11. Casket maker
12. Organist
13. Coroner
14. Cemetery architects and designers
15. Doctor
16. Newspaper writer
17. Personnel in City Hall's Vital Statistics Department
18. Personnel at the morgue
19. Personnel at the crematorium
20. Sympathy card publishers and staff

What is the role of each of the above? How has it changed over the years, and how does it differ depending upon money paid for services?

Watch funeral parties arrive at the cemetery and compare them. Who arrives first? Is there a pecking order of cars? Are people dressed a certain way? What is considered to be proper decorum, or behavior, in this situation? What religious rites take place and what is their significance? Do they tell you anything about the people's religious or ethnic backgrounds? What are the various roles of the grieving and their friends and relatives?

Look at the layout of the cemetery. Who designed it? When was it laid out? Have the needs and therefore the layout changed? Is there a minimum amount of space needed for each dead person? Who owns the cemetery? Are there zoning ordinances? Check with the water department or an engineer for rules governing drainage pipes. Is there a certain pervasion of one color throughout the cemetery? Are there flowers around? What kind? Are they left on special occasions or holidays?

Look at tombstones and notice especially the dates on them. Has the material they are made from changed? What has been the effect of time and weather? Have epitaphs changed? Look at tombstones from the same year. Are there differences in stone or style among them? Did people seem to die at a younger age a hundred years ago? Is there one year that has many deaths? If so, check in City Hall for records of a plague or epidemic. Look at the architecture of large tombs. Can you distinguish differences in religion, social and economic class, and time from the words and the materials? Who composes the message on the tombstone?

How much does death cost, and where can you die? How do you buy a plot, and who buys a plot? For how much? Can you get into a cemetery without a reservation? Are there laws against discrimination? Are there such things as public and private cemeteries? How is a body shipped? Do you have to be a U.S. citizen to be buried here? What laws govern the digging up of a body? Is there insurance to cover burial costs, or can it be covered and paid for by a will?

Who visits a cemetery? What do people do in a cemetery when they visit? Is the cemetery only open at certain times? Is there much vandalism?

WHAT CAN YOU LEARN FROM A CHILD?

Being a child is not easy, you know. I keep changing. Just as I get used to some new part of my body, I find another. You can learn a lot from me. Those first years when I am an infant, you should watch me grow; my muscles and limbs change; I learn to hear and recognize my favorite animals and people; I learn to sit as my back strengthens. When I am young, you could see how my eating habits change, how my need for sleep changes, how I cry for special reasons with special cries.

Talk to my mother, my pediatrician. Compare me to others exactly my age and mark our growth; compare me to what the books say. What month was it when I first saw that mobile? When was the first time I grabbed for it? The first time I could take it to my mouth? The first time I dropped it and was able to remember where I dropped it and then put it where I wanted it?

Look at my eyes and the shape of my head. Compare the proportions of the different parts of my body with the proportions of yours. Watch how my hair and fingernails grow. Did I crawl before I walked? Did I stand before I crawled?

Watch other people's reactions to me. Listen to how they talk to me. Do people talk to me the way they would talk to you, or do they use a special language or tone of voice? Do people bring me up to them, do they come down to me, or do they tower over me?

Where can you find me? I'm next door, at your aunt's, in the room next to yours, at the baby doctor's, in the day nursery, in a kindergarten room, in the park with my mother or babysitter. I can be found in strollers, cribs, playpens, tubs, swingamatics, backpacks, bassinets, and in people's arms.

I'm really pretty wonderful!

Getting the Students Involved in Teaching-Learning

Helaine Dawson

---

from *On the Outskirts of Hope*

Role Playing

At the end of each session, I reflected on and evaluated what had happened. Was I reaching the students? How well were we communicating? Were they listening more? Were they more involved? Did I notice any changes in behavior or habits? Were they developing more hopefulness? Was their span of attention increasing? Was hostility lessening? How could I draw out nonparticipants?

At the beginning of each program I met resistance to my methods. I did not lay down the law, but made them think. I was concerned about giving them opportunities to communicate and express whatever was bothering them. When the students saw how I reacted to their provocativeness and defiance, they accepted me. This might take several weeks.

In order to arouse their attention and sustain it for increasingly longer periods, I experimented with various techniques. Among these was role playing. This served many purposes related to our objectives and to each student's needs. It helped the student to communicate and listen; it made him aware of his relationship to others and of the need to cooperate; and it enabled him to understand himself better. Being able to step outside of himself and see how others look at him was another step on his road to self-development. Role playing could make learning pleasant rather than formidable and boring. It could also be a vehicle for creativity.

Role playing is simply assuming a role. Children often get so involved in role playing that they forget about eating. Psychiatrists call it "psychodrama." Sociologists refer to it as "sociodrama."

The time for introducing role playing will depend on how well you are getting along with your students and how well you are relating. It takes at least five weeks or more to reach the point where role playing can take place. Introducing this activity prematurely may bring about bedlam and consequently destroy its potential value as a teaching-learning technique.

"All right. Today we're going to try something different. We've talked about hair styles, attitudes, and the importance of speech. We've been learning vocabulary each day. Now let's see if we can use some of it." All eyes were focused on me. "We're going to make up our own skit. We'll use no prepared scripts. We won't rehearse. Do you know a word that describes doing something on the spur of the moment creatively?" We learned the words *spontaneous* and *improvise*. "We'll improvise and operate spontaneously."

In the general office clerk program, Wilbert asked, "How do we know what to say?"

"You'll react to each other depending on the situation. You'll respond to the other person. Let's work it out, and you'll see what I mean. We're going to pretend that this is an office." I pointed to my desk at the front of the room. "Make believe this is an IBM office." I wrote it on the blackboard: INTERNATIONAL BUSINESS MACHINES.

"Gee, I never knew it meant that," said Bailey.

"Now, our cast. We need a receptionist. Who wants to be the receptionist at IBM?"

Rosetta volunteered. "What must I do?" she asked. This gave me an opportunity to find out what these students being trained as general office clerks knew about duties of a receptionist.

"Answer the phone," said Susie.

"Smile," said Jim, the gang leader.

"Know the business," said Dick.

"Good. Let's begin with an applicant for a clerical job. Who wants to be the applicant?" Jim volunteered.

"While you're watching, be observing how Jim and Rosetta walk, listen to how they talk and how they answer the telephone if they do. Jot notes down. Then we'll discuss your comments. Remember the criteria we use to come to our conclusions."

The Pacific Telephone Company, through its school department, had loaned us teletrainers. These consisted of a pair of colored telephones with a transmission box and amplifiers that could be operated by plugging in wires to ordinary wall outlets. There were buzzers to buzz the caller, busy-signal devices, and telephone bells. Here was an opportunity for action and speech improvement. I asked Dick, one of the shy members of the class, to be the teletrainer operator. I hoped to ease him into a more active role in subsequent sessions.

Prior to this we had learned the meaning of *criteria* and had discussed criteria that could affect job getting: poor posture, sloppy dress, bad manners, inaudibility, and unacceptable language, for example.

"What criteria will you set up?" This was a form of review.

"Poise and initiative," said Dick.

"Voice and words," said Jessie.

"Manners," said Belle.

"Good. Now we're ready. Curtain." There was still excitement and noise. I waited. They became impatient.

"Shut up. We want to start," said Rosetta.

"May I use your briefcase, Mrs. Dawson?" asked Jim.

"Certainly."

Jim swaggered in, swinging the briefcase. Snuggling up to Rosetta, the receptionist, he said, "Hello, babe, how about it?" Rosetta slapped his face.

"Mrs. Dawson, I was only fooling. Don't count this. Let's do it over."

He walked in again, using his natural gait, which combined the cakewalk with a shuffle. He spoke to the receptionist with his hat on.

"Dope, take off your hat. You're in a office." He quickly complied.

"Good afternoon, Miss Smith. I'm here for a job."

"What kind of a job?"

"A clerical job."

"Wait a minute, please. Do you have an appointment?"

"No."

"Sit down." Rosetta, the receptionist, picked up the phone before Dick had a chance to buzz it on the teletrainer. Laughter broke out. They corrected this. Rosetta continued on the phone. "Mr. Douglas, there's a fellow here for a clerk-typist job. Do we have an opening? OK. I'll give him one. . . ." Turning to Jim, she said, "I'm sorry. There are no openings now. Fill out this application and bring it in tomorrow at 2 P.M." Rosetta kept chewing bubble gum ferociously, while keeping her babushka tied around her head and her coat on.

When it came time to criticize, few said anything. This is the way it was at the beginning of each new program. Later they were able to criticize and accept criticism from each other. We talked generally about what was unacceptable without mentioning individuals. Chewing gum, wearing a coat, and manners were observed. We discussed ways of walking and sitting and how they revealed personality. I demonstrated slovenly sitting and poor posture when walking.

"The way you stand, sit, and walk shows someone observing you how you feel about yourself."

Rosetta's words were slurred, and this I mentioned, but without talking about her. I said that on a clerical job she might be asked to use the telephone. The impression she made on the hearer might have an effect on her employer's business.

"For the first time, you did very well," I told Jim and Rosetta. "It's always most difficult for the first ones. Those who follow learn from the beginners."

I noticed that throughout this first skit the rest had sat

and listened attentively, no one even leaving for the rest rooms. When the bell rang, they were disappointed.

"Can we do this tomorrow?"

"We'll see." I didn't want to overdo any technique. It was much wiser not to allow them to become satiated. "Maybe at least once a week. We'll try various kinds of situations."

Role playing became one of the most pleasurable learning techniques in this first group. In subsequent groups, panels and group discussions were preferred. In role playing they had to listen to each other; they had to think, use their imagination, and plan.

Role Playing: Lesson for Interrupters

If I could get the students to understand what it feels like to be interrupted, maybe they would be more courteous to each other and, by extension, to a supervisor, an outsider, or to me. In each group of general office clerks, therefore I chose the flagrant interrupters for those to be interrupted in role playing, but they were not aware of my purpose.

"We're in the IBM office. I'll select the players today instead of asking for volunteers. Roberta, you will be the supervisor. Susie,[1] you will be the general office clerk. This time I need a few minutes to discuss the role with you privately.

"Roberta, I'll talk to you first." I took her aside. The rest watched interestedly. "Roberta, Susie has been a general office clerk in your department for only three weeks.

---

[1] Susie was a match for Roberta. Throughout the course she was punctual, well groomed, and conscientious. Her voice was resonant. She always had a smile. As a result she was a scapegoat. Her reputation as a "brass polisher" made her the butt of daily attacks, but she was strong enough to withstand them. Her two small children came to school when no baby-sitter was available or when her husband went fishing. They were third-generation welfare recipients. She was most anxious to work and pay back the welfare department, however. Her husband didn't go along with her. He was unskilled but not interested in getting into job training as yet. She hoped to influence him. She wanted a home in the country.

For the first two, her work showed promise. She tried to do everything accurately. She came to work punctually. This past week, however, she seems to be slipping. Her work is sloppy. She has been late several times and has been spending too much time away from her desk. Call her in to discuss this with her. What you say and how you handle it will be up to you." Roberta, as usual, had still not been able to part with her coat or babushka in class. I was curious to see if she would do so in her role as supervisor.

I then called Susie aside, out of earshot of Roberta. "Susie, when Roberta calls you in, don't let her say a word. Interrupt her each time she opens her mouth. I don't care what you talk about. That will be up to you. OK?"

"Well, you know Roberta. She flies off the handle easily."

"I know you can manage. If you were in an office, you'd have to."

"All right," I told the class. "We're ready. Remember to watch for poise, speech, attitude, and manners. Then we'll discuss the presentation. Curtain."

Roberta picked up the telephone on her desk and said, "Miss Susie Smith, please. . . . Miss Smith, will you please come to my office? It's very important."

"Yes, Mrs. Wells," said Susie. Susie got up and went out the imaginary door, walked down the imaginary hall to Roberta's office, and knocked. She was told to come in.

"Roberta," said the supervisor, "You can sit do—"

"Oh, Mrs. Wells, what a lovely coiffeur! You . . ."

"Miss Smith, this is not what I . . ."

"Oh, Mrs. Wells, I like your dress. Is it new?"

"Miss Smith, I just to—"

"What, Mrs. Wells?"

"Miss Smith, I think you're . . ."

"Mrs. Wells, I saw your husband out last night at the dance with another woman." Susie spoke rapidly to get this out before she was interrupted.

"Now, I won't tolerate any more of this." Roberta's

hair, still encased in a babushka, was showing as she shook her head in anger. Her dark expressive eyes flashed, and the group watched me to see what would happen. They knew how volatile Roberta was.

I looked at her and wondered whether to continue or to interrupt. I decided to let her continue, having complete confidence in her ability to handle the situation. It was a test, however. In previous situations she had never allowed anyone to get the better of her. It was fascinating to see what would happen.

Roberta picked up the phone and said angrily, "I want the Personnel Manager. Hello, is this the Personnel Manager? I have something to report . . . a hostile and belligerent employee." With that she slammed the phone down. Laughter.

In the discussion which followed, Roberta gasped, "Gee, Mrs. Dawson, now I get the feeling of what's it like to be interrupted. Is that the way you feel when I interrupt you?"

"Not quite. I don't get excited because I have had more experience in working with people. Roberta, you did admirably. So did you, Susie. They deserve a round of applause." The students applauded loudly for them.

"I thought for a moment Roberta would hit me. She got so mad," said Susie. "Knowing her, I was really afraid. But it worked out all right. Now I have a little more confidence in myself."

If I could change their tendency to attack someone who displeased them, we were making progress. Time would tell.

At this time in the first program, it was possible to criticize individuals without unpleasant repercussions. I asked Rosetta to go to the blackboard and conduct the evaluation of Roberta's and Susie's performances. Rosetta asked the class to give her criteria for their comments. These were reviewed and included manners, dress, posture, walk, use of the telephone, voice, speech, dialogue, ability to listen, and use of vocabulary from previous lessons.

The climax was reached when Roberta's best friend, Cindy, no model of propriety, yelled out, "Did you ever see a supervisor wear a head scarf and coat in a office? You was chewing gum, too. How you expect your employees to act when you don't set a example?"

"Look who's talking," said Roberta. "You always interrupting, so keep your mouth shut."

Progress was being made. Roberta was beginning to substitute verbal responses for violent reactions.

Role Playing: Vehicle for Creativity

At the end of the fourth month of the general office clerk program and a month after the office boys entered, there occurred a spontaneous outburst of self-expression and creativity. By this time I had introduced tours as a regular feature of Personal Development. On this day, however, there was a conflict. Only one class could go on tour, leaving another of my classes at school. At first there was disappointment. But I had told the students about this in advance. I tried never to disappoint them; they had suffered too much frustration in their short lives. I asked them if they wanted to have a joint session with another class or if they preferred to be on their own and see what they could do. I put this to a vote, and the decision was unanimous: "We want to be on our own and show you, Mrs. Dawson, what we can do." I was overjoyed. By this time I had given students opportunities to develop leadership and initiative by letting them conduct vocabulary reviews, chair discussions, and play roles.

When I entered school the next day, several students rushed down and asked, "Mrs. Dawson, have you heard what we did yesterday?" I had not heard. They wouldn't tell me. They wanted me to find out from other teachers first. This was another moment when enthusiasm, so slow in coming, was manifested.

I did hear later. I was told by the administrative staff and teachers that they put on a role-playing situation involving a murder, with a defense attorney, prosecutor, jury, and witnesses. It was so amusing that laughter reverberated to the office above.

They were so busily engaged they never heard the bell —a rare occurrence. This was the goal toward which we were striving: to become so involved that the whole person was called into action.

I began the session with the complimentary remarks I had heard. I let them know how proud I was that they were deriving some enjoyment from learning.

"Mrs. Dawson, we had a wonderful time. You see, we did learn something in this class."

"I would like to sit in the audience as an observer and watch you reenact the scene. How about it?"

"All right," said Jessie, "but Charles, the district attorney, is not here. He drove around again with a revoked license and is in jail. He'll be out tomorrow."

"Someone else can take his place."

Mahalia was chosen director by the group. She went into immediate action.[2]

Mahalia called the cast. Others set up chairs for the jury and placed a chair in front of the group for the judge. They were scurrying and buzzing. Jessie had unanimously been chosen to play the judge.

I sat in the room as an observer. I decided not to interrupt even when unacceptable language was used. This would disturb the creative interaction. Instead I noted what I saw and heard for discussion later.

The group listened to suggestions from each other. It was fascinating to watch them, in perfect freedom, play their roles as judge, defense attorney, plaintiff, defendant, witnesses, and jury so convincingly and so humorously. The way they responded to each other and anticipated actions was a study in behavioral science. They acted as if they had studied Method acting. This illustrated better

---

[2]This was one way of helping Mahalia, shy and inarticulate, become more involved. Heretofore she was afraid to participate. She was willowy and slim almost to the fragile point. Her reading ability surpassed that of the others. In my counseling sessions with her I discovered that she not only was a high school graduate, but had attended junior college for a year. She dropped out to have her first out-of-wedlock child. Her voice was soft and her diction good.

than any textbook exercise or teacher-contrived situation what happens when creativity and freedom of expression are encouraged.

When they finished, several sighed; and Jessie, the judge, said, "Mrs. Dawson, we didn't do as well as yesterday. Yesterday it was funnier, and we had a better time."

That was an astute observation, I thought. It's difficult to recapture the enthusiasm created by novelty, an ingredient of any "first." Jessie's comment, echoed by the rest of the group, revealed something else that was happening: continuing development of ability to criticize and to be criticized. Now they could evaluate themselves and not be afraid to say that they didn't do so well.

After praising each one individually and commenting favorably on specific actions or responses they had made, I asked if we could discuss improvements. This they were happy to do. The story was good; it was theirs. They had suspense and a surprise ending to keep the audience guessing. In fact, I told them that I thought it was so clever and interesting that the other students in the school would want to see it. How would it be, therefore, if they actually put it into better shape and were the first group to present an original offering to the entire student body? At first the actors hesitated. They were afraid they couldn't hold their friends' attention. Then others in the group supplied the moral support needed.

I set the date for a Friday, a month later, to give them the needed time, and said that they could work on the play in our Personal Development sessions.

We talked, and Belle acted as recorder, jotting down a checklist of steps:

1. Director and master of ceremonies
2. Cast
   a. District attorney
   b. Counsel for defendant
   c. Witnesses for defense
   d. Witnesses for prosecution
   e. Guard

    f. Jury (four actors to represent twelve jurors)
    g. Judge
3. Stage setting
4. Evidence—Exhibits A, B, C

I suggested the use of several levels for the performance: the stage for the judge and witnesses, downstairs
in the auditorium for the audience, who unsuspectingly
would be courtroom spectators, and the right front for
the jury. In this way we could involve not only my students but the whole student body. The surprise element
would add to the dramatic effect.

For the next three weeks we allotted a half-hour from
each session for rehearsal. This gave the students added
incentive to study vowel sounds and pronunciation and to
improve language patterns, especially the defense attorney, who sprinkled his remarks with, "Man, I knows. He
be's and I seen him." Such language patterns might not
seem strange to their peers, but it would evoke laughter in
the world outside.

The witnesses were very amusing, especially John,
whose laconic remarks delighted us. When cross-examined
and questioned about how long he had been a practicing
physician, he said, "Fifteen years, seven months, six days,
and four hours." Everyone laughed. They liked John and
looked to him because of his clever repartee and impressive vocabulary.

We discussed the preparation of the program and how
interesting it would be if the students typed it in their
typing class and then mimeographed it themselves. They
could appoint a committee to take charge of this. The
typing teacher gave them permission to do it. Daily they
showed me results which were not satisfactory. I made the
corrections in spelling, design, and cast. Their perseverance and attention to details showed development.

The night before the big event we discussed wardrobe,
props, and responsibilities. By this time they realized their
own interdependence and cautioned those inclined to be
late to be on time. "Show your initiative," said Belle.

I said that I would be the photographer, since I had a

35-mm still camera and would provide the color film. I also would bring in my black raincoat which could be worn backwards as the judge's robe; since Jessie was short and I so tall, it would reach the floor. I also would bring in long rhinestone earrings for Mahalia, a witness—the wife of the physician in the skit—who chose to be the fashion designer for *Ebony* magazine.

The day arrived, and there was great excitement and anticipation. I had invited many staff members from the Center and from the neighborhood community centers. I was anxious for them to see how the students were progressing and their tremendous potentialities. There was a full house. Although there had been rehearsals, there had never been a written script. This would have been contrary to the principle of spontaneity of expression and would have curtailed the flow of creativity.

The stage had been set during the lunch hour. The jury members, who had decided the type of persons they wanted to be, dressed accordingly. Belle was a dignified conservatively dressed vocational nurse, Dick a telephone installer, and John a physician. Jim and Mahalia suggested the evidence: Exhibit A—a black dress; Exhibit B—a drinking glass with lipstick imprint; and Exhibit C—a gun. When we discussed the gun, the students wanted to bring in a real one, loaded. I decided against such realism. I said it was good theater to allow the audience to use its imagination. They chose the title "Woman in Black."

Jim, the defense attorney, would not put on a collar and tie. He was adamant about this in rehearsals.

"I know, Mrs. Dawson, because I been in court enough times. Not every defense attorney wears a white shirt and tie, and I'm one of those that don't. I wears a sport shirt." He had had the experience he mentioned, and I didn't force the issue because he had figured out the kind of defense attorney he wanted to portray.

The skit went over beautifully. The members of the cast responded to each other's dialogue naturally, humorously, and almost professionally. There was little self-consciousness. The students were working as a team.

Their remarks varied daily, as they did at the actual performance. The audience was so amused that there was constant laughter, sometimes uproarious, especially from me. I couldn't help it; I was tickled. Everyone was having such a good time. They had learned so much about themselves, and they projected their delight to the audience. The applause was resounding. I was only disappointed that the Center had not provided the press coverage I had asked for. Now, when the students were showing their capabilities, the bad press they had always received could have been countered.

William said, "Gee, Mrs. Dawson, why can't our class do a scene in a courtroom?"

"You can, but it doesn't necessarily have to be an imitation. Think of another interesting situation. Use your imagination. We'll talk about it later." . . .

LANGUAGE HABITS

Language patterns of young people from poverty areas or ghettoes differ greatly from what the middle-class ear finds familiar. Their "in" language is descriptive and should not be laughed at or ridiculed. Their language patterns may be disturbing. The following examples are typical of their English usage:

1. Double negatives in profusion: "It don't make no difference."

2. Lack of agreement of verb with subject: "He do the work." "I does it that way."

3. Incorrect use of verb tense: "What if he has it did up nice?"

4. Incorrect use of adverbs and adjectives: "He got it quick."

5. Different concept of word meaning: "I was on a job messing with solvents and come home with nasty clothes."

Accept these language patterns as part of their culture. When you and your students are able to communicate with each other, you will find them deeply interested in learning middle-class English if it is taught as a second language. In this way you begin where they are. You bring to their attention better ways or more acceptable ways of expressing ideas.[3] You should not be shocked by their constant use of profanity. Whenever Duke and Wiz used profanity, others told them to hold it and remember where they were. As the course progressed, I never scolded about the use of four-letter words, but I noticed that the students' control over such expletives gradually increased.

As I said earlier, these youths have to be more than bilingual. In many cases they have to be multilingual. I wonder how many of us would fare under such conditions. Whenever they used their own language to express themselves in class, I made notes. I made it a point never to interrupt them in a discussion. This would only have intensified their feelings of insecurity, stupidity, and hopelessness, feelings which I was trying to dispel. They had enough problems to cope with in their environment. I waited until they had finished. Then I called their language to their attention and, phrase by phrase or expression by expression, we examined it and translated it into more acceptable English. They were soon able to correct themselves whenever they heard "in" language. They were also cognizant of language appropriateness.

One of the criteria for evaluating students who participated in discussions or role playing was their language patterns. The tape recorder was an excellent tool for such evaluation. The students' attention span and listening ability increased. They beamed with self-confidence whenever they were able to select more appropriate language structure. No longer were they afraid to criticize each other openly.

"Gee," Ruby said in the duplicating machine class one day. She had just given us her comments on the book *Black Like Me*. We were listening to the tape. "I didn't speak good, huh?" She shook her head and continued. "I sure got to be more alert, huh?" ...

[3]Chapter 4 of *On the Outskirts of Hope* goes into this in more detail.

VOCABULARY DEVELOPMENT

Vocabulary was not taught from lists prepared in advance or taken from textbooks. It developed from discussions, from newspaper reading, or from my own inadvertent use of unfamiliar words. The problem with these students was their not having been taught to conceptualize. Therefore I tried not to assume that concepts familiar to the middle class would be familiar to these young people. I often stopped and asked them if they understood my words. Often they did. When anyone did not, I gave illustrations from their way of life to make the new terms meaningful. Their use of the words immediately indicated their interest. They loved vocabulary after they became accustomed to this method. In fact, I found vocabulary development a most effective tranquilizer.

A few examples of vocabulary development follow.

"When you were talking at once, there's a word that describes the noise and confusion. Anyone know?"

Allen Williams answered, "I got it on the tip of my tongue, but I can't find it."

I wrote C H A O S on the blackboard. Then I pronounced it. I told them its Greek origin. By this time in the program they had become interested in origins of words and expressions. If I omitted to mention a word's origin, students brought it up and tried to guess. They were always pleased when they guessed correctly.

"Suppose you have a meeting of your social club. You're discussing plans for a dance. It's difficult to be heard because several fellows are beating their drum, which they brought for gigging later. Maybe a few others are singing at the same time, while others are carrying on private conversations. Everyone's doing what he wants to without considering anyone else. There is no order. There is great confusion. This is the idea of 'chaos.' Often there appears to be chaos right here." Laughter. " 'Chaos' is a noun. 'Chaotic' is the adjective. There is chaos, but the situation is chaotic. Understand?" A few seemed doubtful. I continued. "After earthquakes, storms, or other disasters, transportation, electricity, and water may be cut off. Houses may be destroyed. The situation can be called chaotic. These disasters are beyond a human being's control. What happens in our classroom we can control."

Chaos proved to be a popular word with all the groups. In the first general office clerk program, when we were discussing what they liked most in Personal Development, Belle said, "Vocabulary. I use the word 'chaos' all the time when I'm home with the baby. 'Emma,' I say, 'don't make so much chaos. One day, Emma was playing with Sarah's baby. Sarah's child screamed and yelled because Emma didn't give her a piece of her candy. Emma said, 'You're making chaos. Stop it.' " We all laughed.

How the youths related their understanding of vocabulary to their way of life was illustrated early in the office boy program. William and Chops had been talking about how they worked together on a dance for their social club. They also entertained by playing drums.

"Do you know one word that can express 'work together'?" When no one answered, I said, "Let me give you another illustration. Then maybe you can guess the word. Suppose Curly and Chops write a song for the next dance. Curly writes the words, and Chops writes the music. We could say that they _____ on the song. Any idea?"

"No, give us a clue."

I put blanks on the blackboard and waited for someone to try to guess the word. Then I filled in several letters:

C O _ _ _ _ R _ _ _

When no one knew, I filled in the blanks:

C O L L A B O R A T E

Then I broke it down into prefix, root and suffix.

COL LABOR ATE

Col was the same as *con*, meaning "with." *Labor* they knew, of course. And the meaning is "to work with" or "to work together."

"Do you understand, or do you want more illustrations?"

"We got it," said Chops. "Me and Curly collaborated to jump Nick."[4]

"Good. You used it correctly, but why always react violently? Can't you think of a more peaceful illustration?" Laughter.

As I said earlier, there was resistance to my methods at the beginning of each Personal Development course. Students equated learning with memorizing, and I was trying to break that identification. They were too impatient to wait for explanations.

During the first two weeks of the framemen program, Wiz frequently said, "You're a good teacher, but your explanations are too long. Give us definitions. That's what other teachers do."

Duke expressed this sentiment, too: "Aw, shee-it, you talk too much. Quit the explanations. Give me the definitions. I'll copy them. Then test me like you wrote them, and I'll know them."

"I will not give you definitions for you to copy. I told you when we began that my methods were different from what you had experienced. I'm more interested in your getting the ideas and feelings expressed by a word. These are different for each one of us, depending on our association with that word. When you understand the idea or the concept, then you can look up the word in the dictionary. It will mean more. Have you noticed how many words you are using to express yourselves in discussions? In this class you have to think, not memorize."

"Yeah, we got a list in high school," said Edward Emile Edlow. "The teacher never explained with so many illustrations. We looked them up in the dictionary, but that still didn't help. Maybe that's why I didn't like to read. I didn't know the words, huh?"

Demo, another member of this frameman group, was as resistant as Duke. When I sensed undercurrents, I said,

---

[4]Nick, one of the docile members of this group, was eager to learn. The only one without a police record, he was the butt of many practical jokes.

"Some of you seem unhappy with the way I introduce vocabulary and explain." Oohs and aahs sounded around the room. "All right. I said on the first day that nothing was taboo for discussion. I mean it. I can accept criticism. Let's discuss it."

We gave Demo the floor[5]. Sprawled out in his seat, he said from the side of his mouth, "What's so wonderful about vocabulary?"

I sat in the circle as an observer. Ali-Tees was moderator.

"What I need vocabulary for?" continued Demo. "All I want to be is the biggest pimp in the world!"

"He means it, too," said Edward Emile Edlow.[6]

"Don't interrupt me," said Demo. "Vocabulary ain't help me get a job."

"How could it?" said Coolsann. "You ain't around enough. You here to learn. Give yourself a chance."[7]

"So, wise guy, where's it get you? You're still here. You ain't got a high job?" This came from Stanford,[8] who was a pal of Demo's and among the four in this class to whom we referred as the perennial resisters or "the opposition." They didn't approve of anything we talked about or the methods we used.

[5]Demo was tall and handsome, with long sideburns and large, dark eyes with very long lashes. He was not well groomed like Duke. His attendance was poor. He attended once a week to sign his weekly allotment form. He seldom was punctual when he did come, but he was quick to pick up information. He was hustling nightly and told me after class that he was too tired to get up in the morning.

[6]Edward, now approaching twenty-three, had spent the years from age sixteen to twenty in an assortment of correctional institutions. His record was full of felony charges, some reduced to misdemeanors. When he entered my class, he had been hostile and had refused to participate. He said that over a period of time he had checked me out, liked the way I operated, and so become one of my unsolicited publicity agents.

[7]Coolsann, twenty-two, with two out-of-wedlock children, was one of the few who had been gainfully employed, in spite of a long arrest record. He worked in a large department store by day while he pimped by night.

[8]Stanford, twenty, also attended once a week, coming on the day to sign for his weekly stipend. I had talked to him frequently after class as I did with Demo, explaining that this was maybe a last chance for a new life. To throw it away wasn't using the intelligence he had. For a few days this had an effect. Then he went back to the old pattern.

Coolsann answered Stanford, "I don't expect a job yet. I got to finish this course first. But I'm developing myself. Like Mrs. Dawson said, she's helping us to develop our potentialities. That's a word I learned, and now I can say things in different ways."

"Man, you fronting, that's what," said Demo. "I'm satisfied with myself, and I sure don't need no vocabulary."

"Yeah," said Stanford. "I know a guy who's deaf and dumb. Vocabulary never helped him. But he's the wealthiest man around. People in the country that never left the country and ain't ever had those big words we getting, knows more than the scientists about the country, see. Vocabulary ain't never help them!"

"You know what else," said Coolsann. "When you're not used to using correct words, but only 'in' language, you may forget on a job and say, 'Yeah, man, I went with a slick broad last night. Sure, plenty of cats around, but we bagging'!"

Now the resisters ganged up on Coolsann. Demo, his eyes flashing, said, "You stupid, man. Don't you think we got more sense than that? We know not to use that 'in' language outside. We'd never use it on a job."

"I still don't see the sense of vocabulary helping me, that's all," said Stanford.

"Let me give you an example," said Coolsann. "Suppose I have to send a telegram some day. You know you pay by the word. So take one of the words we learned. Take 'improvise.' If I remember right without consulting my notes, it means to make something up from the top of your head with no rehearsing. Think of all those words and what it would cost me if I didn't know one word that could say all that—'improvise.' "

"I ain't never send no telegram," said Demo, "and I ain't never gonna. I writes a letter. It's cheaper, see." Laughter.

"Let me say a word," said Stewart.[9] "I had a good job

[9] He had been cooperative from the beginning and tried to influence the others. He was twenty-one, was married and had two small children, and was concerned about supporting his family. He was having marital difficulties, however, because, he told me, his wife listened to her aunt instead of to him.

in a hospital all through high school. I couldn't have kept it if I didn't understand the vocabulary. I'm learning more here than I ever did!"

"Hospital? Who cares about no medicine job? That's for doctors," said Stanford.

"What kind of a job do you plan to get?" asked Stewart.

"Pipefitter," said Stanford.

"Man, that's a technical job. You need learning for that," said his friend, Demo.

"Hell, you don't. My father is a pipefitter, and he can't even count to ten," said Stanford.

"I knows what I wants to be," said another resister. "I wants to be a gangster, but the biggest."

"You can't be that stupid," said Coolsann. "I ain't even answering that!"

"Let's get serious, guys," said Deacon. He usually waited in the discussions until the antagonists were at each other's throats; then he entered cooly and collectedly. "Yeah, let's be serious," others said as each tried to out-shout the others, the noise rose wildly.

Stanford said, "Hey, fellows, cool it. This is plain chaos. I can't even be heard."

"It's friendly chaos, anyway," said Deacon calmly. "Stanford, did you hear yourself? You used a word you learned right here, 'chaos.' " Everyone laughed, including Stanford.

The next morning, Deacon met me before class and said, "You know, Mrs. Dawson, after all that heated discussion yesterday on vocabulary . . . well, in the Reading class, Stanford spoke about something and used five words he had here. I almost fainted. I knew you'd be interested."

Stanford's and Demo's attendance never improved. Stanford was being "kept" by an older woman who let him drive her Cadillac. Neither one made any attempt to change his habit patterns even after being counseled. I understood that not every youth could be reached. I was sorry for Stanford and Demo because they were very bright. If they could only transfer to learning their acumen in hustling!

Creative Teaching

Sylvia Ashton-Warner

from *Teacher*

ORGANIC READING IS NOT NEW

Organic reading is not new. The Egyptian hieroglyphics were one-word sentences. Helen Keller's first word, "water," was a one-word book. Tolstoy found his way to it in his peasant school, while, out in the field of UNESCO today, it is used automatically as the only reasonable way of introducing reading to primitive people: in a famine area the teachers wouldn't think of beginning with any words other than "crop," "soil," "hunger," "manure," and the like.

Not that organic reading is exclusively necessary to the illiterate of a primitive race. True, it is indispensable in conducting a young child from one culture to another, especially in New Zealand where the Maori is obliged to make the transition at so tender an age; but actually it is universal. First words are different from first drawings only in medium, and first drawings vary from country to country. In New Zealand a boy's first drawing is anything that is mobile; trucks, trains and planes, if he lives in a populated area, and if he doesn't, it's horses. New Zealand girls, however, draw houses first wherever they live. I once made a set of first readers on these two themes. But Tongan children's first drawings are of trees, Samoan five-year-olds draw churches and Chinese draw flowers. What a fascinating story this makes!

213

How can anyone begin any child on any arranged book, however good the book, when you know this? And how good is any child's book, anyway, compared with the ones they write themselves? Of course, as I'm always saying, it's not the only reading; it's no more than the *first* reading. The bridge.

It's the bridge from the known to the unknown; from a native culture to a new; and, universally speaking, from the inner man out.

Organic reading is not new: first words have ever meant first wants. "Before a nation can be formed," says Voltaire, "it is necessary that some language should be established. People must doubtless have begun by sounds, which must have expressed their first wants. . . . Idioms in the first state must have consisted of monosyllables. . . .

"We really find that the most ancient nations who have preserved anything of their primitive tongue still express by monosyllables the most familiar things which most immediately strike the senses. Chinese to this very hour is founded upon monosyllables.

"The Chaldeans for a long time engraved their observations and laws upon bricks in hieroglyphics: these were speaking characters. . . . They therefore, at first, painted what they wanted to communicate. . . . In time they invented symbolic figures: darts represented war; an eye signified divinity."

In July, 1857, Tolstoy wrote in his diary:
". . . and the most important of all: clearly and forcibly the thought came to me to open a school for the entire county."

Only two years later, in the fall of 1859, he came close to realizing his dreams. With the same passion with which he did everything, he gave himself to teaching. Almost to the exclusion of all other interests, he gave three years of his life to the peasant children. His work had nothing in common with the standard, well-regulated school systems. Tolstoy wrote that he had a passionate affection for his school. Under his guidance other young people who helped him in his work developed a similar "passionate affection."

As usual he began by discarding all existing traditions and by refusing to follow any method of teaching already in use. First he must fathom the mind of the peasant child, and by doing away with punishments, let his pupils teach him the art of teaching. In his school his pupils were free to choose their own subjects, and to take as much work as they desired. The teacher considered it his duty to assist the children in their search for knowledge by adjusting his method of approach to the individual child, and by finding the best way of proffering assistance in each case.

These free Tolstoy schools, without programmes, without punishments, without rules, without forcing the will of a child, were remarkably successful. The children spent entire days at their studies and were reluctant to leave the schoolhouse.

Fifty years later, Basil Borosov, one of the peasants, said, "Hours passed like minutes. If life were always as gay no one would ever notice it go by. . . . In our pleasures, in our gaiety, in our rapid progress, we soon became as thick as thieves with the Count. We were unhappy without the Count and the Count was unhappy without us. We were inseparable, and only night drew us apart. . . . There was no end to our conversations. We told him a lot of things; about sorcerers, about forest devils. . . ."

And one of the international volunteers in Kabylia in the mountains of Algeria writes:

"About twenty children were sitting in front of the teacher under an ash tree and reading in chorus the name of their village which she had written on a big sheet of paper. They were enormously proud; time and time again they read us the word.

"But the next evening three of the adults came to ask us to teach them to write their names.

" 'Why do you want to write your name?'

"One of them explained: 'To sign at the Post Office. If I can sign my name to collect a registered letter I shall not need to pay the witnesses.'

" 'And do you often get letters like that?'

" 'Sometimes. From my son in France.'

"We went steadily on; but in the evening, instead of resting under the mosquito net, we were all caught up in the fever of fundamental education."

Organic reading for beginners is not new; it's our rejection of it that's new.

THE KEY VOCABULARY

The method of teaching any subject in a Maori infant room may be seen as a plank in a bridge from one culture to another, and to the extent that this bridge is strengthened may a Maori in later life succeed.

This transition made by Maori children is often unsuccessful. At a tender age a wrench occurs from one culture to another, from which, either manifestly or subconsciously, not all recover. And I think that this circumstance has some little bearing on the number of Maoris who, although well educated, seem neurotic, and on the number who retreat to the mat.

Another more obvious cause of the social failure of Maoris is the delay in the infant room. Owing to this delay, which is due to language as well as to the imposition of a culture, many children arrive at the secondary school stage too old to fit in with the European group and they lose heart to continue. From here, being too young and unskilled to do a competent job, some fall in and out of trouble, become failures by European standards, and by the time they have grown up have lost the last and most precious of their inheritances—their social stability.

With this in mind, therefore, I see any subject whatever in a Maori infant room as a plank in the bridge from the Maori to the European. In particular, reading.

So, in preparing reading for a Maori infant room, a

teacher tries to bridge the division between the races and to jettison the excess time.

Children have two visions, the inner and the outer. Of the two the inner vision is brighter.

I hear that in other infant rooms widespread illustration is used to introduce the reading vocabulary to a five-year-old, a vocabulary chosen by adult educationists. I use pictures, too, to introduce the reading vocabulary, but they are pictures of the inner vision and the captions are chosen by the children themselves. True, the picture of the outer, adult-chosen pictures can be meaningful and delightful to children; but it is the captions of the mind pictures that have the power and the light. For whereas the illustrations perceived by the outer eye cannot be other than interesting, the illustrations seen by the inner eye are organic, and it is the captioning of these that I call the "Key Vocabulary."

I see the mind of a five-year-old as a volcano with two vents; destructiveness and creativeness. And I see that to the extent that we widen the creative channel, we atrophy the destructive one. And it seems to me that since these words of the key vocabulary are no less than the captions of the dynamic life itself, they course out through the creative channel, making their contribution to the drying up of the destructive vent. From all of which I am constrained to see it as creative reading and to count it among the arts.

First words must mean something to a child.

First words must have intense meaning for a child. They must be part of his being.

How much hangs on the love of reading, the instinctive inclination to hold a book! *Instinctive*. That's what it must be. The reaching out for a book needs to become an organic action, which can happen at this yet formative age. Pleasant words won't do. Respectable words won't do. They must be words organically tied up, organically born from the dynamic life itself. They must be words that are already part of the child's being. "A child," reads a recent publication on the approach of the American books, "can be led to feel that Janet and John are friends." *Can be led to feel*. Why lead him to feel or try to lead him to feel that these strangers are friends? What about the passionate feeling he has already for his own friends? To me it is inorganic to overlook this step. To me it is an offence against art. I see it as an interruption in the natural expansion of life of which Erich Fromm speaks. How would New Zealand children get on if all their reading material were built from the life of African blacks? It's little enough to ask that a Maori child should begin his reading from a book of his own colour and culture. This is the formative age where habits are born and established. An aversion to the written word is a habit I have seen born under my own eyes in my own infant room on occasion.

It's not beauty to abruptly halt the growth of a young mind and to overlay it with the frame of an imposed culture. There are ways of training and grafting young growth. The true conception of beauty is the shape of organic life and that is the very thing at stake in the transition from one culture to another. If this transition took place at a later age when the security of a person was already established there would not be the same need for care. But in this country it happens that the transition takes place at a tender and vulnerable age, which is the reason why we all try to work delicately.

Back to these first words. To these first books. They must be made out of the stuff of the child itself. I reach a hand into the mind of the child, bring out a handful of the stuff I find there, and use that as our first working material. Whether it is good or bad stuff, violent or placid stuff, coloured or dun. To effect an unbroken beginning. And in this dynamic material, within the familiarity and security of it, the Maori finds that words have intense meaning to him, from which cannot help but arise a love of reading. For it's here, right in this first word, that the love of reading is born, and the longer his reading is organic the stronger it becomes, until by the time he arrives at the books of the new culture, he receives them

as another joy rather than as a labour. I know all this
because I've done it.

First words must have an intense meaning.
First words must be already part of the dynamic life.
First books must be made of the stuff of the child
himself, whatever and wherever the child.

The words, which I write on large, tough cards and
give to the children to read, prove to be one-look words
if they are accurately enough chosen. And they are plain
enough in conversation. It's the conversation that has to
be got. However, if it can't be, I find that whatever a
child chooses to make in the creative period may quite
likely be such a word. But if the vocabulary of a child is
still inaccessible, one can always begin him on the general Key Vocabulary, common to any child in any race, a
set of words bound up with security that experiments, and
later on their creative writing, show to be organically
associated with the inner world: "Mummy," "Daddy,"
"kiss," "frightened," "ghost."

"Mohi," I ask a new five, an undisciplined Maori,
"what word do you want?"

"Jet!"

I smile and write it on a strong little card and give it
to him. "What is it again?"

"Jet!"

"You can bring it back in the morning. What do you
want, Gay?"

Gay is the classic overdisciplined, bullied victim of the
respectable mother.

"House," she whispers. So I write that, too, and give it
into her eager hand.

"What do you want, Seven?" Seven is a violent Maori.

"Bomb! Bomb! I want bomb!"

So Seven gets his word "bomb" and challenges anyone
to take it from him.

And so on through the rest of them. They ask for a
new word each morning and never have I to repeat to
them what it is. And if you saw the condition of these

tough little cards the next morning you'd know why they need to be of tough cardboard or heavy drawing paper rather than thin paper.

When each has the nucleus of a reading vocabulary and I know they are at peace with me I show them the word "frightened" and at once all together they burst out with what they are frightened of. Nearly all the Maoris say "the ghost!" a matter which has a racial and cultural origin, while the Europeans name some animal they have never seen, "tiger" or "alligator," using it symbolically for the unnameable fear that we all have.

"I not frightened of anysing!" shouts my future murderer, Seven.

"Aren't you?"

"No, I stick my knife into it all!"

"What will you stick your knife into?"

"I stick my knife into the tigers!"

"Tigers" is usually a word from the European children but here is a Maori with it. So I give him "tigers" and never have I to repeat this word to him, and in the morning the little card shows the dirt and disrepair of passionate usage.

"Come in," cry the children to a knock at the door, but as no one does come in we all go out. And here we find in the porch, humble with natural dignity, a barefooted, tattooed Maori woman.

"I see my little Seven?" she says.

"Is Seven your little boy?"

"I bring him up. Now he five. I bring him home to his real family for school eh. I see my little boy?"

The children willingly produce Seven, and here we have in the porch, within a ring of sympathetic brown and blue eyes, a reunion.

"Where did you bring him up?" I ask over the many heads.

"Way back on those hill. All by heeself. You remember your ol' Mummy?" she begs Seven.

I see.

Later, standing watching Seven grinding his chalk to dust on his blackboard as usual, I do see. "Whom do you want, Seven? Your old Mummy or your new Mummy?"

"My old Mummy."

"What do your brothers do?"

"They all hits me."

"Old Mummy" and "new Mummy" and "hit" and "brothers" are all one-look words added to his vocabulary, and now and again I see some shape breaking through the chalk-ravage. And I wish I could make a good story of it and say he is no longer violent. . . .

"Who's that crying!" I accuse, lifting my nose like an old war horse.

"Seven he breaking Gay's neck."

So the good story, I say to my junior, must stand by for a while. But I can say he is picking up his words now. Fast.

Dennis is a victim of a respectable, money-making, well-dressed mother who thrashes him, and at five he has already had his first nervous breakdown. "I'm not frightened of anything!" he cries.

"Is Dennis afraid of anything?" I asked his young pretty mother in her big car.

"Dennis? He won't even let the chickens come near him."

"Did you have a dream?" I asked Dennis after his afternoon rest.

"Yes I did."

"Well then . . . where's some chalk and a blackboard?"

Later when I walked that way there was a dreadful brown ghost with purple eyes facing a red alligator on a roadway. I know I have failed with Dennis. I've never had his fear words. His mother has defeated me. During the morning output period—when everyone else is painting, claying, dancing, quarrelling, singing, drawing, talking, writing or building—Dennis is picking up my things from the floor and straightening the mats, and the picture I have of his life waiting for him, another neurotic, pursued by the fear unnameable, is not one of comfort.

Mare resisted any kind of reading vocabulary until one morning when the Little Ones were all talking at once about what they were frightened of he let go, "I shoot the bulldog!" Gay's fear was a dog too. Do we realise just how afraid small children are of dogs?

But I have some dirty, thoroughly spoilt children next door who are never held up with fear. Their Key Vocabulary runs from "Daddy," and "kiss" through words like "truck," "hill," and "Mummy" to "love" and "train." How glorious are the dirty spoilt children.

Out press these words, grouping themselves in their own wild order. All boys wanting words of locomotion, aeroplane, tractor, jet, and the girls the words of domesticity, house, Mummy, doll. Then the fear words, ghost tiger, skellington, alligator, bulldog, wild piggy, police. The sex words, kiss, love, touch, *haka.** the key words carrying their own illustrations in the mind, vivid and powerful pictures which none of us could possibly draw for them—since in the first place we can't see them and in the second because they are so alive with an organic life that the external pictorial representation of them is beyond the frontier of possibility. We can do no more than supply the captions.

Out push these words. The tendency is for them to gather force once the fears are said, but there are so many variations on character. Even more so in this span of life where personality has not yet been moulded into the general New Zealand pattern by the one imposed vocabulary for all. They are more than captions. They are even more than sentences. They are whole stories at times. They are actually schematic drawing. I know because they tell them to me.

Out flow these captions. It's a lovely flowing. I see the creative channel swelling and undulating like an artery with blood pumping through. And as it settles, just like any other organic arrangement of nature it spreads out into an harmonious pattern; the fear words dominating the design, a few sex words, the person interest, and the temper of the century. Daddy, Mummy, ghost, bomb, kiss, brothers, butcher knife, gaol, love, dance, cry, fight hat, bulldog, touch, wild piggy . . . if you were a child,

haka: Maori war dance.

which vocabulary would you prefer? Your own or the one at present in the New Zealand infant rooms? Come John come. Look John look. Come and look. See the boats? The vocabulary of the English upper middle class, two-dimensional and respectable?

Out pelt these captions, these one-word accounts of the pictures within. Is it art? Is it creation? Is it reading? I know that it is integral. It is organic. And it is the most vital and the most sure reading vocabulary a child can build. It is the key that unlocks the mind and releases the tongue. It is the key that opens the door upon a love of reading. It is the organic foundation of a lifetime of books. It is the key that I use daily with my fives, along with the clay and the paint and amid the singing and quarrelling.

It is the key whose turning preserves intact for a little longer the true personality. It is the Key Vocabulary.

MAXIMS
in the preparation of
Maori Infant Reading

The Key Vocabulary centers round the two main instincts, fear and sex.

The Key Vocabulary varies from one locality to another and from one race to another.

Backward readers have a private Key Vocabulary which once found launches them into reading.

The power content of a word can be determined better from a backward reader than from an average reader.

In the presentation of key words to five-year-olds, illustrations are to be shunned rather than coveted.

The length of a word has no relation to its power content.

In all matters in a Maori infant room there is a Maori standard as well as a European one.

Organic Reading

"A child comes up, if at all, in accordance with the law of his own growth."

—Dr. Burrow

It's a sad thing to say of the vocabulary of any set reading books for an infant room that it must necessarily be a dead vocabulary. Yet I say it. For although the first quality of life is change, these vocabularies never change. Winter and summer, for brown race or white, through loud mood or quiet, the next group of words, related or not to the current temper of the room, inexorably moves into place for the day's study.

I tried to meet this division between the climate of a room and an imposed reading book by making another set of books from the immediate material, but all I did was to compose another dead vocabulary. For although they are closer to the Maori children than the books of the English upper-middle class, their vocabulary is static too, and it is not the answer to the question I have asked myself for years: What is the organic reading vocabulary?

At last I know: Primer children write their own books.

Early in the morning this infant room gets under way on organic writing, and it is this writing that I use in relative proportions as the reading for the day; for the children just off the Key Vocabulary with their stories of two words up to those who can toss off a page or so. In this way we have a set of graded brand-new stories every morning, each sprung from the circumstances of their own lives and illustrated unmatchably in the mind.

The new words they have asked for during the morning's writing, and which have been entered in the back of their books, they put up on the blackboard each morning. The words range from one or two to ten or so. They reconsider these words after the morning interval when they come in for the intake hour. They read them and spell them for ten minutes. I don't require that they should all be learned and remembered. If they are important enough they will stay, all right, whatever the length. Neither is it for me to sort out which is important. I never say, "Spell 'pictures.'" I say, "Perri, spell one of your words." Then I get the real word and the right spelling. In fact, this is a thing that I hand to them: hearing each other spell. Sometimes, however, we run over these words before dispersing for lunch, and what they have picked up from the morning's writing and reading of the organic work, in terms of numbers of new words and their varying difficulties is sometimes a surprise.

Each afternoon, however, all the words, whether known or not, are rubbed from the board and each morning the new ones go up. It's exciting for us all. No one ever knows what's coming. Wonderful words appear: helicopter, lady's place, cowboy, sore ear, fish and chips, dirt, Captain Marble, mumps, Superman and King of the Rocket Men. Words following intimately from day to day the classroom mood; echoing the *tangi** in the district, recounting the pictures in the hall the night before or revealing the drama behind the closed doors of the pa.

This is the main reading of the day. They master their own story first, then tackle someone else's. There is opportunity to read out their own story and it is from this reading that discussions arise. And since every background of every story is well known to all, the inner illustration flashes very brightly and the discussions are seldom sluggish.

In reading one another's stories, reference is continually made to the writer for the identification of new words. This hardly hurts the writer. Unwittingly, energetically and independently of me, they widen the intake.

How much easier and more pleasant all this is when the stories are followed with a personal interest, and with the whole of the background seen alive in the mind. The facts of suitable printing, length of line and intelligibility run nowhere in the race with meaning. As for word recurrence, there occurs a far more natural one here than

---

**tangi:* Maori funeral.

anything we could work out. A word recurs as long as they want it and is then dropped cold: a word is picked up like a new friend and dropped when it becomes boring. Which is what I mean when I say it is a live vocabulary. Things happen in it.

Since I take this original writing as a basis for reading, a strict watch is kept on grammar and punctuation. And as for the writing itself, the handwriting I mean, it has to be at least the best that they can do, to save their own faces, when changing books. Which brings one more subject into the vent of creativity: handwriting.

This organic reading, however, is not meant to stand alone: it is essentially a lead up and out to all the other reading, and as a child rises through the infant room, reaching further and further out to the inorganic and standard reading, there is a comfortable movement from the inner man outward, from the known to the unknown, from the organic to the inorganic. The thing is to keep it a gracious movement, for it is to the extent that the activity in an infant room is creative that the growth of mind is good.

THE MECHANICS OF TEACHING ORGANIC SPELLING

After play, at eleven during the intake period, we turn our attention to the new words themselves. The children pick up their books and run to the blackboard and write them up: the words asked for during the writing of the morning. They're not too long ago to be forgotten. Some of them are, when a child has asked a lot, but they ask you what they are.

Since they are all on the wall blackboard, I can see them from one position. They write them, revise them, the older children spell them and the younger merely say them, but each child is at his own individual level and working to his own particular capacity. Some of them read the word to me—if the group is too big for them all to get round the blackboard—but they all hear each other. You obtain this necessary "you and me" again. Of course, there is a lot of noise, but there's a lot of work too.

Sometimes I say, "Who can spell a word?" and I am given from those who can a word that is instinctively within their compass and which, in any case, is a word of meaning to the child himself. He wants to spell it. Moreover, attached to this word is an unaided inner illustration. Spelling evolves easily and cheerfully. True, hard words are abandoned on occasion, according to the relation of the age of the child to the challenge of the word, but often they are industriously learned owing to their emotional value. Words the size of "sky rocket" get themselves spelled from no drive of mine; "skeleton," "lollies" and so on; while few boys do not know how to spell "cowboy." It's not a hard period for the teacher, this one. Taking in seems to be easier than putting out. Besides, the latent energy, the element that so severely opposes a teacher when imposing knowledge, is here turned on what they are doing. It's an energy that is almost frightening when released. True, there is noise to it that some would object to as unprofessional; but when did I ever claim to be professional?

The writing up and spelling of these words take about a quarter of an hour and from here the children run with their books to the ring of small chairs prepared beforehand for the reading and exchange.

THE MECHANICS OF TEACHING ORGANIC READING

About a quarter of an hour for the reading.

You can tell by the state of these books they write daily whether or not the organic reading is going ahead. Contrary to the look of a room, they should end up in tatters. When a teacher handed me a group of books recently in irreproachable condition, I knew that the largest point of the whole organic pattern had been overlooked: the reading of and the discussion of one another's books. All art is communication. We never really make things for ourselves alone. The books are to be read to another.

When I had a junior, she took time off to keep abreast of the mending of these books, and when I didn't have one, I made my morning rounds armed with a roll of Cellotape as well as a pencil, rubber and razor blade and mended as I went. It was hard at first to pass these dilapidated books to an inspector, but I got over it. Once I had some exercise books made at the press, of light drawing paper, with a view to precluding the wear and tear, but although they cost considerably more they tore just the same. The drawing paper should have been of heavier weight. But economy comes into this. However, I have not yet worked out what would be the easier on the committee funds: the outlay on cellotape or on drawing paper. One young teacher practicing the organic work told me that she couldn't go on with it until she had mended her books, little realizing that from her confession I knew that the work was being thoroughly done.

Sitting in their ring of chairs, the children read again their own and then each other's. I regularly invite them to read aloud to the others. But there's got to be a very light hand or the discussion will not follow. And this discussion is the most significant of all. It is the climax of the whole organic purpose. When we are engaged on this, I arrange that the smaller children are outside for games or story with a junior assistant or a senior pupil. For the organic writing itself proves to be a startling point of departure into talk that would not occur otherwise. It leads into revelations that range from the entertaining to the outrageous. But, beyond a normal show of interest, you don't comment. You neither praise nor blame; you observe. You let everything come out, uncensured; otherwise, why do it at all?

About a quarter of an hour for the reading, taking you to half past eleven, then about a quarter of an hour on discussion, on what I call "talk." It may seem a long time for talk in school, but the very least I can say is that I gain knowledge of my material, and the most I can say is that I could never see anything retarding in the "passionate interchange of talk."

The last quarter of the hour from eleven to twelve they read Maori infant readers. It's all intake. I'm not ashamed of eleven till twelve.

MAORI TRANSITIONAL READERS

The Key Vocabulary and the creative writing have shown me into every corner of a Maori five-year-old mind. I feel I know it inside out. I've got books and books written by these small brown people on the subject of themselves. Sentence-length and story-length captions of the pictures within. Not that their writings are the only evidence. Working with them every day as we do we learn their moods, their tragedies and their desires whether we wish to or not.

From this soil the Maori Transitional Readers have grown. And I mean exactly that: grown. Six years of experiment and a hundred other books precede these final four. Many are the times I have put a book with the paint still wet into a Maori hand and watched for the reaction. And on many an occasion I have found myself in a blind alley.

It was the *temperament* of the pa that had to be got into these books. The instinctive living, the drama, the communal sympathy and the violence. Life in the pa is so often a sequence of tears, tenderness, brawls, beer, love and song. I know because I have been part of it all. In the pa tears still hold the beauty and the importance that the European has long since disclaimed.

Why is sorrow in such disgrace in infant-room reading fare? Where are the wonderful words "kiss" and "cry"? The exciting words "ghost" and "darling"? Everyday words in European homes as well as Maori ones. Kingsley's water-baby, Tom, had his despair. Alice in Wonderland found herself in tight corners, and David Copperfield had occasion enough to weep. Why then is the large part of infant-room reading so carefully and placidly two-dimensional? Is there any time of life when tears and trouble are not a part of living? I think sometimes of the children in the slums faced with these happy smooth books, and feel the same about them as I do about Maori primers. Do the word experts who assemble these books assume that by putting peaceful books into the hands of children they will be an influence for peaceful living? When I see children turning from the respectable, rhythmless stories that parents think it wisest to give them to the drama and violence of comics I think it might be the other way.

Sometimes I relax the children with eyes closed to dream. When they awake I hear these dreams. The violence of those has to be heard to be believed. A lot of it is violence against me—which they tell me cheerfully enough. I come out very badly. My house has been burnt down, bombs fall on me, I'm shot with all makes of guns and handed over to the gorilla. Presumably it's the authority and discipline which I represent.

The distance between the content of their minds, however, and the content of our reading books is nothing less than frightening. I can't believe that Janet and John never fall down and scratch a knee and run crying to Mummy. I don't know why their mother never kisses them or calls them "darling." Doesn't John ever disobey? Has the American child no fears? Does it never rain or blow in America? Why is it always fine in primer books? If these questions are naïve it must be because of the five-year-old company I keep. Heaven knows we have enough lively incident in our Maori infant rooms. The fights, the loveships, and the uppercuts from the newcomers. I see the respectable happy reading book placed like a lid upon all this—ignoring, hiding and suppressing it.

Into the text and pictures of these transitional books I have let a little of the drama through. A few of the tears. A good bit of the fears, some of the love, and an implication of the culture. From the rich soil of the Key Vocabulary and the creative writing I can do no less. Even if I did deplore dramatic living, which I don't. To me it is life

complete with its third dimension and since Beethoven
and Tchaikovsky see it the same way, I am this time in
more august company.

Nevertheless I gladly acknowledge the place of the
"Janet and John" books in a Maori infant room. But their
presence there is not the issue. The issue is simply the
transition of a Maori at a tender and vulnerable age from
one culture to another, from the pa to the European
education.

A five, meeting words for the first time and finding
that they have intense meaning for him, at once loves
reading. And this is the second issue. Love of reading.
Love of a book. When I have observed my Maori fives
stalling on the opening "Janet and John," I have seen in
my mind simultaneously the lifetime of comic-book reading to follow and the delinquency beyond. However good
a book is it can't supply the transitional needs unless it
is in sympathy with the Maori children, has incident which
they understand and temperament which they sense. Only
in a familiar atmosphere can reading be evolutionary, in
much the same way as the Key Vocabulary is organic, and
it is to supply these needs that the pa or Transitional
Books have been composed.

Since their purpose is to bridge a gap (a gap of two
thousand years between the races) rather than to teach
English, I use the pa vernacular as an overlap.

The word "eh?" so heavily used in Maori speech is a
carry-over from the Maori language, from *nei?* used constantly in Maori chat at the end of a sentence, the equivalent to our "Isn't it?" "Don't we?" "Haven't they?" "Don't
you think?" and like phrases. Maori children begin sentences with it sometimes: "Eh, Mrs. H.? We're going to
the river, eh?" It's one of the necessities in the text of a
Maori Transition Book. And to hear Maori children read
these sentences with "eh?" is reward enough for the ex-
penditure of courage in writing it. "We play, eh?" "Me
and you, eh?" "You stay by me, eh, Daddy?" A sound
for sore ears. Where has droning got to? Get them to read
"Let us play. They are at home. Mother is in the house."

I see in a current supplementary for primers the conversation of Quacky the Duck.

"I do not like the pond. I do not want to live here."

Has the compiler never heard of the word "don't"? Who in heaven—or in hell, for that matter—speaks like this? *Cadence!* Has no one heard of the word? Does no one read poetry? Why must reading be made harder for fives by the outlawing of cadence? I do not know, I do not know, I do not, I do not.

I don't delay the delivery of a thought by saying "He is not naughty," but say "He's not naughty." "Where's Ihaka?" "He'll get a hiding." "Kuri's at home." "Pussy's frightened." "I'll come back." In grown-up novels we enjoy the true conversational medium, yet five-year-olds for some inscrutable reason are met with the twisted idea behind "Let us play." As a matter of fact, Maoris seldom if ever use "let" in that particular setting. They say "We play, eh?"

These allowances of the natural dialogue preserve cadence and are no harder to learn than any other words. A little easier possibly since cadence is the natural outcome of the running conversational style, the style that is integral. Which brings me back to the consideration of reading books as an integral factor in a child's life.

In word recurrence, sentence length and page length I have only open admiration for the American work. And I follow it respectfully and slavishly in the Maori books. The framework, like so much else that is American, is so good. It's only the content that is slightly respectable for Maoris and me.

How the schematic level of illustration came about is more a matter of evolution than of reason. A matter of instinct maybe. A matter of revulsion possibly against respectability and the "right thing" that Maoris and I find so intimidating. I can illustrate on the representational level but I like the schematic. And another thing I have found out in this byway of art is that a schematic drawing can convey much emotion. I have illustrated delicate adult poetry this way. And Maori infants in all their candour have never yet challenged this frivolity.

Maybe schematic drawing is a language of their own that they reciprocally understand. I have some books at school illustrated by the children themselves. Fascinating, to make an absurd understatement. Anyway an illustrator can hardly help his style, and it's the children who are the judges. I feel that when I come down to their level in text it's a matter of harmony to come back to their level in drawing too. At its worst it honours their own medium, and is the converse of the adult who laughs at children's efforts. And at its best it's a tongue with which to say what I want to.

Speed has pressed this style into curves. There's no time to attend to straight lines when illustrating stories on the blackboard as you tell them or picturing books in a hurry. However, so far there has been no accusation from my judges.

I know hardly anything about colour, but after illustrating dozens of books the urgency of the pace has pressed out, like the curved lines, a simple formula. I should be ashamed to fall so far out of step with my five-year-olds as to see a tree as green and a sky as blue. In the Maori infant rooms over the years I have been brought up amid black roofs, orange houses, green ears, yellow faces, purple trucks and turquoise rain, so if I am charged with riot in colour it's the company I keep. How they draw I draw and what they write I write.

In the familiar setting of the Maori Transitional Books a Maori child may accomplish the mechanics of reading, simultaneously realizing that reading means something personal. At this preliminary stage he has a chance to believe in reading and from his experience he can carry within him a confidence to any other reading book; with or without the natural dialogue, with or without the third dimension, with or without the pa temperament and with or without turquoise rain. He is equipped with a little reading ability and a measure of confidence, and under these conditions the "Janet and John" books can be a step of delight.

All of which brings me to another thought. It is possible that the transitional reading, easing as it does the whole reading process, may have some bearing on the length of time a Maori spends in an infant room, given good attendance. Those of my children who attend regularly do make it in two years but I'm wary of spectacular results in experiment. So do some other Maoris in other infant rooms clear the primers in two years. Transitional reading however could help to forestall the situation arising at the top of a school: the familiar picture of fourteens and fifteens too old to go to high school, too young and untrained to do a skilled job, holding an authentic grudge against European education and ripe for delinquency. Even if this preliminary conditioning of the transitional reading helped to take even one year off the Standard 6 age it would not be wholly futile.

How important is this early approach to reading? Can it be, in any unseen way, related to many a Maori's aversion to reading anything beyond comics in later life? Possibly not. I think that's a matter of racial development.

The Maori Transitional Books are used not as a substitute for the American books but as a lead up to them. They condition a Maori child to be able to use the "Janet and John" series more wholly. They have been designed to help bridge the breach between the races and are a modest contribution towards the preservation of a Maori's social stability in later life. I know they differ from the current literature of an infant room on some controversial issues, but so are Maoris different from us. The thing that is so constantly forgotten by the majority race in judging Maori life is that there is a Maori standard as well as an European one.

Nevertheless it is to the standard of Maori five-year-olds that I have measured these books.

Fannie R. Shaftel and George Shaftel

from *Role Playing for Social Values*

THE CHILD'S OPINION OF HIMSELF

A child sees himself, to a large extent, through the opinions of him reflected by the people around him. If an individual is warmly regarded as estimable and competent by his teachers and friends, his self-esteem is likely to be high. It is important, therefore, to maximize the opportunities for individuals to earn the respect of peers and teachers.

If an individual is underappreciated in his group, a planned sequence of role-playing[1] can do much to change his status with his peers. The teacher can give such an individual opportunities to play roles quite different from the ones assigned him by his peers, roles in which the undervalued person can demonstrate a wider range of skills and perceptions and qualities than the group ever permitted him to exhibit. And in this process, not only is the individual's status among his agemates changed but, if he receives a supportive response from his group, his self-concept also is altered for the better. The result is often a significant improvement in his learning achievement.

The undervalued member of the group may be the butt of jokes and pranks on the part of the others, or he may be simply ignored, always left out, treated as if he didn't

[1]Role-playing is a group of problem-solving procedures that employs all the techniques of critical evaluation implied in the terms "listening," "discussion," and "problem solving," and is akin to the research procedures which behavorial scientists term *simulation* and *theory of games.* Role-playing, as do simulation and gaming, utilizes a symbolic model (verbal rather than physical or mathematical). Role-playing (as do the others) proceeds into problem-definition, delineation of alternatives for action, exploration of the consequences of those alternatives, and decision-making.

exist. Role-playing, in which leading offenders are placed in the role of a person who is jeered at or pushed aside, often results in an awakening of sensitivity that changes scorn for the scapegoat or pariah into the beginnings of sympathy and acceptance.

The story of "George" provides an example. George was a "left-out" who was venting his anger and frustration so actively that he had become a nuisance and a disrupting influence. He was small for his age even in his class of first-graders. He was sullen, angry, and a problem.[2]

George teased, punched, kicked, scribbled on other children's papers for no apparent reason. "He hurt me, and I didn't do anything to him," was heard all day long. Talking to him didn't help, for although he seemed to understand what I was saying, he was unable to express more than the simplest thoughts in his new language. Nor did other plans to help him control his aggression, to give him status in the group, to find him a friend of his own. After several weeks of trying we reached an impasse. George continued to be George, and the children were as one in their refusal to have anything to do with him.

Then one day I had an opportunity to watch him on the playground. There were the usual hopscotch and four-square games, cowboy-and-Indian and first-grade "chase" games. George stood on one side watching but going through the motions of the games. He ran along with the cowboys but a little distance away, until they were lost in the other activities. Then he wandered to the sandbox, the sparkle replaced by his more usual serious expression. He built sand castles which were knocked down by unobservant children. The third time he built his castles he saw a trio running toward him. What was in his mind I'm not sure, but as they approached he laughed and kicked over his own buildings. They charged on through as if he didn't exist. He stood quietly for a little while, then

[a]Marie Zimmerman Solt, "George Wanted In," *Childhood Education*, April, 1962, pp. 374–76. Quoted by permission.

joined a group of children admiring another boy's new top. In a matter of seconds he found himself on the outside of the circle of boys. He stepped back, fury on his face, and kicked two little girls who were walking by.

"Teacher, George kicked me and I didn't do anything to him."

"George wants friends. He wants to be a part of the fun. Being ignored is what he can't stand." But how to break this continuing downward spiral of rejection—aggression—rejection? The previous year his kindergarten teacher told me that he had tried to play with the other children, but they couldn't understand him nor could he communicate with them. So they went their way and he either annoyed them or played by himself. George, with his limited English, had established a pattern of behavior which was going to be difficult to change.

But what about the rest of the class? Could they be helped to understand—to feel as George felt? Perhaps the medium of role-playing could help to put them in George's shoes.

The next day I told the class a story—a story without an end. I asked them to pretend that they were the children in the story and decide how it should be ended. It concerned Johnny's move to a new house, the loneliness he felt when he went out to play and saw no one he knew. They solved Johnny's dilemma very nicely by acting out the neighborhood children's inviting Johnny to play The whole class agreed that this was good. A few days later I tried again, this time moving Johnny across the country. However, the story was complicated by the fact that the children were playing a game that Johnny didn't know. When he tried to play he made mistakes. Solutions offered were having him go away because he ruined the game and showing him how to play. These were acted out without any comment from me. The class decided that the second solution was better because it helped Johnny feel better. This indicated to me that most of the children identified with the boy in the story. The next week we talked about Johnny again. This time the setting was across the ocean in Germany, not questioned in our army-centered town. The first day he went to school he felt very lonely because they were playing games he did not know and speaking a language he did not understand. He asked to play and one of the children laughed at him. Then Johnny hit him because he didn't know what else to do. Now what?

There were different ideas. "Johnny shouldn't have hit the other boy—it only made him madder."

"Well, Johnny was mad, too. The other children shouldn't have laughed."

One solution tried was ignoring Johnny, but this didn't help him. The class recognized that. They also tried having a child explain the game, but the group protested— "Johnny couldn't understand him."

Then someone suggested that a child could show him what to do without talking. They tried this and decided it would work. Johnny could play and wouldn't feel like hurting anyone.

During this acting-out I weighed the children's feelings. They seemed ready to understand George, to realize their part in his problems, and to find some directions for helping him. I waited for a good day—a day when other things were favorable. Sunny weather to play outside, a day successful in other undertakings, a day when George had created a number of problems but none too serious. He left the room on a pretext arranged with the office. Then I told the class we were going to have another unfinished story—this time a true story.

The Johnny in today's story was born in Japan, a country far away. He had a big brother and sister who helped him learn many things, especially games that Japanese children like to play. They also taught him the games they learned at the schools on the army base—games that American children played. He knew London Bridge, Farmer in the Dell, and Cowboys and Indians. Then just before he was to go to school the family was transferred to America. Johnny wasn't worried. He knew all about American schools from his brother and sister. It would be fun—with lots of children to play with and wonderful things to do.

But it didn't work out that way. First there was no one to talk to, because no one spoke Japanese. When he tried to join the cowboy games he couldn't say whether he was a "bad guy" or a "good guy." The fun went on and he could only stand and watch. He knew how to play cowboy—he even brought his gun—but they didn't give him a chance. One day he felt so angry and unhappy that he used his gun—the wrong way—and the teacher took it away. He couldn't tell her what was wrong—that he only wanted to play.

Each morning he cried because he had to go to school. His father talked to the teacher and then told Johnny that if he didn't hit the children they would play with him and he would have a good time at school. He couldn't explain to his father that he had tried and it hadn't worked.

Then came first grade: learning to read and write and do arithmetic. It was better, but there was still no one to play with at recess. The boy who sat with him at his desk always turned around to talk to the girls on the other side, and he only turned back if Johnny pinched him.

About this time the story was interrupted by a quiet question. "Is this story really about our Georgie?"

"Yes, the little boy in the story is George. How did you know?"

"It sounds like him."

"George has been very unhappy since he came from Japan. He's unhappy most of the time."

"But he's a pest. He hurts us all the time and we don't do anything to him!"

"Let's see if you can tell why he hurts you." And I read the notes I had taken the day George had been in the sandbox.

"This is George's unfinished story. How do you suppose we can end it for him?"

"He can play with us. We're playing cowboys."

"We're playing kickball. He can play with us."

Out of the many responses I suggested the group I knew George wanted to play with most. When George returned to class, for the first time he was greeted with, "C'mon, George. We're going to play tether ball and if we don't hurry the courts will be gone." The smile on his face was a beautiful and fitting end to a long, unfinished story.

It was worth noting the academic success that followed on the heels of George's social success. In September he had tested high average on the Lee-Clark—even in the vocabulary—although I seldom heard him speak. He was in the lowest reading group because he simply did not respond to reading instruction. He either bothered everyone near him or stared into space. It was January before we finally were able to help him. At that time he was just starting the preprimers. He indicated that he wanted to join the top group with his new friends. They were half way through the primer. This posed a real problem, which I thought would be solved by having him visit. Within a few days I realized he was reading with them.

By the end of the year there was no difference between his work and theirs. He is now in third grade and has retained his place among the best in the class. Many times the sight of George running with his friends on the playground revives my sinking spirits in the morass of difficulties which face us each day.

Improving The Emotional Climate Of The Classroom

Sometimes the various individuals and factions in a classroom are so hostile to one another that much disruptive clash of feeling and byplay occur, to the degree that learning is impaired. Role-playing can offer significant help in bringing harmony to the stormy atmosphere. Not a single session but a well-planned series of sessions is usually necessary.

Preliminary analysis of the group structure of the class is helpful in determining the causes of dissension. Identification of the individuals who are key persons in the tangle of hostilities is also a necessity. Role-playing can then be structured to show the class the results of their disruptive activity, the reasons for it, and ways of solving the issues that are making pupils lash out at each other. Such experiences can do much to bring calm and team-work into the classroom.

Occasionally, in a classroom group, certain members who are outside the influential cliques are given no respect by their age-mates. In discussions, when these fringers make suggestions, their ideas are either ignored or mocked. An effective technique in such a situation is to bring aware-ness of what is happening to the group by playing a taped recording of a discussion in which the fringers' responses, although worthwhile, win no recognition from their classmates. A role-playing session then, in which influential members of the group (perhaps the actual of-fenders) take the roles of the individuals whose sugges-tions are ignored or belittled, can do much to help the offenders discover how their behavior is affecting the vic-tims. The class is helped, too, to realize that they have all suffered by not utilizing the worthwhile ideas presented by the unpopular members of the group.

Sometimes a committee does not function well. A role-playing session, in which other people portray the com-mittee in action, can do much to make the individual committee members aware of why they have not worked together well, of who have been disrupters and obstruc-tionists and noncooperators, and can help the committee members learn to cooperate productively.

Sometimes a fight occurs on the playground, or a group of pupils get into a brawl over taking turns in the use of play equipment. After an incident of this kind, the teacher can bring the class to a focus on the problem of their behavior through discussion. Then the teacher can have the group re-enact the whole incident just as it occurred. Further discussion can analyze the causes of the rumpus, the lack of consideration shown by individuals involved, the errors in tactics committed by even the well-mean-ing participants. Discussion can then turn to sensible ways in which the problem could have been handled—and those ways can be tested out in role-playing that puts good sense and consideration for the other fellow into practice.

Another area in which role-playing can be a potent instrument for growth is in helping a group to learn to appreciate individuals who are different. Often young people need to be guided to awareness that everyone has something to contribute to the group. In fact, the odd-ball may have something very important to contribute.

Role-playing sessions can be set up to show, for example, that the shy, soft-spoken individual in the group who never pushes himself into prominence, never interrupts when someone else is sounding off, may be the person who has special knowledge needed by the group. If given a chance, he would share it; but he needs special consideration from the others before he can speak up. The youngster who has trouble speaking good English may be a newcomer from a foreign country who could teach the other children much about skiing or fishing with a butterfly net or gathering sea shells or what the ruins of Pompeii look like or what you can see from the Tokyo Tower or how the Haida Indians make canoes or dig for "gooeyducks" or how you feed silkworms and treat cocoons to get the silk fibers or how sea shell is carved into cameos. The boy who limps because he had polio before the vaccines were developed may not be much of a runner when playing baseball but he may be a Dead-Eye Dick with a bow and arrow or a radio ham who talks to other hams a thousand miles away. Until you really get to know another person, you may be unaware of the talents he possesses; and when a group neglects or derides or rejects an individual who is in some way "different," it may be that the group is depriving itself of unsuspected riches. Role-playing can demonstrate this possibility to the class.

But, even more importantly, children must be helped to see all individuals as of worth, just because they are people, with feelings and desires, not alone because they have talents that may serve special causes. Everyone can contribute to and enrich life, in the cohesive group (Crosby, *Reading Ladders in Human Relations,* 1963).

PARENT-TEACHER CONFERENCING

Parent conferences can be prepared for through role-playing sessions. This is skills training for teachers. It can be done even as rehearsal for discussion with specific parents about the problems of a particular student. The young teacher who is shy, who tends to become tongue-tied with impressive people, who is naturally casual or brusque or sparing of words, can profit from role-playing with colleagues the act of greeting parents, of putting them at ease, the tactful presentation of the particular problems of classroom achievement their offspring is encountering. Such practice can be very helpful in learning how to win parents' understanding and cooperation in dealing with pupils' difficulties in the classroom.

HELPING A TROUBLED SECOND-GRADER

The following account shows how role-playing can be used to relieve a disturbing situation in a classroom, to bring help to a individual child, and to aid a whole class grow in tolerance and understanding.

Mrs. Nichols, who taught first and second grade in a suburban school, had nine-year-old Marilyn in her group. The girl should have been in the fourth grade, but had been put here in a combined first and second grade because she couldn't do fourth-grade work—and because the principal believed that Mrs. Nichols had the patience and warmth of personality to cope with Marilyn.[3]

On the playground, Marilyn was always a focus of trouble. She was the butt of playground mischief. Inside the classroom, she was still a center of furor: a disruptive clown, who would go through all kinds of antic

[3]The teacher in this true account of creative work is Mrs. Hildred Nichols of the Montebello Public Schools, Montebello, California. (See also H. Nichols and L. Williams, *Learning About Role-Playing for Children and Teachers.* Association for Childhood Education International, Washington, D.C., 1960.)

movements with her hands and face and body, cavorting and mugging for laughs. She couldn't concentrate on work, and she kept the other children from doing so by annoying and distracting them until they lashed out at her in irritation.

Marilyn was deaf.

And the only talk of which she was capable was gibberish.

She had been almost totally deaf from birth, and had never learned to talk so that she could be understood.

She was not a drab, apathetic child but a bright and lively youngster acrackle with energy, keenly alive to sensation and impulse. The trouble was, of course, that her energy and curiosity had no constructive outlet. Frustrated, it found expression in mischief. She acted the fool. She stole things. Inside the classroom or out on the playground, she was always embroiled in excitement, either upsetting other children or being the butt of teasing that almost drove her into screaming hysterics.

Mrs. Nichols could have asked that Marilyn be removed from the class. But she knew that if this were done, Marilyn would be permanently excluded from school, for she had a record of trouble making. In the school which she had previously attended, she had repeatedly rebelled by running away. Several times she had not been found until help from the police had been enlisted. Here, Mrs. Nichols realized, with her, was Marilyn's last chance for an education. Her parents, with five other children to support, were too poor to provide special schooling for Marilyn.

Mrs. Nichols decided that she would *have* to help Marilyn become a cooperative member of the class.

But how?

First of all, Mrs. Nichols got the P.T.A. to buy Marilyn a hearing aid. For the first time in her life, then, Marilyn could really hear.

Next, Mrs. Nichols asked for help from consultants in the office of the County Superintendent. It was arranged for Marilyn to have some special tutoring in speech and reading at home.

Marilyn's problem, however, was not merely to become able to learn, but to become accepted by her contemporaries and to become a functioning and cooperating member of the class.

Mrs. Nichols decided to use role-playing to help her with this problem. She then discovered that the materials she needed did not exist at first- and second-grade level.

So Mrs. Nichols created them.

She wrote a series of two-minute stories on the general theme of "How it feels to be different." She selected the kinds of happenings which intensely arouse the feelings of children, the kinds of pressures which make them behave explosively and unacceptably. And this series of stories —over a period of several months—she read aloud to the youngsters seated on the floor in a circle before her.

The first story, "Play Ball," told about a crippled boy who could not run. He did take part in the ball games, however, for his classmates ran for him. They liked him, and they respected him: he was very skillful at making model planes.

Another story she wrote for her circle of rapt listeners was "A Big Boy Like You," about a child who was so shy and got so fussed when grown-ups questioned him that he couldn't answer. And she read to her class the story "There's No Room," telling how a child felt when he wasn't wanted, as Marilyn so often had felt. Mrs. Nichols read "The Lost Ring," about a girl who sometimes stole things—though she didn't really intend to: the act was unpremeditated, and afterward she was just sick over having committed it.

"Have you ever felt badly about not getting something you wanted very much?" Mrs. Nichols asked her youngsters before reading "What Did You Get?" The story was about a boy whose family gave no presents one Christmas because of lack of money. Meeting his friends, the boy lied about what wonderful gifts he'd received. "Why do you suppose Johnny did that?" Mrs. Nichols asked the class.

Usually, after reading a story, all she had to do was ask a question to release a flood of reactions.

Discussion would be excited and eager as the children

told details from their own experiences or from those of friends. Mrs. Nichols achieved several goals simultaneously: as the weeks passed, she made the point—established and reinforced it, driving it home—that people may suffer not only from handicaps like a crippled leg which prevents running, but from other types of handicaps too, like shyness, or not being wanted, or not having money. Moreover, she was guiding the children into sharing experiences and feelings and ideas. Not only through discussion, but through role-playing.

Often she had the youngsters dramatize one of the stories, and act out roles in it, spontaneously, without structuring or rehearsing, just improvising as they went along.

They stepped into the story characters' shoes. They stepped into Marilyn's shoes. They "identified" with Marilyn, gradually and increasingly. They learned how much she wanted to be liked. They didn't know the words, but they grew aware of the frustration, the feelings of rejection and shame, which so often Marilyn had felt.

They made growth. Learning how Marilyn felt, they began to sympathize with her. It was only natural, then, that they began to ease up on her. They stopped teasing and prodding her into screaming outbursts. Instead, they began to accept her. They started including her in games. She was chosen on teams.

The result was, finally, that she—belonged.

All the careful work Mrs. Nichols had done paid off!

She had her class plan a culminating program for the end of the year, to which they invited the principal.

They showed him the things they had made in a construction unit. The pupils ran the whole show themselves. First and second graders! One would begin, would tell what he had made, how he had built it, and what tools he had used. Finished, he would call on another child to rise and perform.

And Marilyn took her turn with all the others.

Marilyn—the nine-year-old who hadn't been able to hear, at the beginning of the school term; who had been the disruptive element in the classroom, the child who

had to vent the frustrated life within her in making
trouble, the pathetic one who had run away when her
helplessness got too intense for bearing—Marilyn rose
when called upon, and took a turn like all the rest in
explaining her project. She didn't mumble it, didn't do a
fragmentary job, but gave a clear and logical presentation
which the principal could easily understand. Marilyn
could communicate now. Marilyn could talk intelligibly.
When her turn was over, she called upon the next child
and sat down. Just like anybody else.

Marilyn was no longer painfully "different."

An interesting footnote to Marilyn's story is worth adding. At the end of the year, Mrs. Nichols told the children
that all had passed, and all were being promoted. "Me,
too?" Marilyn demanded. "Yes," Mrs. Nichols assured
her. And Marilyn wailed, "But I don't *want* to leave the
first grade!"

Not only did Marilyn profit by this venture in teaching
for better human relations, but the whole class was helped
to grow in insight and sympathy. The effort Mrs. Nichols
had made, to mold attitudes and values, *did* carry out
of the classroom and onto the playground and into
neighborhood and home.

Role-Playing With Mentally Retarded Children

In the course of a research project in Special Education
(Daley and Cain, 1953) it was decided to try role-
playing with a group of mentally retarded ninth graders.
The teachers concerned were devoted and conscientious,
and eager for any help which held promise for their
students. They were, however, frankly dubious about role-
playing. They doubted that it was practical with their slow
learners. They believed that any presentation which called
for more than six or eight minutes of concentration on the
part of their students would not work. The consultant
urged them to try it, saying that she believed, out of
her experience with the problem-story procedure, that

even mentally retarded pupils would be able to participate for considerable periods.

The consultant came to one of the special classes, in a big city junior high school. The teacher was a skilled, sensitive person who had encouraged his students to develop spontaneity through use of a homemade puppet theatre.

He introduced the consultant by saying that, since they had had so much fun making up stories for their puppets, he thought that they'd like to hear another kind of story that Mrs. Jones had been using with other boys and girls.

The consultant set the stage for "Clubhouse Boat." This problem-story had not been tailored to meet the specific needs of mentally retarded students in junior high schools but was written for average fifth- and sixth-grade students.

Nevertheless, these members of the special class gave the consultant their full attention as she read the story. It took twenty minutes to tell, with some dramatics and elaboration of detail. No pupil became overtly restless. Many of the young people expressed their feelings, during the presentation, in whispers and quiet comments.

When the consultant stopped, and asked, "What do you think Tommy will do?" there was a long moment of silence. Then the students began to talk.

These mentally retarded youngsters had ideas. They explored the consequences Tommy would face if he kept the money. With a little encouragement, several students got up and role-played a solution to the dilemma. Even a brain-injured girl who, the consultant had been warned beforehand, was often irrelevant in her comments, made pertinent remarks.

The class not only offered as many real solutions as "normal" classroom groups, but added considerations the consultant had never before been given. Further discussion revealed that these mentally retarded youngsters understood the story dilemma very well—*because they had held jobs and had actual experience of similar conflicts themselves.*

The adults present who were observing, and who knew

these young people well, were surprised and delighted at the amount of participation in both role-playing and discussion which this session brought forth.

Moreover, instead of showing an attention span of just six or eight minutes, this retarded group participated in the role-playing for almost fifty minutes. This tended to confirm the belief among the adults that mentally retarded youngsters have abilities that have not been tapped for lack of media that release their powers.

When the period ended, several students came to the consultant and told her, "That was a good story!" and they asked her to come back after lunch because they wanted to put on a puppet show for her.

At one o'clock she came back to the classroom. At the suggestion of their teacher, the group put on a puppet version of "Clubhouse Boat." And it was good! They recalled every significant element of the problem-story. In fact, they even inserted a scene which had been merely implied in the original. Their production was complete, the dialogue natural, and they acted out a sensible solution. And these were retarded youngsters!

When given material that touched upon the problems that were real for them in terms of the life situations they knew, they demonstrated a level of practical judgment that was considerably above the ability which the school had been able to elicit from them before. Role-playing, when structured through the problem-story, enabled them to perform in terms of the daily life experience they knew, and they had the exhilaration of success rather than the frustration encountered so often when dealing with academic materials.

EASING OUT-OF-SCHOOL PROBLEMS THROUGH ROLE-PLAYING

A teacher who works with role-playing for some time finds that she has released unexpected potentialities in her pupils which can help them to deal with some of their out-of-school problems.

For example, it was suggested to the members of two classes who had considerable experience with role-playing that they might like to write their own problem-stories.

The results were very satisfying. Pupils produced stories that were informative about the young people themselves, and therefore of help to the teachers in understanding their students. Some of the stories were used for role-playing. The two classes were so pleased with the results that they planned to do more writing.[4]

One of these stories is reproduced below, with a record of how one class role-played one of the narratives.

ROCK HAPPY JUDY

I was out in the backyard, playing with my friend Jack . . . . When my sister came up and hit me with a rock, and she ran around the house. Mother called Judy into the house and asked her if she hit me with a rock, and she said she didn't. There was a big argument between Judy and me. She said that somebody else must have thrown the rock from behind me. I didn't believe a word Judy said because it was all a lie. Of course just because Judy is a girl, I guess Mother took her word, and told me to go outside and play and forget it. So I went outside and began to play, when up came my sister again and hit me. Then my friend and I went into the house together and told Mother. Mother called Judy in again and we had a nice little argument and Mother still wouldn't believe us. Now you try to solve this case for us. . . .

The classroom teacher, although in most cases not trained as a guidance worker, inevitably does much to counsel her pupils, both in individual instances and as a group. Role-playing can aid her in various ways: for diagnosing tensions and sources of strain in the classroom group, for helping individuals to become more self-assured, for helping the group to learn to accept and sup-

[4] Guided and supervised by Barbara Celse Hunt, Supervisor, Orange County Schools, California.

port the individual who is "different," for improving the emotional climate of the classroom.

A child builds an image of himself from the reflected opinions about him of others around him. It is important, therefore, to maximize the chances for individuals to earn the respect of peers and teachers. Role-playing can provide opportunities for the underappreciated individual to improve his status with his age-mates; and such improvement often not only betters a pupil's self-esteem but significantly improves his learning achievement. Role-playing, too, can help to build heightened sensitivity in the group for the feelings of the individual who is the butt of jokes, for the fringer and the isolate, and thereby can increase their chances for acceptance in the group. When cliques and factions cause a stormy emotional climate in the classroom, role-playing in which the effects of such strife are portrayed, and in which consciousness of the feelings evoked is awakened, can do much to produce peace in classroom relationships.

Role-playing can help the teacher in such aspects of guidance work as parent-teacher conferencing. The inexperienced teacher can *practice* consultation with other teachers, in order to acquire some skill and confidence.

Making Letters

John Holt

from *What Do I Do Monday?*

In our work with children, there are a couple of good rules to keep in mind. One is that it is always better to say to a child—instead of "Do it this way"—"How many ways can you think of to do it?" The other is to let children find, by experiment, trial and error, and imitation, which of the possible ways of doing a thing is best for them. This best way may often be our way, the way we would have "taught." This is what Dennison means by "the natural authority of adults." But even if in the end children do come to *our* way of doing things, we should let them do so in *their* way. Some might say, "Why waste time? If we know that a given way of doing things is best, why not just tell the children to do it that way?" But our way may not be the best way, but only the way we are used to. Also, the best way for us, or for some children, may not be the best way for all. Finally, it is *always* better, if he can do so at not too great cost or risk, for a child to find out something for himself than to be told. Only from making choices and judgments can he learn to make them better, or learn to trust his own judgment.

A scene comes to mind. While I was visiting a college, giving several talks and observing different parts of the school's work with children, someone asked me to come to a seminar, run by some operant conditioners, behavior reinforcers. In general, I don't like this way of dealing with children, or for that matter people of any age. This seemed all the more reason to see some of what they were doing. Perhaps what they were doing was better than it had sounded. Perhaps it was worse.

The leaders of this seminar were telling about some of the work they had done teaching four- or five-year-olds to write—that is, to make letters. They explained reinforcement theory and their own methods. I believe they generally gave the children tokens or points. Soon one of the leaders said, "Now the first thing we have to do is teach the children the right way to hold the pencil." We all nodded agreement. But then, as they told about the prizes they gave to children who held their pencils correctly, I began to wonder. Suppose we *didn't* teach children how to hold the pencil? What would happen? And then an even more subversive thought crept in. Is it really true that the way we all hold our pencils is the only way, the best way? Might some other ways not work as well? So, sitting on the floor in my corner of the room, I began to experiment. Soon I found five other ways of holding a pencil. One was at least as good as the conventional grip. The others were a bit awkward, but with them I could make a legible handwriting recognizably my own. Switching to the left hand, where I was starting from scratch with all grips, I found one of my new grips much more comfortable for me than the conventional grip, though it made my handwriting slant the other way.

Now, as I write, I have done the same experiment again. Results are the same. There *are* other ways to hold pencils, and some of them, for children with small and weak fingers, might at first be a good deal better than the one we try to teach them. Given the right kind of pencil or pen (like a ball-point), it is really very easy to write with the pen gripped in the whole fist. Writing with the left hand, for me at least, the fist grip is considerably easier and more controllable. Also, my hand doesn't have to touch the paper, which might do away with the problem of smearing the ink. I suspect that the fist grip might be much less cramping and tiring for little children. But anyway, why not let them learn to hold a pen the way they learn to ride a bike or whistle or do a thousand other things far more complicated and difficult than holding a pen? Children want to learn to write—watch any two-year-old with pencil and paper. If we give them pencil and paper, they will try out different grips to see which works best for them. They will certainly look to see how we do it, and will probably do it our way if they can. But if something else is more comfortable for them, where's the harm?

I did not raise this issue at the seminar. I had come to hear their story, not to tell them mine. I left the meeting feeling as strongly as before (and much more strongly now) that getting children to do things by rewarding them every time they do what we want is unneccessary, harmful, and even in its own terms inefficient.

Men, and above all little children, have much more intelligence than, say, pigeons, and it seems unwise, to say the least, to treat them the same. Even if efficiency is all we are interested in—and it ought not to be—the efficient way to teach any creature is to make the fullest possible use of his capacities.

We have such a passion for uniformity and control! One might think we had all come off one of our own assembly lines. In classrooms all over the country we can see, tacked up over the chalkboards, the same letter chart —on green cardboard—capital and lower case A, then capital and lower case B, then C, and so on. On some of these charts, and these I would really like to rip off the wall, there are even little arrows and numbers to show in what direction and in what order the child must make the strokes of the letter! Must children feel that they have to make their letters in *exactly* the shape they see on the chart? This might make sense if it were true that only the exact shape of the A could be recognized by other people as an A. But this is not true. Even the books in our classrooms have many different kinds of A's. Typography is one of the great crafts or even arts, with a long history of its own. Why not give children a glimpse of this part of the continuum of experience? Why not get, from any maker of type, or printer, or commercial artist, or art supply store, some sheets of samples of type faces, so that children can see some of the many ways in which we make our letters? Better yet, why not invite the children, using old newspapers, magazines, labels, and so on, to find as many different kinds of A's (or other letters) as they can?

By the way, we ought to make sure to use the words "capital" and "lower case" instead of words like "big" and "little" or "large" and "small," or anything else suggesting that the difference is a matter of size. The difference is a matter of shape; size has nothing to do with it. We can make any capital or lower case letter as small or as large as we wish. Some of the children may ask why we call some letters Capital and other Lower Case. The word "capital" may come from the fact that the Romans (who invented our alphabet) used those letters on the capitals, that is, across the tops, of buildings. I'm not sure of this. Lower case has to do with the ways in which printers arrange letters in a font, or case, of type. If there is a printing shop around that you can visit, the children can see what lower case means. Or perhaps someone could bring a font of type to the class for the children to look at. And this raises other questions, to which I don't know the answers. Who invented lower case letters, and for what reason or purpose? When did men start using capital letters for the rather special purposes for which we now use them, with lower case used most of the time? Do other alphabets, and if so which, make the distinctions we do between capital and lower case letters?

We might start everyone thinking about the number of ways we can make a capital A. We could make it tall and thin, or short and fat. We could make it slant to the right or to the left. We could make the strokes thick (heavy) or thin (light), or a mixture of the two. We could put feet (serifs) on the legs, or leave them off. We could put the bar high in the letter, or low in the letter. We could weight the lefthand stroke, as in the type face Ultra Bodoni. Or we could weight the righthand stroke. We could make our strokes hollow, or fill them with cross-hatching, or dots. We could make our strokes out of wiggly lines, or right-angled steps, or dots, or short dashes. Or we could make our strokes out of the letter A itself, or some other letter—why not an A made out of B's, and a B made out of A's? Children like such novelties. They suggest that the world is a fascinating place, full of possibilities. Why not tempt children with the idea of making A's (or other letters) in as many different ways as possible? Making letters would then be an exploration, an adventure, not a chore. The chances are that they would make a great many more letters. Also, by making a variety of shapes they would train and coordinate the writing muscles of <u>hand</u> and arm far better than they could with the old, laborious, wrinkled-brow, tongue-sticking-out-of-the-corner-of-the-mouth drill.

This is just a beginning. Suppose we have a collection of A's. There are at least two things we can do with the collection. We can consider for each pair of those A's what the significant variable is. An example will make this clear. In the first pair of A's the variable might be called Proportion—the ratio of height to width. (Some good new words here—as I say elsewhere, the idea of ratio is fundamental to the idea of number.) In the second pair of A's the variable is the direction of slant—Right or Left. Another variable could be the amount of slant. Who can draw the slantiest A? In the next pair the variable might be called Weight (or Thickness) of Stroke. Naming the variables may suggest new variables to us. Or it may suggest ways in which we can combine variables. Thus, we might have an A which is thin, slightly slanted, slanted left, and heavy stroked. Children play a lot of these classifying or categorizing games in school as it is—why not combine them in an interesting way with the world of letters? For older children there are mathematical possibilities in this that I won't even go into here—the total number of kinds of A's you could make combining all these variables, and so on.

Another game would be, given a particular A, to make a similar B, or C, or some other letter. (Again, we are in the field of likes and differences.) Or make an entire matching alphabet. Or, given a certain A, make a B in all respects the opposite—given a Heavy, Right Slanting,

Fat A, make a Light, Left Slanting, Thin B. We might put these letters on cards and have various ways of sorting them—put similar letters together, or opposite together, or all the ones together that have a given variable in common. We might play with these letters some of the kinds of matching and sorting games found in the excellent piece of classroom equipment called Attribute Blocks (McGraw Hill Corporation, Webster Division, St. Louis, Missouri). Or we might invent a color code, assigning a color to each variable. Thus if to the variable of Proportion we gave the color blue, and agreed that a large number indicated a tall thin letter, and a small number a short, fat letter, we could use color and number to designate a certain kind of A. How might we designate slant by using a number? What do people mean when they say a highway has a slope of 1 in 10? What kind of people, in the course of their work, have to interest themselves in such matters? What is the steepest grade usable for a railroad? An auto road? Or we could use degrees to measure slant, and thus introduce children to the protractor, and also to another part of mathematics, the measurement of angles in degrees.

Children can make letters out of other things than pencil and paper. Why not letters you can feel as well as see? There can be many advantages in this. Children who have become so anxious about reading that they can hardly even *see* letters, let alone tell one letter from another— see my remarks about this in *How Children Fail,* or Dennison's moving description of José trying to read in *The Lives of Children*—can regain their sense of the shape by feeling it. The Montessori schools have letters made of sandpaper or cardboard or wood backing, which the children feel, and learn to know by touch. A good idea; but like much Montessori equipment the letters are expensive, and because sandpaper is hard to cut, they are hard to make. We can find cheaper and easier ways to do the same thing. How about gluing heavy twine to cardboard to make the shapes of letters? How about putting rough crepe paper, or perhaps strips of masking tape, on a background of glossy paper? How about using double-sided

Scotch tape, and then putting salt or sand on the top? How about pegs in a pegboard, or round-headed map pins pushed into cardboard? How about letters made of grooves pressed into clay, or out of glass beads pressed into clay?

Recently I visited the Children's Community Workshop School in New York City, a wonderful independent public school—that is, a school open to all and charging no tuition. Many of the children in one of the early age groups were sticking oranges full of cloves, to make a scent ball to hang in a clothes closet. As I helped one little boy with his clove orange (he asked me to), an idea came, and I stuck cloves into an orange to make my name, J O H N. Quite a number of children came round to watch as I made those letters. It seemed hardly possible that one *could* make letters with cloves and an orange—letters were made with pencil and paper—and yet, there they were. The boy asked me if he could keep the orange. I said sure, so at the end of the day he took it home, wrapped up—bundled up might be a better word —in tissue paper.

Why not mobiles of letters? Letters hanging from the ceiling? It would be easy to make them of pipe cleaners. Or papier-mâché, on a core of rolled or crumped paper. What could be more handsome than papier-mâché letters, printed in bright colors? Or we might make letters of the cardboard cylinders in paper towels. Or letters of rubber tubing. Or of spaghetti, bent when wet and then allowed to dry. Of plasticene or clay. Of wire from coat hangers, or, for schools in farm country, of baling wire. Of cloth cylinders stuffed with more cloth. Huge letters, tall as a child.

Another project. Using only one sheet of paper, how big a letter can we write? How big, if you can use more than one sheet? What is the largest letter that can be made, keeping inside the classroom? Outside the classroom? In the schoolyard, can we draw huge letters with chalk? Write them in the snow? Make them out of snow? Or could we make letters out of children themselves, like marching bands at a football game? If the school building has several floors, someone might take photos of these child-letters from an upper window. Which letters can we make with our fingers? I don't mean drawing with the fingers, I mean using the fingers themselves for the parts of the letter. Some letters are easy—T, C, etc. Others are not so easy. Can we make them all? How many letters can we make, using our whole body—arms, legs, etc.? If two or more children work together on this, how many can they make? Can you have a dance of letters? Children might be interested to know that in many languages all words have gender, that is, are boy-words or girl-words. If letters had to be boy-letters or girl-letters, which would be which?

We might show children how to use the lettering rules that draftsmen use to get uniform lettering on their drawings. From these, a child would learn through his hand, his muscles, what it felt like to make a letter of a certain shape. Stencils, rubber letter blocks, any kind of printing material, are all popular with children. Let children who are starting to make letters begin by tracing. Write a letter with heavy strokes, using a black felt-tipped pen; then let them put it under their paper and trace from it, over and over, perhaps in rhythm, until they get the feel of it. From drugstores, get Magic Writing Pads—write on one, lift up the paper, and the letter disappears. This is good for beginners—if they make a bad one, they can get rid of all traces of it immediately. No erasing, smudges, holes in the paper. In certain kinds of import stores, more on the coasts than further inland, we can often get the kind of small slates that all children use in countries where chalk is cheap and paper scarce. Children like to write on these, and again, erasing is easy, which is important for nervous beginners.

From these beginnings, I am sure you can think of many more ideas of your own. I have written at such length on a very simple subject to show that *nothing,* not even a task as seemingly cut-and-dried as making letters, needs to be monotonous, frightening, dull, cut off from the rest of learning and of life, or from the possibility of imagination, experiment, invention, play.

Teaching Children to Think

Joseph Featherstone

from *Schools Where Children Learn*

Discontented people in Britain sometimes make polemical use of an imaginary land called America, where everything is democratic and efficient. My purpose is not to create another, equally useless myth for the comfort of disheartened American educators. There is nothing utopian about the good British schools I am describing. Teachers are, by American standards, underpaid (salaries start at $30 a week). The turnover in staff is rapid, and schools receive pittances for buying equipment and books. Teaching is often a flat business and always a tough one. It is of immense practical significance that in the flat, tough world of overworked teachers and daily routines, substantial numbers of British primary teachers are organizing their classrooms in a way that really does promote individual learning, that allows children to develop at their own pace in the early years of school.

As examples of this kind of approach, I've described how children learn to read and write, and the careful way in which they are introduced to mathematics. These methods are not guaranteed to make bad teachers, or people who dislike children, into good teachers. But they are more suited than formal methods to the nature of small children and to the kinds of subjects that should be taught in primary school; and they encourage many ordinary teachers, who find that they are happier using them and less likely to spend all their time worrying about discipline. Such methods assume that children can re-

260

spond to courteous treatment by adults, and that to a great extent they can be trained to take the initiative in learning —if choices are real, and if a rich variety of material is offered them. As the Plowden Report concedes, these assumptions are not true for all children (some will probably always benefit more from formal teaching) or for every child all of the time. But the Report is itself testimony to a growing conviction in Britain that these assumptions can provide a workable basis for an entire nation's schools.

Are they a workable basis for American schools? The task of creating American schools along these lines will be formidable, to say the very least. This isn't the place to rehearse the institutional and cultural obstacles to change in American education, but I want to anticipate some of the most serious questions that may be raised about the kinds of schools I've talked about. In reform, as in anything else, there must be priorities, and the first priority is simply to see clearly.

Some Americans acknowledge that good British schools are doing better work than good American schools, but they are reluctant to admit that this is because, among other things, children are given freedom to choose from among selected activities in the classroom and to move around the room talking to each other. If they are teachers, they may react to such a proposition with contempt, because they know how hard it is to maintain classroom discipline. Where the class is taught as a unit, and every child is supposed to pay attention as the teacher talks, discipline can be a serious matter; it is even more so when the class splits into groups for reading aloud, as any first-grade teacher knows. Quick children get restless; slow children dread the ordeal, and act accordingly. Any teacher who can keep order under the circumstances has a certain amount of talent, however wasted. Tony Kallet, a perceptive American who worked as an advisor in Leicestershire, has written of the difficulties in maintaining control of the class in the good, but very formal, American school in which he apprenticed. Some children managed quite well, he recalls, but others, especially the "problem children," found the discipline too much, too little was permitted them, and "their problems were, in part, being created, rather than mitigated by control." After working with English classes, he saw matters in a different light, but, for all the time he was in an American classroom, "it did truly seem that every single control imposed was necessary if anything was to be accomplished," a view with which many American teachers will sympathize.

Watching children in British classes working diligently on their own prompts another question: are British children fundamentally different from Americans, and are there critical differences in national character? No doubt there are differences; and yet middle-aged English visitors to the informal schools often react with the same disbelief as American visitors; they find it hard to credit British children with so much initiative and so much responsibility. Also, formal schools in Britain have many discipline problems. American teachers working on their own —and how lonely they seem—have succeeded with approaches similar to those of good British primary schools. Herbert Kohl ran a sixth-grade class in Harlem along fairly free lines and his book, *36 Children,* includes extraordinarily powerful samples of the children's free writing. A British teacher from one of the good local authorities came to a large American city to teach a demonstration class of eight- to eleven-year-olds in a slum school. Before leaving England, he was assured—by Americans—that he would find American children as different from British as day is from night. Yet, the American children reacted exactly as English children to a classroom thoughtfully laid out to permit choices. At first they couldn't believe he meant what he said. After a timid start, they began rushing around the room, trying to sample everything fast, as though time were going to run out on them. Then they "settled remarkably quickly to study in more depth and to explore their environment with interest and enthusiasm." The teacher noticed that for the first two weeks no one did any written English or math, and when he asked them why, they said they hated those subjects. Eventually, he got more and more of the class interested in free writing, but he never could get them interested in mathematics. The schools had permanently soured them on math.

Another argument one hears against this kind of education is that it won't prepare children for life. The answer the Plowden Report makes to this seems to me sensible: the best preparation for life is to live fully as a child. Sometimes this fear takes the reasonable form of a parent's question: will these informal methods handicap a child if he moves on to a school run on formal lines? It is a real question in Britain as children move from good infant schools to old-fashioned junior schools, or from informal primary school to rigid secondary school. I went to a parents' meeting at one superb infant school; the parents were completely won over by the methods of the school, but they were nonetheless apprehensive of what could become of their children in a new situation. The head of the school said that the children did in fact do well in the formal junior school, which was true. There was only one repeated complaint about them: they were not very good at sitting still for long periods of time. In general, an ability to write and to understand mathematics—to say nothing of an ability to work on their own—stand children in good stead, whatever school they later attend. Heads of good schools insist that children are more adaptable than most parents imagine—and one indication that the problem of switching from one school to another is not crucial is that most principals in good local authorities agree with the Plowden Report's recommendation for another year of the informal methods of infant school: with an extra year, most of them think, they could lick their remaining reading problems, and the transition will be even easier.

Another pressing question Americans ask is, oddly enough, historical. It is said that these kinds of classes were tried in the progressive era of American education, and found wanting. This is one of those historical lessons we cling to, and, since nothing is as treacherous as our sense of recent history, it bears looking into. Progressive education, like the progressive movements in thought and politics, was woven from many different, often contradictory threads. It evolved against a background of the great shift in the function of American secondary schools, a change from elite preparatory institutions to mass terminal institutions; just as in the 1950s, when our present picture of progressive education was firmly etched in the popular mind, many high schools were turning into mass college preparatory institutions. The radical attempt to give secondary education to the whole American population was an important aspect of progressive education, just as the reaction against it was appropriate to an era when nearly half the students in secondary school would go on to college.

As a movement, progressive education reflected a new concern for science brought to bear on society. In the schools this meant educational psychology, tests, and the cult of research. Another element was a concern with social reform: John Dewey's vain hope that the schools could in some way become centers for the continuous reconstruction of society. A distinct, if sometimes related strand, was an emphasis on individual growth and development. This last, in particular, was reflected in the practices of a number of American private schools in the 1920s and 1930s. Good and bad, these schools tended to see children through ideological lenses: they were followers of Freud, at least to the extent that they thought repression wicked, and some idealized children as participants in the artist's historic struggle against bourgeois society. The best of the "child-centered" private schools based much of their teaching on the idea that children come to understand the world through active play; they tried to get students to take part in the running of the school; they broke down barriers dividing one subject from another, often making the surrounding community and its life part of the school curriculum. These seem today the sounder aspects of their work. The ideological emphasis on liberating the child now appears less useful. In some progressive schools, the energies of staff and children were wasted in testing the limits of permissible behavior, a procedure that was almost forced on the children by an abdication of adult authority. It is not strange that this abdication did not always lead to more freedom: in practice, freeing children from adult authority can mean exposing them to the tyranny of their peers; eliminating "external" rules can mean setting up subtle and unacknowledged rules that are just as ruthless and, even worse, vague and arbitrary.

There isn't much evidence that the classroom practices of the progressive private schools which stressed individual growth ever spread far and wide. The emphasis on cooperation and adjustment to the group was shared by the public school, but it took a different turn: preaching adjustment and "Americanization," the public schools were playing one of their traditional roles—taming objectionable outsiders, shaping them to fit into society, making sure that immigrants and lower class people made the minimum of trouble. The public school wing of the progressive movement in education was thus deeply conservative; obsessed with reform of school administration, putting the operations of the schools more in line with the principles of scientific management espoused by Frederick Taylor and his disciples. (It says much about a misunderstood period that the idea of a school managed as a business was more powerful than the idea of the school as a model civic community, though of course social science, civics, and other shattered fragments of John Dewey's dream did enter the curriculum for better or worse.)

With certain notable exceptions, what we call progressive education was seldom tried in American public schools. In practice, progressive education in public schools meant secondary education for all, and, perhaps, more educational opportunity; more courses, especially in high school, of the life-adjustment variety; more time given to extracurricular activities; more grouping by ability; more emphasis on testing; some "project work" that was no doubt a welcome relief from the textbooks; some more or less important changes in the textbooks themselves; professionalization; new degrees and credentials for educators; and reform in the management of the schools, often based on inappropriate models from the world of business.

What wisps of the vision of education as individual growth trailed into the public schools were largely rhetorical. In their famous study of "Middletown" (Muncie, Indiana) in 1925, Robert and Helen Lynd described the classroom: "Immoveable seats in orderly rows fix the sphere of activity to each child. For all from the timid six-year-old . . . to the . . . high school senior . . . the general routine is much the same." When they returned to Middletown ten years later, "progressive education" had arrived. There was talk of growth, personality development, and creative self-expression: ". . . the aim of education should be to enable every child to become a useful citizen, to develop his individual powers to the fullest extent of which he is capable, while at the same time engaged in useful and lifelike activities." Along with the new rhetoric, the Lynds noted, went increased stress on administration. There was no basic change in methods of teaching or classroom organization. Their report can stand as a paradigm of what progressive education amounted to in most American schools. Education that treats people as individuals had become a cliché without ever being reality.

There are parallels here with the primary school revolution in Britain. It, too, is distantly tied to the changing role of the secondary schools, and certainly much of its rhetoric is reminiscent of our progressive-education movement. British schools certainly share the concern with individual development of the good American progressive schools. And yet the differences in the two movements are profound. Although the British schools stress cooperation, and children are encouraged to teach each other, there is no abdication of adult authority and no belief that this would be desirable. The role of the teacher as active catalyst and stage manager is central. The idea of giving children choices is a considered judgment as to how they best learn. The teaching of mathematics, as described, illustrates how intent these schools are on teaching children to think; they have no particular ideological interest in turning children into social saviours or artistic rebels against bourgeois conventions, or whatever. It is this deep pedagogical seriousness, the attention paid to learning in the classroom, that makes the British primary school revolution so different from American progressive education, which was all too often unconcerned with pedagogy.

This pedagogical focus and what it means can be seen in the way informal British schools are solving the problem of grouping children into classes according to abilities —what the British call "streaming," and what we call "tracking." In both countries it is customary for larger schools to track students so that there are A, B, C, and sometimes D or E classes in a supposed order of ability and intelligence. (And within a class there are slow, average, and fast reading groups.) On the whole, teachers in Britain and America favor the practice, and it is easy to see why. When you deal with the class as a unit, when learning is done by groups, it is less grueling if the group is of roughly similar abilities, and, within limits of conventional instruction, tracking does enable children to go at something closer to their own pace. Tracking, or streaming, is a heated subject in Britain, as it is in America. The spread of informal methods of teaching is calling its utility into question, and many of the schools run on freer lines are abandoning the practice. The Plowden Report, which favors "unstreaming," cites a survey of tested differences between formal and informal schools. It suggests that in terms of measurable achievement, children in tracked schools do slightly but not much better than children in informal schools where tracking has been abandoned. There are, as I have mentioned, grounds for discounting this finding: formal schools train children to take achievement tests, whereas informal ones teach more important things, and we have evidence that the differences in test scores wane as the children grow older.

In England, as in America, there are many reasons why a practical alternative to tracking would be desirable. Tracking in a primary school brands certain children as stupid at an early age, with profound and unhappy effects. "I'll never forget the look on the faces of the boys in the lower stream," an East London junior school head told me. His school has successfully abolished the practice, but he is unable to forget the look: "I still see it when my boys in the lower streams of secondary modern school come back to visit." Tracking has an abiding effect on teachers, too: it tempts them to think that a single pattern of instruction can be applied to a whole class, and it increases the odds that they will deal with their children in terms of abstract categories, IQ, racial stereotype, or whatever. In England, as in America, the upper tracks of a school tend to be middle class, which makes the school even more an instrument for reinforcing social inequity. In America, tracking is commonly a means of maintaining racial segregation within a supposedly integrated school.

After watching British classes, another defect of tracking occurs to you: it ignores the extent to which children learn from each other, slow children learning from the quick, and the bright ones, in turn, learning from the role of teacher they must adopt with the slow. This is most evident in the small number of schools that use family, or vertical, grouping where there is not only no grouping by ability, but no grouping by age, and every class is a mixed bag of older and younger children.

Yet it makes little sense to condemn tracking unless teachers can be shown alternatives to formal classroom teaching. This is where the pedagogical bite of the primary school revolution is so impressive. When a British school stops tracking today, it is not simply returning to the past; it is shifting to a different definition of the roles of teacher and student, and setting up a new kind of classroom in which students are trained to work independently. With the blessing of the Plowden Report, fewer and fewer infant schools track, and it is more and more common for junior schools to abandon tracking in the first two years, and in some cases in the third. How far this trend will go depends on the impact the primary school revolution makes on the secondary schools. One survey in the Plowden Report shows that teachers who used to be overwhelmingly in favor of streaming as a general policy for primary schools are coming to approve of unstreaming. The reason, clearly, is that they are beginning to see workable alternatives.

Tracking is regarded as a necessary evil in America, as are IQ and standardized achievement tests, formal class teaching, specified curriculum materials, set hours for set subjects, fixed ages for entering school, being promoted, and so on. Of course, teachers and administrators realize that children's intellectual and emotional growth varies just as widely as their physical growth, yet they seldom feel able to act on their understanding, to treat each child differently. The good British schools raise serious doubts as to whether these evils are in fact necessary. In America, as in England, there is a growing, and on the whole healthy, skepticism about education. People are questioning the standard methods, and they are becoming realistic about the limited extent to which any school can be expected to pick up the marbles for the rest of society. (One interpretation of the Coleman Report would be that it calls into question all our standard techniques of education, in slums as well as suburbs.) No approach to teaching will solve America's historical and social problems, but, as far as education can make a difference, the work of the British schools in many different kinds of communities suggests practical, working models of individual learning. For those who believe that what American education needs is not more of the same, it suggests alternatives.

The forces that might help bring about similar changes in American schools are few. To some extent the best of the American curriculum projects—such as the Educational Development Center—are pushing schools in the right direction. Good, open-ended materials are often in themselves a kind of retraining course for willing teachers, helping them become more confident about trying informal methods. Curriculum materials are by no means being abandoned in the British schools, but they are making different use of them. Curriculum materials must give teachers and students freedom to use them in a variety of ways; the best materials are often simply handbooks and guides to new approaches, rather than set lessons. Good materials become even more important in the later years of school. Geoffrey Caston, of the Schools Council, worries that the successful methods of the infant schools, where, of course, the curriculum is largely generated by the students' own activities, will prove less successful when widely applied to older children by teachers of varying abilities. This may or may not be true. I saw junior schools where the free methods of the infant schools were being triumphantly vindicated, but I saw others that were very sleepy and could have used the stimulation of good materials. It is unlikely that curriculum projects can make much difference in America until they find a way of engaging ordinary teachers in creating materials. Americans should profit from the British understanding that the valuable and enduring part of curriculum reform is the process of creation and thought; unless you let teachers in on that, the stuff is likely to be dead. The American curriculum projects and some school systems might help set up equivalents to the advisory centers in good British authorities, teams of teachers and others whose only task is to work in the field with classroom teachers, spreading new ideas. Jerrold Zacharias once proposed display centers that would act as supermarkets for teachers interested in new ideas and techniques. (One role of the advisors in England is to take over classes for teachers so they can attend courses and displays.)

Certainly, useful work could be done developing new kinds of tests in the United States. The IQ and standard achievement tests are not the bogies they are made out to be—I suspect that schools use tests as an excuse to keep from having to try out anything new—but the likelihood of change would be increased if their grip on the minds of school administrators and parents could be loosened. Tests that reflect an ability to express oneself in writing or to reason mathematically would be a help: the problem is to persuade Americans to consider the relevance of standards other than the ones now used. Clearly new tests alone won't solve that. Techniques, particularly when devised by outsiders, are never going to be enough.

It is within the schools that change has to come. Yet

the prospects are dim. American private schools that once promoted progressive education are now largely formal in their methods; many are test-ridden, catering to parents who want solid evidence that a second-grade performance will lead to Harvard. They invite John Holt's gibe, "A conservative is someone who worships a dead radical." There are American communities in which principals and teachers are confident of their relationship with parents, and in such places, schools could begin to work along individual lines. Good suburban schools, able to withstand the possibility of slightly lower achievement test scores, also exist, but they seem to be getting rarer. Some of the better Headstart programs may influence the schools to make the first few years of learning more flexible, and perhaps some cities where education has reached a crisis point can be prodded into setting up some freer demonstration classes.

A new class of schools in the United States likely to be interested in informal learning are the community schools which are beginning to appear in a few cities. Yet they have the burden of working out another, perhaps more important, educational problem: how to get parents to participate in the life of the school. This is hard enough, without trying simultaneously to change traditional patterns of classroom teaching. Parents in community schools, like parents everywhere when they face schools, lack convincing models of how things could be different, and they are rightly suspicious of theories and experiments.

This is the point: we lack actual classrooms that people can see, that teachers can work in, functioning schools that demonstrate to the public and to educators the kind of learning I have described. These must be institutions that develop and grow over time, not just demonstration classes. (New York City has tried out every good idea in educational history—once.) To make any impact, such schools will have to be very different from the private experiments of the 1920s and 1930s, with their ideological confusions and their indifference to public education. The temptation is to say America needs many such schools, and we do. But a tiny number of infant schools pioneered the changes in Britain. Careful work on a small scale is the way to start a reform worth having, whatever our grandiose educational reformers might say. In the end, you always return to a teacher in a classroom full of children. That is the proper locus of a revolution in the primary schools. . . .

WHY SO FEW GOOD SCHOOLS?

I've used examples in writing, math, and the arts to show some of the work done in good junior British schools. But why are there so few of them? I can only hazard a few guesses.

The Plowden Report described a survey made some years ago, which said that as children went from the infant to the junior level there is a

narrowing of opportunities, a tendency toward regimentation, a substitution of group or even class teaching for individual work. Many children tackled less difficult work and wrote less in their own words than they had done some months before. The libraries in the youngest junior classes were often inferior in quality and range to those the children had left behind in the top infant classes, and children spent more time on "readers" and less on real books. Individual interests in music and art and craft had petered out. Some boys whose ability and attendance were average or poor had fallen back in almost every respect when seen four months after transfer. They made little perceptible headway by the end of the year.

This is probably less true today, for more junior schools have altered their ways. Many of the junior schools I saw were at least struggling to change, if not always with great success. But in others, the danger signals the Plowden Report cites in another context were too evident: "Fragmented knowledge, no changes in the past decade, creative work very limited, much time spent on teaching, few questions from the children, too many exercises, too many rules, frequent punishments, and concentration on tests."

One important reason for the rigidities of junior schools is the secondary schools they serve. What is wrong with British secondary schools is a long, long story, but in general they are even more meritocratic than American high schools; they brand more kids as failures; they are as prone to teach a curriculum and set subjects that don't make sense to a lot of their students. What the system does to failures is obvious. It may be even more illuminating to note what it does to successes. Richard Hoggart has described the state of mind of the scholarship student, the product of the upper reaches of the British system. It may have a familiar ring to American readers:

He begins to see life, for as far as he can envisage it, as a series of hurdle jumps, the hurdles of scholarships which are won by learning how to amass and manipulate the new currency. He tends to over-stress the importance of examinations, of the piling-up of knowledge and of received opinions. He discovers a technique of apparent learning, of the acquiring of facts rather than of the handling and use of facts. He learns how to receive a purely literate education, one using only a small part of his personality and challenging only a limited area of his being. He begins to see life as a ladder, as a permanent examination. . . . He becomes an expert imbiber and doler-out; his competence will vary, but will rarely be accompanied by genuine enthusiasms. He rarely feels the reality of knowledge, of other men's thoughts and imaginings, on his own pulses; he rarely discovers an author for himself and on his own. In this half of his life he can respond only if there is direct connection with the system of training. He has something of the blinkered pony about him; sometimes he is trained by those who have been through the same regimen, who are hardly unblinkered themselves, and who praise him in the degree to which he takes comfortably to their blinkers . . . . As a result when he comes to the end of the series of set-pieces, when he is at last put out to raise his eyes to a world of tangible and unaccommodating things, of elusive and disconcerting human beings, he finds himself with little

inner momentum. The driving-belt hangs loosely, discon-
nected from the only machine it has so far served, the
examination-passing machine.*

The ethos Hoggart captures so vividly is surely part of
the reason why excitement wanes in the later years of
school. All schools mirror their social order. All, in addition to teaching rudimentary skills, and passing on certain
elements of a common culture, socialize children to adult
society and sort them out socio-economically. As the children grow older—as they reach the secondary schools—
the curriculum is increasingly narrowly defined, in academic terms, and there is more and more pressure on the
schools to serve one particular function: to provide the
credentials that justify separating out those who make it
from those who don't. This is the great barrier to further
reform; it may mark the outer limits of the possibilities of
school reform in a fundamentally unequal society. Indeed, the interesting thing about the British example is
that they have been able to go as far as they have toward
making the early years of schooling decent and humane,
despite the overwhelming class biases of the educational
system.

The slowness of change in junior schools can also be
accounted for by the fact that reform has seeped upward
from nursery and infant schools, whose methods were
worked out over thirty years. There isn't the backlog of
traditions and materials that many of the infant schools
now have. Older children need a large amount of open-
ended curriculum material, too. A lot of junior classrooms
look starved for books and stuff.

It may be particularly unlucky that the spread of informal methods from infant to junior schools has been
occurring at a time when primary education in Britain is
badly understaffed and underfinanced. The cumulative
neglect of the primary schools—the Cinderellas of the
system—is fascinating and depressing, since they are by
far the most creative and important part of British educa-

*Richard Hoggart, *The Uses of Literacy*, London: Chatto and Win-
dus Ltd., New York: Oxford University Press. Reprinted by permission.

tion. In a number of places I visited, a junior school that was accounted pretty good two or three years ago was no longer considered worth looking at. Turnover of staff had completely altered the picture. Arthur Razzell has described how a principal feels who has developed some good teaching only to watch his staff disappear, to be replaced by people who have never worked informally before:

> Either I had to revert to a more formal and directed system of teaching until my colleagues had settled down and were in a position to try out new ways of working, or else I had to plunge straight on, giving all the support I could, and hope that they would be prepared to tackle informal teaching. Whichever course I took it was clear that our experimental work had come to an end too early for us to judge whether it was effective or not.

Thus, many fear that inadequate funds and staff will check the progress of a reform that has made such impressive gains in the infant schools. One or two of the gloomier, older veterans, about to retire, worry that the Plowden Report could become the highwater mark of a progressive movement that is already spent.

Yet the movement seems far from spent in the authorities where change has spread farthest, and where the sort of thing I have been describing is flourishing. I imagine that in Leicestershire and Oxfordshire there will be more and more examples of this kind of teaching—in schools staffed by ordinary teachers. It is especially moving to visit an authority like the West Riding, where, in the face of incredible staffing problems and poverty, reform still spreads. There, harassed school authorities and teachers keep a vision of what good teaching can be. In such areas, it is hard to believe that the secondary schools can remain unchanged against the force of their vision.

It is as a first step toward such a vision that I've tried to give concrete examples, to arrive at some specific notions of what a good job looks like. It seems to me that the time has come to stop endlessly asserting objectives— discipline, the liberal arts, the three Rs, basic education, even freedom and spontaneity—without being specific about how the objectives are reached.

Let me conclude this brief account of some British schools by returning to the specific. Talk of children's writing may seem far-fetched, like giving IBM typewriters to monkeys, until you see schools where children *are* writing. Then a number of things occur to you about what should be going on in schools. Writing is a good way to learn, because an emphasis on written expression makes it more likely that children will build on the mastery of language they already possess, instead of having it destroyed, which is what so many American reading programs end up doing. This is not an argument for a crash program of three hours of writing every morning; writing can't be taught in isolation as a separate subject. There must be something to write about. There have to be books of all sorts available (who wants to write about Dick and Jane?), and there has to be talk.

If many people write most freely about their own experiences, then a priority in organizing the school day becomes providing a setting for experiences out of which writing and other kinds of expression can come. (They can, of course, be vicarious and imaginative experiences in realms far removed from everyday existence.) You can't, in most cases, get writing from children by command, but the more varied things there are to do and to choose from, the greater the likelihood of engaging children with diverse interests. This ought to be the start of a new curriculum.

There is something else about writing. It offers the teacher the possibility of playing a different role from the conventional one. There isn't a correct answer, for one thing. (Not that there's anything wrong with learning that sometimes there is one right answer, but the schools have beaten that point into the ground.) Since the experience is the child's own, he has to stick to it if the writing is to be honest. The teacher can't know more about it than the student; the teacher can be catalyst, editor, audience, guide, drawer-out, but she has to work with what the child gives. The student and teacher can both be—I wouldn't say on equal terms, for that is fairly rare —sharing a concern for the piece of writing and what it says. Thus there is a basis for a conversation, something that is fairly unique in most schools. In a different context, talking about science, David Hawkins has described this as an "I-thou-it" relationship—teacher and student seeing each other in mutual, working relationship to some portion of the world around them, a pendulum, a tube filled with glycerine, soap bubbles, and, I would add, some writing or clay sculpture. Until a child is working on something, a teacher has little to go on. Once there is something both are preoccupied with, the ground is laid for a man-to-man discussion. My impression of one kind of awful classroom reinforces this: far from being impersonal, the room is filled with everybody's consciousness that a scary relationship exists between students and teacher. There is nothing but this relationship, and nothing gets learned. In good classes, relationships between students and teachers grow out of common interests. Cultivating these interests is the job of teaching.

Also, a teacher working with a child on a piece of writing can perform a real service—encouraging expression, helping the child improve. Both the teacher and the child sense this; it colors the relationship. A deep, unstated problem of the schools, a problem that gets worse as children grow older, is that what teachers have to teach is frequently not worth learning. One reason teachers in the early years of school seem happier than most is that they are teaching something that matters, reading. In later years teachers are apt to be shaky about the value of what they're doing, with good reason. In writing, as in other areas, the work of the English schools I've described is focused on things that most teachers and children would consider worth the effort. The contrast with the sludge of memorized trivia in the later years of our primary schools is stunning.

Learning from British Teachers

To what has been said here about British schools, some points of special interest to teachers and administrators may be added:

1. Although I don't wish to present the methods described simply as a better way to learn the three Rs, I do want to note that there are few reading problems in good British schools; and heads of schools predict that the few remaining problems will diminish when the informal methods of the infant schools are extended for another year.

2. British teachers, like teachers everywhere, pray for small classes, but informal methods work in classes of forty children. It would clearly be better for the teachers if numbers were smaller, yet the methods do succeed, and some teachers I spoke with argued that they make it easier to teach large classes.

3. Tracking is not necessary in primary schools where the emphasis is on individual learning: British teachers are coming to see workable alternatives to ability grouping.

4. Informal methods work well not only with young children in the first years of school, but with older children, too. There are problems: the junior schools are slower to change, partly because they stand closer to the rigid secondary schools, and partly because it takes time and much experimenting to develop the kind of rich background of materials and methods the infant schools now possess. British curriculum projects are creating good open-ended materials, especially in science and math, for individual learning. Whatever the difficulties, it is clear that the junior schools are at their best when they continue along the freer lines of good infant schools.

5. Since nothing in schools happens in isolation, patterns of individual learning can develop in one area of the curriculum and spread to others. Thus for some British

schools, art was the first subject in which children were encouraged to work on their own; others experimented with individual movement and mime and interpretive dancing in their physical education classes; some introduced the musical instruments devised for children by the German composer, Carl Orff; many schools are now discovering that mathematics is a great catalyst for change.

6. Everything depends on the teacher's confidence that children can learn with these methods. Where teachers and children are used to a strict timetable and traditional classroom instruction, it is best to proceed gradually: successful small steps are the only way to gain confidence. Wise heads of schools making the transition from formal to informal methods often start with a pair of willing teachers—with the idea that two people encourage each other, help create materials, and cheer one another up when things go badly. Many teachers begin by allowing the children one free period in the day, when free writing, painting, and working with mathematical apparatus is encouraged. As the children get used to working on their own, the teachers gradually extend the free period and start altering the layout of the classrooms. In schools where math is the focus for change, a teacher will introduce a free math period—usually Friday afternoon—in which different kinds of mathematical apparatus and homemade materials are set up for the children to tinker with. After some of these free math periods, teachers often find the children becoming interested in recording the results of their activities in pictures, charts, graphs, and essays—this last introducing English in the form of free writing on mathematics. Teachers may decide that one period is not enough for the children, and so they extend the time to let them pursue a piece of work to the end. Teachers can wean themselves and the children from textbooks in a variety of ways: one is to start using the textbook selectively as problems arise in the classroom from the children's tinkering. Thus, if a child playing with liquids and containers raises a question about volume, the teacher can direct him to a relevant section in a

standard arithmetic book. Another bridge between conventional instruction and a much freer approach is provided by assignment cards.

7. It would be a mistake to try to copy the techniques of an informal classroom without understanding the spirit behind the techniques: If it is desirable to let children choose their activities within the selected environment of the classroom, teachers have to be given choices as well. Within the British schools now making the change from formal to informal methods, you find teachers, some of them very talented, who don't approve of the new methods. On the whole, their preferences are respected, and this, in itself, is an important key to the character of the primary school revolution. The kinds of classrooms described will come slowly to the American schools, if they come at all; and they will come only when teachers believe in them.

Albert Cullum

from *Push Back the Desks*

THE RENOIR ROOM

We turned our sixth-grade classroom into a Renoir Room! How exciting it was to step into the unknown world of this great French painter.

After emptying the room of all vestiges of school life —textbooks, bulletin boards, announcements, school menus, and the wastepaper basket—the magic began. Slowly but delightedly the students hung the first Renoir painting, and then the next, and the next, until fifty-four reproductions of Renoir paintings were displayed on the four classroom walls. Some were small, some large, some first-rate Renoirs, others not so good, but a magic was there, a greatness was there, and that's all that mattered for the moment.

The desks were out in the hallway, and the chairs were arranged for a public school art gallery, that is, they were placed in small groups of threes and fours facing clusters of Renoirs.

Now we had a Renoir Room with no textbooks and no desks. No learning? Wrong! We had created the type of learning situation that really counts—a type of learning situation that helps a student to grow and at the same time proves to him the value of his skills and of learning to read.

The purpose of this project was to have students enter the world of Renoir through the beauty of his work, to engage in independent research to discover the man Renoir, and to digest and share this newly found world with the rest of the school.

The students ventured into the world of Renoir through

281

intensive reading and research in the school library, the public library, and books at home and in the local bookstore, The Lighthouse. They pored over art books, biographies, and references. At one point the public librarian complained that too many students from my class were in the library and that it didn't have that many books about Renoir.

A whole new world of words opened up to them—impression, spontaneity, inspiration, technique, contemporary, classical, realism, modern, creative freedom, palette, influence, neo-impressionist, opaque, original, vigor, sensibility, dynamic, master, exquisite, salon, composition, texture, bourgeois, progressive, austerity, chromatic, post-impressionism, and many, many more. What a wonderful new wealth of words the students learned, used, and understood.

The fifty-four Renoir paintings became more meaningful as each day progressed. The life of Renoir became alive. His rich, creative life became known to the entire class because, to be thoroughly prepared to talk about Renoir, students had to read more than the school's encyclopedia. That's why students come to school—not to learn how to read, but to read, to explore new worlds through reading, to digest challenging material, and to gain pleasure and enjoyment.

Once all the data had been accumulated by individual note-taking (no notes were scrutinized by me), the class had to determine what facts to use for the lectures they intended to give. The children had to decide how best to hold the attention of the various groups to whom they would talk about Renoir. What would be interesting for a sixth-grade class might not be of interest to a first-grade group, and then there was the problem of how to approach adult groups who were coming after school. As it turned out, not too many adults attended, for they did not fully grasp the importance of their roles in this lecture series.

It is not an easy matter to decide how to adjust a lecture to various age levels. As teachers we must give students every opportunity to organize and decide on their own. The classroom teacher sets up the structure—in this case the Renoir Room—but the students must make all the decisions. They decided with whom they would work, they decided what phase of Renoir's art they would emphasize, they decided to what age-level group they would like to lecture, and they decided if they wanted to volunteer to participate in the project.

The day arrived when Ann and Louise were ready to give the first lecture to a third-grade group. It was Miss Hall's class, and her youngsters were quite excited as they entered a classroom that was an art gallery—a new world for them. Good schools introduce students to as many new worlds as possible.

The third-graders were initially startled by the fifty-four paintings. After they were seated the lecture began. The two girls were nervous at first because they were not quite sure if they could capture the interest of these eight-year-olds. Soon, however, they perceived a quiet attentiveness in the room as the lecture progressed, and then they knew that those twenty-four third-graders were with them.

Louise left the makeshift rostrum and, with a pointer in hand, circulated about the gallery pointing out various masterpieces such as "Two Girls at the Piano," "Madame Charpentier and Her Daughters," "Luncheon of the Boating Party," "The Swing," "The Bridge," and so forth. As she was talking, Louise sensed which paintings were favored by the group and which paintings did not impress them. After she finished her tour, Ann completed the lecture with some final comments about their being such respectful guests and reminded them to be sure to circulate about the Renoir Room and make any comment they chose to. Also, cookies would be served! The idea of cookies pleased everyone, and it was most interesting to observe the youngsters nibbling cookies and commenting about the art work:

"His women are fat!"

"I like his clouds."

"I don't like any of them."

"He's my favorite painter now."

"I like the boy writing the best."

"How much do they cost?"

"That woman is wearing a funny hat."

Then it was time for Miss Hall's children to return to their classroom. They thanked the two lecturers and filed out. That afternoon after school five third-graders returned to visit the Renoir Room—and only one asked for a cookie.

The Renoir Room lasted for two weeks during which many lectures were presented to all age groups. Every lecture was a success. The idea spread. The Midland School librarian allowed us to set up in her library a Picasso Palace that consisted of fifty Picasso paintings representing his five periods. At Osborn School the librarian began a program of lending reproductions for a week.

Children were being exposed to greatness, and they were responding positively.

Did every class visit the Renoir Room? Of course not! Why? It was not in the curriculum, and besides, how could a second-grader possibly understand Renoir? My answer was quite simple—"They would understand Renoir as a second-grader could understand Renoir." I reminded the skeptics how, in response to a question about the meaning of his abstract works, Picasso once replied to the effect, "How does one explain the song of a bird? I paint for all ages, not just twenty-seven-year-olds."

Out of the Renoir Room came a love of a particular painting entitled "The Skiff." Jimmy loved this painting so much that he requested that it be one of his Christmas presents, and I believe it is now hanging in the family living room. Also out of that Renoir Room came reading that would make the reading workbooks blush . . . dictionary work that made sense and was practical . . . speeches and recitations that had a purpose and were not just parrot work. Writing took place . . . writing ads to publicize the Renoir Room . . . writing opinions of the work of Renoir. The students fed on Renoir—they feasted on this touch of greatness!

What does turning a classroom into a Renoir Room or a Cezanne Cellar have to do with school work? As one father so aptly expressed it, "I want my kid to go to school to learn . . . yeah, even Renoir and all that crap!"

My phrasing is not quite that direct. I simply want children to be exposed to as many things as possible in all elementary grades. Sometimes at this level a tremendous impact occurs between student and greatness! Greatness can exist every day in each classroom—not only in the room of the specialists, but in every everyday classroom with every everyday teacher.

If a teacher doesn't like the soft pastel world of Renoir, then why not turn the classroom into a Chagall Chamber, or a Degas Den, or a Modigliani Mansion? But do turn your classroom into something and at least once a year expose your students to an unknown quantity. Step back and let the students explore. Step way back, and let the experience be their success, not something you taught them. When children achieve success on their own, a love of the subject develops and they have an exhilarating sense of fulfillment that never fades away.

Prints needed for a classroom gallery are not expensive. Don't wait for petty cash or school board approval, or your gallery will never open. Prints can be purchased in almost any book store for about $2 each, or they can be borrowed from most local public libraries. Obtain the cardboard prints for they are more receptive to rougher handling.

Why wait until students go to the art teacher to be exposed to a great painting? The same is true with music. Why wait till the music period? When children enter an everyday classroom in the morning, why shouldn't Toscanini be conducting?

If the excitement of greatness does not exist in your own school, create your own room of greatness. Of course you can't do it all by yourself, but you can obtain all the help you need from the painters of the world and the composers and the writers. Children grasp greatness very quickly!

Through the art projects in class, I gained a knowledge of various art works and techniques. I also was inspired to create my own opinions and interpretations of the paintings. I have never since had the opportunity to absorb so much information about art in a classroom.

Sherry Hensley, 1963

I still have the painting "The Tragedy" by Picasso.

Gary Gilch, 1961

I first saw Da Vinci's "Mona Lisa" in your classroom and learned the complexities of her smile. The other various paintings you put up I still keep coming across and probably always will.

Jim Hadley, 1961

Frequently people will ask what was my most enlightening school year. When I answer "fifth-grade," people sometimes appear surprised, but in my case fifth-grade was the most challenging and rewarding year. To this day I often find myself browsing through art books or walking through museums, happy that I can recognize certain artists, while my mind is being flooded with fifth-grade memories.

Teddy Martin, 1960

I also found the identification of famous paintings very interesting. I still remember some of the famous scenes and their artists.

Bill Cornelius, 1959

I still have the painting "Portrait of a Girl" by Modigliani in my room.

Ira Shuman, 1960

KING TUT'S TOMB

It was frightening at times to stumble accidentally face-first into a cobweb, but it certainly made learning the basic skills of arithmetic much more palatable. Problem-solving, double division, or inverting fractions in the basement of St. Luke's Chapel choir room made arithmetic a fascinating "happening."

What do cobwebs and excitement, and even flashlights, have to do with learning arithmetic? Everything!

When I was a fifth- and sixth-grade teacher at the old St. Luke's School in Greenwich Village, I was assigned the room known as the choir room. The choir room had a trap door. Of course the class opened the trap door and climbed down to explore the cellar, which some have considered to be part of the old burial ground of St. Luke's Chapel. It was dark and damp down there, and the children hoped someone would actually find a human bone. This is where the arithmetic "digs" originated.

Approximately once a week, I opened the trap door so that the children could explore for arithmetic problems. The night before I had visited the "tomb" and had scattered problems about. The arithmetic challenges were typed on index cards of different sizes, and each card was labeled according to the difficulty of its problem. As the children wandered about, they inadvertently stumbled upon index cards and commenced to work the problems and the puzzles. Everyone loved arithmetic!

The cellar was spooky, but not so spooky that the students couldn't concentrate. When a child had solved his problem, he scrambled up to daylight and presented me with a dusty but completed problem. Some problems were worth as much as fifty points.

All digs were successful, for each student had his or her own level of competence, and each decided what his level of success would be for each day. This technique seemed to relax everyone, for some days one would be more ambitious than others.

Drilling and reviewing seem to take up so much time in elementary classrooms, but they do not have to be boring. Children learn better when they're excited and talkative rather than composed and quiet. Opening that trap door in the St. Luke's Chapel choir room exposed the children to a fresh breath of a mysterious damp, stale air, but arithmetic was learned!

Years later when working as a fifth-grade teacher at Midland School in Rye, I did not teach arithmetic one session. Miss Mones, the teacher across the hall, did teach it, and she seemed to be searching for a new approach to arithmetic review. My memory was refreshed by that breath of fresh, damp, stale air. I mentioned to Miss Mones the success I had with my St. Luke's School arithmetic digs, and she, a courageous soul, was willing to gamble. What was there to lose? Nothing really.

This was the beginning of King Tut's Tomb. At first the tomb consisted of some sheets hung over a string attached to the walls with nails in a corner of the back of the room. All the time we were frightened that the project might be canceled because of the edict, "No nails in the walls!"

However, the principal of Midland School came to the rescue by helping develop a permanent structure for the tomb. The walls and roof consisted of large mattress boxes nailed and stapled onto a light weight wooden framework; a low door was cut through on one side. Life-sized figures, about six-feet high and made by the children, guarded the tomb. Each figure was beautifully detailed in the ancient Egyptian art form with modern poster paint, and the walls too were brightly painted. The entrance to the tomb was covered with a piece of black cloth.

The boys and girls were excited, just as the St. Luke's youngsters had been excited, just as any elementary school kid in any country would be excited. It's fascinating how a change of pace can intrigue the elementary school child, how a fresh breath of stale damp air in the atmosphere can cause a stir of wonder.

Did you ever hear of fifth-grade students working on math problems during their free time? It happened. Excitement built up while the tomb was being constructed. The class read about Egyptian tombs and discussed Egyptian treasures and curses. Their imaginations were stirred to become archeologists.

What was the reason for a King Tut's Tomb? Math problems, puzzles, arithmetic challenges, graphs, and other items dealing with numbers and numerals were the treasures within King Tut's Tomb. The "archeologists" dug for the solutions.

Who was eligible to dig? Everyone. To become an archeologist and be able to dig in King Tut's Tomb one had to have the right attitude. What was the right attitude? The right attitude was the ability to be reliable and to be able to work independently.

The "cut-ups" presented something of a problem—would they be able to handle themselves properly inside the dark tomb? Could they conduct themselves as archeologists? Would they pinch, kick, or strike their colleagues in the dark or would they be so fascinated searching and stumbling for mathematical excitement that they would not be tempted to be unruly? I am happy to report that everyone behaved in an exemplary manner.

The mechanics of operating King Tut's Tomb were simple:

1. Problems for each dig were written on cards and tacked inside the tomb.
2. Each problem was given a point score, which was noted on the card. The more difficult or time-consuming ones were worth more. Since this project was not designed solely for able students, problems included simple computations as well as involved and difficult problems. There were puzzles, construction problems, and all types of odds and ends. Here are some examples:

$\dfrac{3}{4} \times 1 = ?$ $\dfrac{5}{16}$

$\begin{array}{r} 3469 \\ 2187 \\ 3412 \\ +\ 6110 \end{array}$

Factor 1870 into prime factors.

How many hockey teams can be formed by the fourth-, fifth-, and sixth-grade boys' gym class if there are 58 boys in the class?

In the decimal numeral 4659.67:
  a. the 7 represents ———
  b. the 4 represents ———
  c. the 9. represents ———

Represent 43 using Egyptian symbols.

What is the sum of CCCLXXVI and MDCCL?

Can you tell why zero is a multiple of every whole number?

3. Each problem was numbered and stayed in the tomb for others to "discover." Dig answers had to be turned in with a number; otherwise it became too complicated to score. The answers were deposited in a box designed as a sarcophagus. The reason for scoring was that to receive credit for a dig, each archeologist had to acquire a certain amount of points within the time of that particular dig.

4. Wrong answers were returned to be worked again if the students so wished.

5. A dig generally lasted about two weeks, and then the cards were taken down. Sometimes a difficult card that had stumped several kids stayed up for another dig.

6. After each dig, answers were discussed, and ways of approaching problems were exchanged. This was the valuable aspect of the project.

7. At the end of the year very fancy certificates were presented to the active, hardworking archeologists.

King Tut's Tomb captured the fancy of the children. Archeologists would drop in with flashlights, paper, and pencils and before entering King Tut's Tomb, each one was required to bow respectfully three times before the entrance. There were very few that didn't feel the spirit and catch the excitement. For some it was a temporary excitement; for others it lasted the whole year. Some just sensed the excitement in being admitted to the tomb by going through the rigmarole required to enter; others accepted the challenge of delving into a mystery. Some were reinforced by the majestic appearance of a King Tut's Tomb and were able to step into the unknown.

With the aid of flashlights and some synthetic grains of sand, students emerged from the tomb not only with a solved arithmetic problem but with another facet of their personalities successfully exposed.

The opening of the tomb for the first dig was announced over the school's loud speaker. This was done before each dig. The times when the tomb would be opened were announced. To accommodate eager diggers, the tomb was opened for digging before classes began in the morning, during class whenever anyone had some free time available, and after school.

After three o'clock was a busy time! Not too many teachers allowed their children to leave their respective classrooms during the day to visit the tomb, so those after-school archeologists made up for lost time. After bowing down on hands and knees, he or she would crawl into the tomb. Remember the entrance was low! No one could enter the tomb without performing the ritual. No one could enter who wouldn't comply with all the rules and regulations.

Teachers came from other schools to see what was happening. Some caught the spirit and bowed three times before entering; others, however, could not capture the world of make-believe, and they were not permitted to go in.

It was dark inside the tomb, darker than outside. Flashlights were used although they were not always essential.

On winter afternoons though, the late diggers really did need them. They loved to work when it became dark. However, work on the problems could be done at home or at school or whenever an archeologist had time.

The back of the classroom always had an archeologist or two working on a problem. Some would always stay to watch Miss Mones empty the sarcophagus.

Parents began stopping by to see what this tomb was all about, for their youngsters were most involved with math puzzles, looking things up in the almanac, making hourglasses that ran for five minutes, and coming home with slightly soiled clothes. A few parents even bowed three times and crawled into King Tut's Tomb.

There were no grades connected with King Tut's Tomb —only a child's interest and perseverance were valued. Consequently the children worked independently. They chose their own problems, persisted if they were so inclined, or dropped the project.

The St. Luke's Chapel choir room still exists, but it is no longer used as a classroom, for St. Luke's School has a brand-new building. The Midland School King Tut's Tomb has been discarded, but there are a few hundred students throughout the country whose nostrils are still sensitive to a fresh breath of damp, dark, stale air.

Whether it be new math or old math, permit this fresh breath of damp, dark, stale air to enter your classroom.

The tomb made math fun and challenging, and something you didn't do just for grades or tests. Maybe this is one of the major reasons why math is my favorite subject today.
                                                    Beth Pomerantz, 1962

Before you went in, it was essential *that you bowed three times. This was for the benefit of King Tutankhamen himself. Getting help from other people was taboo; this was a do-it-yourself project. Even now I sort of feel a thrill when I think about the tomb, the darkness, and quiet inside penetrated by several flashlights. I'm sure I'll never forget it!*

                                                    Jon Lawson, 1962

Classroom Meetings

William Glasser

from *Schools Without Failure*

This is about classroom meetings, meetings in which the teacher leads a whole class in a nonjudgmental discussion about what is important and relevant to them. There are three types of classroom meetings: the *social-problem-solving* meeting, concerned with the students' social behavior in school; the *open-ended* meeting, concerned with intellectually important subjects; and the *educational-diagnostic* meeting, concerned with how well the students understand the concepts of the curriculum. These meetings should be a part of the regular school curriculum.

SOCIAL-PROBLEM-SOLVING MEETINGS

The many social problems of school itself, some of which lead to discipline of the students, are best attacked through the use of each class as a problem-solving group with each teacher as the group leader. Teachers in their faculty meetings will do essentially the same thing that each class does in the classroom meeting: *attempt to solve the individual and group educational problems of the class and the school*. When children enter kindergarten, they should discover that each class is a working, problem-solving unit and that each student has both individual and group responsibilities. Responsibility for learning and for behaving so that learning is fostered is shared among the entire class. By discussing group and individual problems, the students and teacher can usually solve their problems within the classroom. If children learn to participate in a problem-solving group when they enter school and continue to do so with a variety of teachers throughout the six years of elementary school, they learn that the world is not a mysterious and sometimes hostile and frightening place where they have little control over what happens to them. They learn rather that, although the world may be difficult and that it may at times appear hostile and mysterious, they can use their brains individually and as a group *to solve the problems of living in their school world.* Over and above the value of learning to solve their problems through class meetings, students also gain in scholastic achievement. . . .

School children have many social problems, some of which may call for discipline, some not. Under ordinary conditions, because there is no systematic effort to teach them social problem solving, school children find that problems that arise in getting along with each other in school are difficult to solve. Given little help, children tend to evade problems, to lie their way out of situations, to depend upon others to solve their problems, or just to give up. None of these courses of action is good preparation for life. The social-problem-solving meeting can help children learn better ways.

Working with an eighth-grade class of an elementary school, I recently held a social-problem-solving meeting that can serve as an example. Although I do conduct social-problem-solving meetings, they are more difficult for an outsider such as I to hold than for the classroom teacher; students usually feel that someone who doesn't know them well has no business probing into their problems. In terms of Reality Therapy, before one can successfully change behavior, one must be involved. It is difficult for a class and a total stranger to become sufficiently involved with each other to make the meeting successful enough to serve as a demonstration. In contrast, the other kinds of meetings, open-ended and educational-diagnostic, are very easily led by someone the class does not know because these meetings do not present nearly the threat of the social-problem-solving meeting.

A serious problem with the eighth-grade class in the spring of 1967 was truancy. On some of the warmer days, as many as six or eight out of a class of thirty-five would be absent from school. The same children were not absent every day, although some missed school more than others and some always came to class. I was asked to focus on truancy during the meeting. Although no one expected that one meeting would solve such a serious problem, my goals were to get the class to think both about their own motives in cutting school and about some ideas that might help the whole class toward better attendance. The meeting started with my asking the class if everyone were present that day. There was considerable discussion, timid at first but shortly more frank, revealing that about eight students were absent and that those present knew that most of the absentees were not ill that beautiful spring day. When I asked whether some of the students present also frequently skipped class, many admitted that they did. The students sensed that I was nonpunitive and that I was inquiring because I was concerned about their not coming to school.

We discussed at some length what they gained by cutting school and what problems it was causing. We also discussed the school's methods of handling truancy and their parents' reactions to these methods. The students maintained that school was dull and that they saw little sense in what they were learning. They gave the impression that their lives were so full of interesting things to do outside of school that they didn't feel they could attend regularly. They rationalized their position by saying that this year was the last time they would have a chance to cut because next year, when they entered high school, they would have to toe the mark. Questioning their rationale, I said that I doubted that they would attend high school any more regularly. I added that I did not believe that the things they complained about in the eighth grade would be much different in high school. As we continued to talk, most of the students admitted that the reference to high school was rationalization; from their experience with sisters, brothers, and friends, truancy was just as common in high school as in the eighth grade.

At this point we had accomplished what in Reality Therapy would be called exposing the problem for open, honest discussion. My warm and personal attitude helped the class to open up. Talking only about the present problem, we got it out on the table for everyone to examine. Getting this far probably would have been sufficient for the the first of a series of meetings aimed at a real solution to the truancy problem. Because the meeting was a demonstration, however, I wanted to go further, and I started pressing the class for a solution. I asked them if they would talk to the absent students to try to get them to stop cutting and to attend school regularly. I knew that unless the students made a value judgment that going to school is worthwhile, they would not attend regularly. It was clear that the statements they made about the value of school were merely lip service. Unless their attitude toward school could be changed, I or anyone else faced an impossible task in trying to get them to come regularly. The relevance of the school work must be taught, and where too much irrelevant material is in the curriculum, it must be replaced by material more meaningful to the children.

I attempted, nevertheless, to get from the students present a commitment to attend school the next day. Their wariness toward me and toward anyone who suggested change was apparent in their refusal to make this commitment. The refusal was also a perfect example of the difficulty we have in getting students to participate in irrelevant education. They gave every reason they could think of why they might not be in school the following day. To end the meeting and to help the students understand the importance of making a commitment, I introduced a technique that sometimes works even when a value judgment has not been made: I asked the class to sign a statement promising to come to school the next day. About one-third of the twenty-nine students were willing to sign the statement. The others were very leery about it, giving all kinds of excuses such as that they might be sick or they might be run over on the way to school. They did not want to do anything as binding as signing a piece of paper saying they would attend school. To the nonsigners I said, "If you won't sign a paper stating you will come to school tomorrow, will you sign a paper stating that you won't sign a paper? In other words, will you put your lack of commitment in writing?" After much heated discussion, about one-third more said they would sign the second paper. Although signing this paper did not commit them to come to school, it might still help them to understand the commitment process. One-third of the students remained who refused to sign either paper. I asked them if they would sign a paper stating that they would sign nothing, but they were too smart for me and still refused to sign. I said, "Under these circumstances, will you allow your names to be listed on a piece of paper as students who refuse to commit themselves in any way regarding truancy?" I would put their names on the paper; they would not have participated in the commitment process in any way. To this they agreed, and we obtained the three lists at the end of the meeting.

One meeting with little involvement, no real value judgment, and weak commitment produced, as I expected, no improvement in attendance. There was, however, much discussion not only among these students but also in the entire seventh and eighth grades concerning the class meeting. I had set the stage for a series of meetings to attack the problem of truancy. If this first meeting could have been followed with regular meetings several times a week, the students could have discussed the importance of attending school and been led toward value judgments, plans, and commitments. In class meetings teachers must listen to the reasons given for poor school attendance. When reasons with some validity are given, we must consider changing our teaching to make the school worthwhile to the students where it is not. In addition, we must teach the value of school.

Social-problem-solving meetings such as the one just

described are valuable to students and to the school. I suggest that all students in elementary schools wishing to implement the meetings meet regularly during the week for a reasonable time to discuss the problems of the whole class and of individual students within the class. Both students and teachers should consider the class meetings as important as reading, history, or math. . . . Although better guidelines may be developed as the meetings progress, the following should give a good start.

All problems relative to the class as a group and to any individual in the class are eligible for discussion. A problem can be brought up by an individual student about himself or someone else, or by the teacher as she sees a problem occur. In a school with a unified faculty involved with each other and with all school problems, subjects for discussion can be introduced in any class by any student or any teacher, either directly by a note to the group or indirectly by an administrator with knowledge of the problem. In addition to school problems, problems that a child has at home are also eligible for discussion if the child or his parents wish to bring them up. . . .

The discussion itself should always be directed toward solving the problem; the solution should never include punishment or fault finding. The children and the teacher are oriented from the first meetings in the first grade that the purpose of the meeting is not to find whose fault a problem is or to punish people who have problems and are doing wrong; rather the purpose is to help those who have problems to find better ways to behave. The orientation of the meetings is always positive, always toward a solution. When meetings are conducted in this way, the children learn to think in terms of a solution—the only constructive way to handle any problem—instead of the typical adult way soon learned by school children —fault finding and punishment. . . .

Meetings should always be conducted with the teacher and all the students seated in a tight circle. This seating arrangement is necessary if good meetings are to occur.

Classroom meetings should be short (10 to 30 minutes) for children in the lower grades and should increase in length (30 to 45 minutes) as the children grow older. The duration of a meeting is less important than its regular occurrence and the pertinence of the problems discussed.

Children who must be excluded from class because their behavior is not tolerable to the teacher or the students will have a better avenue for reentry into the class through the use of class meetings than they have at the present time. Under ordinary school procedures, a principal dealing with a problem child who has been sent out of class finds himself meting out some sort of punishment. He usually swats the child, lectures him, calls in his parents, excludes him from school, or assigns detention time after school or during school. These procedures tend to work less well each time they are applied to any individual child. When the classroom meetings are a part of the school program, the principal has an important added wedge in working with the child. He asks the child sent to his office what he was doing and helps the child understand that *what he did* caused him to be excluded. The principal conducts the discussion with a goal of sending the child back to a class meeting in which the same points will be pursued. The principal counsels the individual child in a way that emphasizes what the child did. In an atmosphere of problem solving instead of punishment, the child usually will discuss his part in whatever happened. The principal then asks the child whether he has any plan to go back to class. Working with the principal, the child is asked to make a plan to get back into his class. If he does not want to go back, he is told that the class will nevertheless try *to help him* the best they can without him. He is asked to work out his plan in some detail, which usually does not take much time. For example, the boy may have been fighting with another boy so much that the teacher finally sends him out of the class. In a school where he is not threatened with punishment, he will admit to the principal that he was fighting and, after a while, admit the part he played in the fight. The principal then asks him to think about how he could stop fighting. Usually he says he would do better away from the other boy. This discussion sometimes takes a little time; maybe the other boy has to come in so that they can agree together on a plan to stay apart for a while. Both boys take the plan back to the class and the class may agree to help by not egging them on. In future meetings the class can work on the underlying problem, which may be jealousy, and the teacher can work on the boys' failure in school, which usually is a part of behavior problems.

The principal works with the child in a nonpunitive, problem-solving way. Using the class meeting, the child has a built-in entrée to return to class. As the procedure becomes operational and the children see that it works, they are happy to use it because it makes their lives easier. The whole disciplinary structure of a school should revolve around the class meeting. Individual discussions with children concerning their problems should be directed toward individual, and then group-accepted, solutions.

As time goes on, fewer and fewer disciplinary problems arise, so that class meetings about behavior disturbances become infrequent. Children learn through problem solving in the group how to avoid trouble in school and sometimes at home, although it is the rare home where children are encouraged to solve problems by discussion and planning. If they learn to do so in school, however, the knowledge will prove of value all their lives. Although social-problem-solving meetings often deal with behavior problems, many other subjects can be discussed: friendship, loneliness, vocational choice, and part-time work are examples.

In my experience, much of which has been in schools where discipline was a prime concern, I have found that direct disciplinary meetings are often ineffective in getting children involved with each other in a warm, positive way. They gain *positive involvement* more quickly through meetings in which they discuss ideas relevant to their lives. Earlier in the book I discussed the irrelevance of much of education to the lives of the children in school. I made the point that behavior disorders and educational failure were directly related to this irrelevance. Here it can be shown that classroom meetings, initiated to solve disciplinary problems, can be used effectively to gain and to sustain educational relevance. To understand how this is done, we need to describe two additional kinds of classroom meetings, neither of which directly relates to behavior problems.

OPEN-ENDED MEETINGS

Probably the cornerstone of relevant education is the open-ended classroom meeting. It is the type of meeting that should be used most often, even where behavior problems are common. When behavior and other social problems are minimal, social-problem-solving meetings will be used infrequently. The open-ended meeting, however, is always applicable; the more it is used, the more relevance can be added to education. In the open-ended meetings the children are asked to discuss any thought-provoking question related to their lives, questions that may also be related to the curriculum of the classroom. The difference between an open-ended meeting and ordinary class discussion is that in the former the teacher is specifically not looking for factual answers. She is trying to stimulate children to think and to relate what they know to the subject being discussed.

For example, in meetings with second-grade classes, I have introduced the subject of blindness. In answer to my question, "What is interesting to you?" one class said they would like to talk about eyes and ears. Although the five senses are not a specific part of the second-grade curriculum, from this introduction an open-ended meeting was held that provided a way for the students to gain greater motivation to read and to take more interest in the world around *them*. . . . I asked the children what they did with their eyes, and they all said, "See"—a good, simple, factual answer. In a discussion with small children, it is best to let them begin at a simple level where they have confidence in their ability to give a good answer.

Going to a more complex question, I asked, "What do you see with your eyes?" They mentioned many things, including "the words in our books." Again they were succeeding in answering a question; they enjoyed it and were becoming involved. At the same time, I was able to direct them toward books and reading in a way new to them. Children are just as stimulated by new approaches as we are, and they are just as bored with sameness as we are. One value of the open-ended meeting is to give new ways a chance to be used. I then asked them about people who can't see, and they said, "They are blind." A short discussion on what blindness means followed. Despite an apparent understanding of blindness, most of the children believed that blind people could really see if they tried hard. We worked at length before everyone understood that blind people could not see at all. The children closed their eyes tight and kept them closed. Slowly, through this participation and discussion, it began to dawn on the class that if you are blind, you cannot see.

By now the children were all involved, but so far they hadn't done much thinking or problem solving. It was important at this time to introduce a problem related to their school work that they could solve if they worked hard. I asked, "Could a blind man read?" The reaction I received from the second graders was laughter, puzzlement, and incredulity. To think that a blind man could read, after they had just confirmed that a blind man couldn't see, was absurd. I asked them to keep thinking to see if someone could figure out some way that a blind man could read. Of course, I implied that there was an answer. I wouldn't ask second graders a question that had no answer, although in this case the answer was not easy. I insisted that they keep trying to solve the problem; their first reaction when the going got tough was to give up. In school the children had rarely used their brains to solve problems. Accustomed to simple, memorized answers, they gave up when these answers didn't work.

The discussion so far had piqued the children's interest and awakened their faith in their brains. They kept trying, but they were in trouble. The leader must judge when to give them help; he must not do so too soon. I decided to help them at this time by asking if someone would like to take part in a little experiment. We had an immediate raising of hands; they were all eager to help, partly because they sensed that the experiment was a way to keep the discussion going. I selected a boy who, I detected, was not one of the better students or better behaved members of the class. He was waving his hand, eager to volunteer. Calling him over, I told him to shut his eyes very tight and hold out his hands. I asked him if he were peeking; he said, "No." Putting a quarter in one of his hands and a dollar bill in the other, I asked him if he could tell me what I had put in his hands. The entire class was now glued to the experiment. Some of the brighter students immediately began to glimpse the idea. The boy was able to tell me what was in his hands. I asked him how he knew. Although he wasn't very verbal, he finally said that anyone could tell a dollar bill from a quarter. When I took the dollar bill away and put a nickel in his hand instead, he was still able to distinguish the nickel from the quarter. I then asked him to sit down. Again I asked the class, "How could a blind man read?" Thoughtful students now began to express the idea that if a blind man could feel the letters on a page, he might be able to read. I said, "How could he feel the letters on a page? The page is smooth." And I ran my fingers over a page. One bright child said, "If you took a pin and poked it through the page, you could feel where the pin poked through." From that, most of the class—and they were very excited—was able to get the idea: you could feel the letters on a page! . . .

Later the class asked what books for the blind look like. They wanted the teacher to bring some in, which she promised to do.

In the discussion after the meeting with the class teacher and several other teachers who were observing, I noted that the meeting could be used as a way to stimulate children to learn to read. The teacher could point out, or have the children point out to her, the advantage of having eyes; reading, difficult as it is for many of these children, is much easier for them than for the blind. The children were deeply involved in the meeting, enjoyed it, and used their brains to think about and solve what seemed at first an insoluble problem. They experienced success as a group and success as individuals. Meetings such as this one in the second grade can be used as motivators in many subjects of the curriculum. In addition, a class that is involved, thinking, and successful will have few disciplinary problems.

In the lower grades, the open-ended meeting may have to be related to the curriculum by the teacher; in the higher grades the class can make the connection. Having a thoughtful, relevant discussion on any subject, however, is more valuable than forcing a connection to the curriculum. In fact, if enough thoughtful discussions are held on subjects not in the curriculum, we should study the curriculum to see where it should be changed.

Educational-Diagnostic Meetings

A third type of class meeting, the educational-diagnostic, is always directly related to what the class is studying. These meetings can be used by the teacher to get a quick evaluation of whether or not teaching procedures in the class are effective. For example, in an eighth-grade class in another school district, I was disappointed to find that the students, despite studying the Constitution for a semester and a half, seemed to know very little about it. Although they had studied its clauses and many of them could recite certain sections from memory, the students had a nonthinking view of the Constitution. . . .

My first question to the class was, "What is the Constitution?" The class seemed to be taken aback by this question, but I repeated it several times, adding, "I just want to know if anyone here can tell me what the Constitution is." Looking for some sort of definition or description to start the meeting, I saw immediately that the students were in trouble. It had never occurred to them that anyone would ever ask them what the Constitution is; assuming that everyone, including themselves, knew, they hadn't bothered to think the idea through. The best answer I could get was that the Constitution is something written in books to be studied. I asked them, "Does the Constitution exist? Is there a Constitution on a piece of paper nailed to a wall somewhere that people can see?" The class doubted that it existed in the form I had described. Finally I had to tell them that the Constitution did exist and that people could go to Washington, D.C., and see it. (I usually don't give answers, but I was filled with frustration at this point.)

From this small factual start, I went on to see whether the students understood the ideas of the Constitution. Following their assurance that they had studied it in detail, I asked them to name some of its important features. When they mentioned the Bill of Rights, I said, "Do these rights pertain to you?" It took some time before they understood what I meant and more time to agree that in fact the Bill of Rights did pertain to the students sitting there. Some of them thought the Bill of Rights did pertain to them, while others thought that it was just for adults. To some extent the latter group was correct because, until the recent Supreme Court decision in the Gault case, minors had almost no protection under the law. Of course they had not learned this in their study of the Constitution.

The key question, however, which brought on a discussion confirming my doubts about the students' understanding of the Constitution, was, "What happens if you do something on your own property that is against the law? For example, may you drive a car on your own property even though you don't have a driver's license and are too young to drive? May you drink a can of beer in your home if your father offers it to you, even though you are legally too young to drink?" I don't know the correct legal answers in these two examples, but that was not the point of the questioning. There was heated discussion. Many of the students suggested that you have no right to break the law on your own property and that you should be punished if you do. I then raised the question of how you could be caught. "Do the police have the right to spy on your house and then come in and arrest you if they think you are drinking beer with your father?" The class said they thought the police did have the right and should do so. I then asked them how the police would know whether a child was having a glass of beer with his father. Although they said that this would be hard to discover, they did have some constructive ideas. One of them was that the police should have a television set focused in everybody's home and, as soon as the police saw anyone doing anything wrong, they should come and get him! Many in the class agreed with this idea and no one disagreed strongly. At that point we dropped the discussion.

It was clear that the discussion was provoking individual thinking about the Constitution. My affirmation of the existence of the Constitution in Washington was the only time during the discussion that I corrected the class or offered them a right answer. In the educational-diagnostic meeting, the leader should not incorporate value judgments into the discussion. The students should feel free to voice their opinions and conclusions in any way they see fit. The teacher learns points of weakness that require additional teaching by her and additional study and discussion by the class. In memory education, where discussions probing understanding rarely occur, students may get answers right on tests and still have no working, living knowledge of something as important as the Constitution and how it pertains to them. Unless the teacher takes a completely nonjudgmental attitude, however, she will never discover these distortions. Cueing to her judgments, students see no reason to discuss their own ideas and opinions.

It is hard for a teacher to conduct an educational-diagnostic meeting because of her involvement with the subject and consequent possible inability to recognize the points that the class may have missed. To see more clearly what a class knows, therefore, teachers might sometimes exchange classes to run these meetings. The blind spots could thereby be eliminated. The educational-diagnostic class meeting should never be used to grade or evaluate the students. It should be used only to find out what students know and what they don't know.

I have described the three kinds of class meetings that I have used during the past several years in my work in the schools. These meetings have proved interesting to students and teachers alike. The technique is not easy for teachers to learn because the required class leadership is not ordinarily taught. Few teachers will conduct meetings without some guidelines, some chance to observe a group, and much approval and encouragement from their superiors. Successful meetings occur only through practice, through evaluating what happens, and through following the guidelines given earlier in the chapter. Unless the meetings are nonjudgmental and open-ended, they will fail.

Enough teachers are conducting class meetings now so that some feedback is available. Many teachers are starting to use some of the techniques involved, especially the circle and the open-ended question, in regular teaching. Going from the open-ended question to some factual material, they encourage students to use judgment and to give opinions. As I write this book, however, most teachers in the schools in which I work have not incorporated classroom meetings into an integral part of their class program. Unfortunately, it is usually isolated from regular teaching. Most teachers conduct meetings one, two, or three times weekly; some report successful, continuing meetings every day. Although some teachers, despite their principal's permission to conduct meetings, still feel guilty about "wasting time" or "playing games," the success of the meetings is slowly winning them over. Students have responded very favorably in every class. Reminding the teacher when a meeting is due, they become involved quickly in the meetings. Because the students don't know that it is hard to have a good meeting, they soon have good meetings, especially in the lower grades. They are eager to participate in discussions relevant to their lives.

When one asks students whether their school work is in any way related to their lives outside of school, most of them reply incredulously, "Of course not." By the tenth grade, students are firmly convinced that school is a totally different experience from life. One learns to live and, completely separately, one learns at school. The three types of class meetings described herein can provide a stable bridge across the gap between school and life.

For the meetings to be most beneficial, they should be used by a majority of the teachers in the school. Children need experience in problem solving and in relating education to life throughout the elementary school period. Learning to think thus builds from year to year. The children gain the important beliefs that they can control their own destinies and that they themselves are a vital part of the world they live in. These beliefs are rarely acquired at present. When I have asked students whether their ideas or interests are important in school, I have been told vehemently in meeting after meeting that, "Our interests have no value in school."

Class meetings keep a class together because the more and less capable students can interact and because students can always succeed. In a meeting, no one can fail. One person's opinion is just as good as another's; there is no right and wrong. The only "wrong," perhaps, is not to participate at all, and this has been a minor problem where meetings are held regularly and with enthusiasm. Overparticipation and talking out of turn are much more common. When, in the open-ended meetings and, to some degree, in the educational-diagnostic meetings, the child succeeds in the eyes of his peers and his teacher, he becomes motivated to do some of the less exciting fact finding necessary to make the judgments and decisions that may evolve from the meetings. If meetings become important and facts become necessary to successful meetings, then it is worthwhile learning facts. The meetings provide the internal stimulus missing from an education that too often starts and ends with facts.

Although I suggest that class meetings be held at a regular time at least once a day in elementary school and perhaps two or three times a week in high school, there is no reason that teachers cannot use the technique for arithmetic, history, science, and other subjects. Whole-class teaching reduces isolation and failure. We use large, cooperative groups in most of the extracurricular subjects. The team, for example, is the basis of competitive athletics. But in the class curriculum, where it could be equally effective, it is little used. By treating the whole class as a unit, the same spirit of cooperation can arise as arises on athletic teams. By eliminating failure, by accepting each child's thinking (at least during the time of the meeting), and by utilizing his mistakes as a basis for future teaching, we have a way of approaching the child that supports him. The present system of accentuating his mistakes tears the child down and makes him unable or unwilling to think.

Another advantage of class meetings is the confidence that a child gains when he states his opinion before a group. In life there are many opportunities to speak for oneself. The more we teach children to speak clearly and thoughtfully, the better we prepare them for life. When a child can speak satisfactorily for himself, he gains a confidence that is hard to shake.

So What Do You Do Now?

Neil Postman and Charles Weingartner

from *Teaching as a Subversive Activity*

You are a teacher in an ordinary school, and the ideas in this book [*Teaching as a Subversive Activity*] make sense to you . . . what can you do about it, say tomorrow?

1. Your first act of subversion might be conducted in the following way: write on a scrap of paper these questions:

> What am I going to have my students do today?
> What's it good for?
> How do I know?

Tape the paper to the mirror in your bathroom or some other place where you are likely to see it every morning. If nothing else, the questions will begin to make you uneasy about shilling for someone else and might weaken your interest in "following the syllabus." You may even, after a while, become nauseous at the prospect of teaching things which have a specious value or for which there is no evidence that your anticipated outcomes do, in fact, occur. At their best, the questions will drive you to reconsider almost everything you are doing, with the result that you will challenge your principal, your textbooks, the syllabus, the grading system, your own education, and so on. In the end, it all may cost you your job, or lead you to seek another position, or drive you out of teaching altogether. Subversion is a risky business—as risky for its agent as for its target.

2. In class, try to avoid *telling* your students any answers, if only for a few lessons or days. Do not prepare a lesson plan. Instead, confront your students with some sort of problem which might interest them. Then, allow them to work the problem through without your advice or counsel. Your talk should consist of questions directed to particular students, based on remarks made by those students. If a student asks you a question, tell him that you don't know the answer, even if you do. Don't be frightened by the long stretches of silence that might occur. Silence may mean that the students are thinking. Or it may mean that they are growing hostile. The hostility signifies that the students resent the fact that you have shifted the burden of intellectual activity from you to them. Thought is often painful even if you are accustomed to it. If you are not, it can be unbearable.

There are at least two good accounts of what happens when a teacher refrains from telling students answers. One of them appears in Nathaniel Cantor's *The Dynamics of Learning;* the other, in Carl Rogers' *On Becoming a Person.* You may want to read these accounts before trying your experiment. If you have any success at all, you ought to make your experiment a regular feature of your weekly lessons: one hour every day for independent problem solving, or one hour every week. However much you can do will be worth the effort.

3. Try listening to your students for a day or two. We do not mean reacting to what they say. We mean listening. This may require that you do some role playing. Imagine, for example, that you are not their teacher but a psychiatrist (or some such person) who is not primarily trying to teach but who is trying to understand. Any questions you ask or remarks you make would, therefore, not be designed to instruct or judge. They would be attempts to clarify what someone has said. If you are like most teachers, your training has probably not included learning how to listen. Therefore, we would recommend that you

obtain a copy of *On Becoming a Person* by Carl Rogers. The book is a collection of Rogers' best articles and speeches. Rogers is generally thought of as the leading exponent of nondirective counseling, and he is a rich source of ideas about listening to and understanding other people. You probably will not want to read every article in the book, but do not overlook "Communication: Its Blocking and Facilitation." In this article, Rogers describes a particularly effective technique for teaching listening: the students engage in a discussion of some issue about which they have strong feelings. But their discussion has an unusual rule applied to it. A student may say anything he wishes but only after he has restated what the previous speaker has said *to that speaker's satisfaction.* Astounding things happen to students when they go through this experience. They find themselves concentrating on what others are saying to the point, sometimes, of forgetting what they themselves were going to say. In some cases, students have a unique experience. They find that they have projected themselves into the frame of mind of another person. You might wish to make this special listening game a permanent part of your weekly lessons. But, of course, you ought to try it yourself first. An additional aid to you in your efforts at listening will be "Do You Know How to Listen?" by Wendell Johnson. The article appeared in *ETC.* In autumn 1949. This publication is edited by S. I. Hayakawa, and we enthusiastically suggest that you become a permanent subscriber.

It is important for us to say that the principal reason for your learning how to listen to students is that you may increase your understanding of what the students perceive as relevant. The only way to know where a kid is "at" is to listen to what he is saying. You can't do this if you are talking.

Invite another teacher to observe your class when you are experimenting with listening. After the lesson, ask your colleague this question: On the basis of what you heard these students say, what would you have them do tomorrow, or next week? Perhaps your colleague will then invite you to observe her class while she experiments with listening. After a while, both of you may find that you are becoming increasingly more effective at designing activities based on what students actually know, feel, and care about.

If you are somewhat uncertain about how to start your students talking, look back at the chapter "What's Worth Knowing?" Several of the questions listed there will trigger enough student talk to challenge your powers as listener.

4. If you feel it is important for your students to learn how to ask questions, try this:

Announce to the class that for the next two days, you will not permit them to make any utterances that are not in the form of questions. Then, present the class with some problem. Tell them that their task is to compile a list of questions, the answers to which might help in solving the problem. If your students require an inducement, tell them you will reward (with A's, gold stars, or whatever sugar cubes you conventionally use) those students who produce the most questions. At this point, you need only be concerned with the quantity of questions, not their quality. Your students probably have had very little experience with question-asking behavior (at least in school), and the primary problem is to get them to begin formulating questions. Later, you can have them examine their questions in an effort to determine if there are certain criteria by which the quality of a question can be evaluated. (For example: Does the question contain unwarranted assumptions? Does it leave important terms undefined? Does it suggest some procedure for obtaining an answer?)

You might use some such problems as the following depending on the age of your students:

Suppose we wanted to make the school the best possible school we can imagine, what would you need to know in order to proceed?

Read the following speech (for example, by the President). What would you need to know in order to evaluate the validity of the speech?

Suppose our job was to make recommendations to improve the traffic problem (or pollution problem or population problem or whatever), what would you need to know in order to suggest a solution?

5. In order to help yourself become more aware of the subjectivity of your judgments, try this experiment:

The next time you grade your students, write down your reasons for whatever grade you assigned to a student. Then, imagine that you are the student. Study the reasons that your teacher gave to explain your grade. Ask yourself if you can accept these reasons and reflect on what you think of a teacher who would offer them. You might discover that your basis for assigning grades is prejudicial to some students, or lacks generosity, or is too vague. You might also discover, as some teachers have, that the conventional grading system is totally inadequate to evaluate the learning process. Some teachers have grown to resent it bitterly and have been driven to invent another system to complement the one they are forced to use.

Another experiment that might be helpful: Each time you give a grade to a student, grade your own perception of that student. The following questions might be useful:

1. To what extent does my own background block me from understanding the behavior of this student?

2. Are my own values greatly different from those of the student?

3. To what extent have I made an effort to understand how things look from this student's point of view?

4. To what extent am I rewarding or penalizing the student for his acceptance or rejection of my interests?

5. To what extent am I rewarding a student for merely saying what I want to hear, whether or not he believes or understands what he is saying?

You may discover that your answers to these questions are deeply disturbing. For example, you may find that you give the lowest grades mostly to those students you least understand, in which case, the problem is yours—isn't it?—not theirs. What we are driving at is this: too many teachers seem to believe that the evaluations they make of their students reflect only the "characteristics," "ability," and "behavior" of the students. The teacher merely records the grade that the student "deserves." This is complete nonsense, of course. A grade is as much a product of the teacher's characteristics, ability, and behavior as of the student's. Any procedure you can imagine that would increase your awareness of the role you play in "making" the student what you think he is will be helpful, even something like the following:

Keep track of the judgments you make about students. Every time you *say* words such as right, wrong, good, bad, correct, incorrect, smart, stupid, nice, annoying, polite, impertinent, neat, sloppy, etc., keep a record. Do it yourself or have a student do it. You can simply make a check on a sheet of paper that has been divided in two, with one column marked "+" and the other marked "—." Beyond the verbal judgments, you might keep track of the judgments you make that are made visible nonverbally, through facial expression, gesture, or general demeanor. Negative judgments are, not surprisingly, impediments to good learning, particularly if they have the effect of causing the learner to judge himself negatively.

Positive judgments, perhaps surprisingly, can also produce undesirable results. For example, if a learner becomes totally dependent upon the positive judgments of an authority (teacher) for both motivation and reward, what you have is an intellectual paraplegic incapable of any independent activity, intellectual or otherwise.

The point to all of this is to help you become conscious of the degree to which your language and thought is judgmental. You cannot avoid making judgments but you can become more conscious of the way in which you make them. This is critically important because once we judge someone or something we tend to stop thinking about them or it. Which means, among other things, that we behave in response to our judgments rather than to that which is being judged. People and things are processes. Judgments convert them into fixed states. This is one reason that judgments are commonly self-fulfilling. If a boy, for example, is judged as being "dumb" and a "nonreader" early in his school career, that judgment sets into motion a series of teacher behaviors that cause the judgment to become self-fulfilling.

What we need to do then, if we are seriously interested in helping students to become good learners, is to suspend or delay judgments about them. One manifestation of this is the ungraded elementary school. But you can practice suspending judgment yourself tomorrow. It doesn't require any major changes in anything in the school except your own behavior.

For example, the following incident—in this case outside of a classroom—is representative of the difference between a stereotypic and a suspended judgment.

A man and his seventeen-year-old son on Monday evening had a "discussion" about the need for the son to defer his social activities on week nights until he has finished doing all of the home work he has for school the next day.

It is now Wednesday evening, 48 hours later, about 7:30 P.M.

Father is watching TV. Son emerges from his room and begins to put on a jacket.

FATHER: Where are you going?

SON: Out.

FATHER: Out where?

SON: Just out.

FATHER: Have you finished your home work?

SON: Not yet.

FATHER: I thought we decided [*that's the way parents talk*] that you wouldn't go out on week nights until you'd finished your home work.

SON: But I have to go out.

FATHER: What do you mean you "have to"?

SON: I just do.

FATHER: Well, you're not going out. You just have to learn to live up to the terms of the agreements you make.

SON: But . . .

FATHER: That's all. I want no back talk.

MOTHER: Please. Let him go out. He'll be back soon.

FATHER: I don't want you butting in.

MOTHER: [*to son*]: Go ahead. It will be all right.

[*Son exits.*]

FATHER [*in a rage*]: What the hell do you mean by encouraging his impertinence. How do you expect him to learn responsibility if you side with him in an argument with me? How . . .

MOTHER [*interrupting*]: Do you know what tomorrow is?

FATHER: What the hell has that got to do with it? Tomorrow's Thursday.

MOTHER: Yes, and it's your birthday.

FATHER: [*Silence.*]

MOTHER: Your son has been making a birthday gift for you at Jack's house. He wanted it to be a surprise for you tomorrow morning. A nice start for the day. He has just a bit more work to do on it to finish it. He wanted to get it done as early as possible tonight so he could bring it home and wrap it up for tomorrow. And then he'd still have time to do his home work.

Well, you see how easy it is to judge someone as something on the basis of *x* amount of data perceived in one way while simultaneously they are not only not that, but are something quite different.

Judgments are relative to the data upon which they are based and to the emotional state of the judge.

Learning to suspend judgment can be most liberating. You might find that it makes you a better learner (meaning maker) too.

6. Along the lines of the above, we would suggest an experiment that requires only imagination, but plenty of it. Suppose you could convince yourself that your students are the smartest children in the school; or, if that seems unrealistic, that they have the greatest potential of any class in the school. (After all, who can say for certain how much potential anyone has?) What do you imagine would happen? What would you do differently if you *acted* as if your students were capable of great achievements? And if you acted differently, what are the chances that many of your students would begin to act as if they *were* great achievers? We believe that the chances are quite good. There is, as we have noted, considerable

evidence to indicate that people can become what others think they are. In fact, if you reflect on how anyone becomes anything, you are likely to conclude that becoming is almost always a product of expectations—one's own or someone else's. We are talking here about the concept of the "self-fulfilling prophecy." This refers to the fact that often when we predict that something will happen, the prediction itself contributes to making it happen. Nowhere is this idea more usable than in education, which is, or ought to be, concerned with the processes of becoming.

A *warning:* you will have great difficulty in imagining that your students are smart if you hold on to the belief that the stuff you know about, or would like to know about, constitutes the only ingredients of "smartness." Once you abandon that idea, you may find that your students do, in fact, know a great deal of stuff, and that it is easier than you supposed to imagine they are the brightest children you ever had.

7. The extent to which you can try the following experiment depends on the degree to which the administration and the school community are rigid. In its most effective form, the experiment involves telling your students that all of them will get A's for the term and, of course, making good on your promise. At first, the students will not believe you, and it has sometimes taken as long as four weeks before all the students accept the situation. Once such acceptance is achieved, the students can begin to concentrate on learning, not their grades. There is no need for them to ask, "When is the midterm?" "Do we have to do a paper?" "How much weight is given to classwork?" and so on. If such questions do arise, you can reply, honestly, by saying that the questions are not necessary since the grades have already been given and each student will receive the highest possible grade the system allows. (We can assure you that such questions will come up because students have been conditioned to think of education as being indistinguishable from grades.) The next step is to help the students discover what kind of knowledge they think is worth knowing and to help them

decide what procedures can most profitably be used to find out what they want to know. You will have to remind your students that there is no need for them to make suggestions that they think will please *you*. Neither is there any need for them to accept your suggestions out of fear of reprisal. Once they internalize this idea, they will pursue vigorously whatever course their sense of relevance dictates. Incidentally, they are likely to view your proposals not as threats, but as possibilities. In fact, you may be astonished at how seriously your own suggestions are regarded once the coercive dimension is removed.

If you are thinking that students, given such conditions, will not do any work, you are wrong. Most will. But, of course, not all. There are always a few who will view the situation as an opportunity to "goof off." So what? It is a small price to pay for providing the others with perhaps the only decent intellectual experience they will ever have in school. Beyond that, the number of students who do "goof off" is relatively small when compared with those who, in conventional school environments, tune out.

There is no way of our predicting what "syllabus" your students will evolve. It depends. Especially on them, but also on you and how willing you are to permit students to take control of the direction of their own studies. If you, or your administration and community, could not bear this possibility, perhaps you could try the experiment on a limited basis: for example, for a "unit" or even a specific assignment.

8. Perhaps you have noticed that most examinations and, indeed, syllabi and curricula deal almost exclusively with the past. The future hardly exists in school. Can you remember ever asking or being asked in school a question like "If such and such occurs, what do you think *will* happen?"? A question of this type is usually not regarded as "serious" and would rarely play a central role in any "serious" examination. When a future-oriented question is introduced in school, its purpose is usually to "motivate" or to find out how "creative" the students can be. But the point is that the world we live in is changing

so rapidly that a future-orientation is essential for everybody. Its development in schools is our best insurance against a generation of "future shock" sufferers.

You can help by including in all of your class discussions and examinations some questions that deal with the future. For example:

> What effects on our society do you think the following technological inventions will have?
> *a.* the electric car
> *b.* the television-telephone
> *c.* the laser beam
> *d.* the 2,000-mph jet
> *e.* central data storage
> *f.* disposable "paper" clothing
> *g.* interplanetary communication
> *h.* language-translation machines
>
> Can you identify two or three ideas, beliefs, and practices that human beings will need to give up for their future well-being?

In case you are thinking that such questions as these are usable only in the higher grades, we want to assure you that young children (even third-graders) frequently provide imaginative and pointed answers to future-oriented questions, provided that the questions are suitably adapted to their level of understanding. Perhaps you can make it a practice to include future-oriented questions at least once a week in all your classes. It is especially important that this be done for young children. After all, by the time they have finished school, the future you have asked them to think about will be the present.

9. Anyone interested in helping students deal with the future (not to mention the present) would naturally be concerned, even preoccupied, with media of communication. We recommend to you, of course, the books of Marshall McLuhan, especially *Understanding Media*. We think that the most productive way to respond to McLuhan's challenge (as he has suggested) is *not* to examine his statements but to examine the media. In other words,

don't dwell on the question "Is McLuhan right in saying such and such?" Instead, focus on the question "In what ways are media affecting our society?" Your answers may turn out to be better than McLuhan's. More important, if you allow your students to consider the question, *their* answers may be better than McLuhan's. And even more important than that, the process of searching for such answers, once learned, will be valuable to your students throughout their lives.

Therefore, we suggest that media study become an integral part of all your classes. No matter what "subject" you are teaching, media are relevant. For example, if you are a history teacher, you can properly consider questions about the effects of media on political and social developments. If you are a science teacher, the entire realm of technology is open to you and your students, including a consideration of the extent to which technology influences the direction of the evolutionary process. If you are an English teacher, the role of media in creating new literatures, new audiences for literature, and new modes of perceiving literature is entirely within your province. In short, regardless of your subject and the age of your students, we suggest that you include the study of media as a normal part of the curriculum. You might bear in mind that your students are quite likely to be more perceptive and even more knowledgeable about the structure and meaning of newer media than you. For example, there are many teachers who haven't yet noticed that young people are enormously interested in poetry—the poetry that is now on LP records and sung by Joan Baez, Phil Ochs, and Bob Dylan; or that young people are equally interested in essays of social and political criticism—as *heard* on records by Lenny Bruce, Bill Cosby, Godfrey Cambridge, Mort Sahl, et al.

10. Before making our final suggestion, we want to say a word of assurance about the revolution we are urging. There is nothing in what we have said in this book that precludes the use, *at one time or another,* of any of the conventional methods and materials of learning. For certain specific purposes, a lecture, a film, a textbook, a

packaged unit, even a punishment, may be entirely justified. What we are asking for is a methodological and
psychological shift in emphasis in the roles of teacher and
student, a fundamental change in the *nature* of the classroom environment. In fact, one model for such an environment already exists in the schools—oddly, at the
extreme ends of the schooling process. A good primary-
grade teacher as well as a good graduate-student adviser
operate largely on the subversive assumptions expressed
in this book. They share a concern for process as against
product. They are learner- and problem-oriented. They
share a certain disdain for syllabi. They allow their students to pursue that which is relevant to the learner. But
there is a 15-year gap between the second grade and
advanced graduate study. The gap can be filled, we believe, by teachers who understand the spirit of our orientation. It is neither required nor desirable that *everything*
about one's performance as a teacher be changed. Just the
most important things.

11. Our last suggestion is perhaps the most difficult. It
requires honest self-examination. Ask yourself how you
came to know whatever things you feel are worth knowing. This may sound like a rather abstract inquiry, but
when undertaken seriously it frequently results in startling
discoveries. For example, some teachers have discovered
that there is almost nothing valuable they know that was
told to them by someone.

About the Authors

Gordon Ashby lives in Marin County north of San Francisco where he works as an environmental designer. He is married and a father. His family is one of those involved in developing the school described in the book *Rasberry Exercises* by Rasberry and Greenway.

Sylvia Ashton-Warner left New Zealand, the locale of her work in *Teacher*, to teach in a private school in Aspen, Colorado. While there she completed *Spearpoint*, her newest book.

Bruno Bettelheim is Professor and Director of the Orthogenic School of the University of Chicago. He is the author of a number of books, among them *Love Is Not Enough* and *Children of the Dream*.

Albert Cullum is a Professor of Education at Herbert H. Lehman College of the City University of New York. He is an active lecturer at teacher training workshops and has written four other books with specific dramatic and language materials. He previously taught in the public schools for twenty years.

Helaine Dawson lives in San Francisco with her husband. She still sees many of the pupils she describes in her book *On the Outskirts of Hope*. She has also conducted teacher training courses and has concentrated recently on projects concerning the Chicano community.

Sunny Decker. In *An Empty Spoon*, Mrs. Decker describes her first year of teaching in a large inner city high school. She has since helped compile *The Yellow Pages of Learning Resources,* also represented in this anthology.

George Dennison was a teacher and founder of the First Street School in New York City. His book, widely admired, deals with the children of that school.

Daniel Fader is Professor of English at the University of Michigan. His latest book is *The Naked Children.*

Joseph Featherstone is an Englishman whose original reports about the British Infant Schools were published in the USA in *The New Republic* in 1967. His accounts are among those credited with awakening an enormous interest in open classrooms in this country.

Hans Furth is Chairman and Professor of Psychology at Catholic University in Washington, D.C. He specialized in the field of intellectual processes in relation to linguistic development. On sabbatical, he spent a year studying with Jean Piaget.

John Gardner is President of Common Cause in Washington, D.C., a peoples' lobby for lawful political change. He is past president (1955) of the Carnegie Foundation and was former U.S. Commissioner of Education. He has written many well-known books, among them *Excellence: Can We Be Equal and Excellent Too?*

William Glasser is heavily involved in teacher training with his own consulting firm in Southern California. The Ventura School, a part of the public school system of Palo Alto, California, is run on his principles and is open to visitors by appointment.

Carol Guyton Goodell taught in elementary schools for ten years, tutored extensively and founded a tutoring service, and worked for a year at Portola Institute in Menlo Park. She and her colleagues Dennis Dobbs and Robert

Hill design simulation games and have done teacher workshops on gaming at University of California and at Stanford. They formed a consulting business, Real World Learning, Inc., in San Carlos, California. She is married and the mother of two children.

Paul Goodman, poet and critic, the author of *Growing Up Absurd*, died in 1972. He had lectured widely on the subject of education.

Harold Hart is the publisher of the original works of A. S. Neill, of which *Summerhill* is a classic and a benchmark for educational discussions. *Summerhill: For and Against* is a compendium of opinions about the work of A. S. Neill, of which five were excerpted as examples.

Fred Hechinger is the Education Editor of *The New York Times*.

James Herndon is a junior high school teacher in a suburb of San Francisco. He is married and the father of two sons. His first book, *The Way It Spozed to Be*, written ten years ago, received national acclaim.

John Holt is the best-selling author of books on education and a prime mover personally in encouraging reforms and innovations in education. He is a former teacher. *What Do I Do Monday?* deals with specific techniques which teachers can use as models, or which they may find give them new ideas.

Virginia Cary Hudson did not live to see her essays in book form. It is thanks to her daughter, Virginia Mayne, that they survived an attic fire and reached a publisher. *O Ye Jigs and Juleps,* published in 1962, was reprinted for the twenty-second time in 1971, winning new admirers every year.

Lenore Jacobson is the Principal of Ponderosa Elementary School in South San Francisco, California. She has been an educator for two decades, has a doctorate in curriculum from UC Berkeley, and won the Cottell Fund Award of the American Psychological Association First Prize in 1967 for *Pygmalion in the Classroom*.

Herbert Kohl has been actively involved in the alternative schools movement, working mainly on the frontlines in Berkeley. His first book, *36 Children*, was a story of his initial experiences as a teacher in Harlem, and subsequent books have dealt with evolutionary stages in his educational thinking and techniques.

Elton McNeil is Professor of Psychology at the University of Michigan.

Ashley Montagu, the author of over forty books on widely ranging subjects, is currently on the faculty of Columbia University. Some of his books are: *The Natural Superiority of Women; Immortality, Religion, and Morals;* and *Man's Most Dangerous Myth: The Fallacy of Race*.

Neil Postman is a Professor at New York University. He has traveled extensively since the publication of *Teaching As a Subversive Activity* and is frequently a keynote speaker at educational conferences and workshops. He recently coauthored *The Soft Revolution* with Charles Weingartner.

Max Rafferty is presently Alabama Superintendent of Public Instruction although he was in the same position in California when his section was written. He is an articulate conservative in education as explained in his book *Suffer Little Children*.

Robert Rosenthal is Professor of Social Psychology at Harvard University. His book *Pygmalion in the Classroom* won the Cottell Fund Award of the American Psychological Association First Prize in 1967.

Fannie Shaftel is Professor of Education at Stanford. She was their first recipient of the Distinguished Teaching

Award. Her special area of expertise is in sociodrama and related techniques. She is married to George Shaftel and is the mother of one son. She will retire in 1974.

George Shaftel is an educational writer specializing in books on history and on science. He is married to Fannie Shaftel and the father of a grown son. They live in Menlo Park (Ladera), California.

Mark Terry, a young writer and teacher, is the author of *Teaching for Survival,* published in 1971.

Leo Tolstoy is best known as a nineteenth-century Russian novelist, historian, and scholar. For three years, however, he experimented with a school for peasant children. His record of this experience heavily foreshadows *Summerhill* in some ways, and certainly contradicts any claim modern educators might have for the invention of open classrooms or the inquiry method. *Tolstoy On Education* was translated from Russian by Leo Wiener.

Charles Weingartner is Associate Professor of Education at Queens College in New York. He was formerly a high school teacher. After co-authoring *Teaching As a Subversive Activity* with Neil Postman, they collaborated again with *The Soft Revolution.*

Richard Saul Wurman is associated with GEE!, Group for Environmental Education, Inc., and the architecture and planning firm of Murphy Levy Wurman in Philadelphia.

Selected Bibliography

A *Selected* Bibliography means that I left in the books I remember and thought were worthwhile, that there are a lot I have forgotten or haven't read that I should have read, and/or that there are references mentioned in the separate selections for this anthology which may not be in the Bibliography. In short, the term "selected" gets me out of any inferred promises that this is the complete be-all-and-end-all bibliography on education, but it surely is a damn good beginning. You'll notice that there is only one book per author, or at the most two, but this doesn't mean I haven't read any others. It does mean that I figure you'll make it to the library to get the others yourself.

The best printed bibliography that you can buy reprints of is available from *The New School Exchange Newsletter*, 301 East Canon Perdido, Santa Barbara, California 93101. It is good but not perfect, and is aimed at a humanistic emphasis in education, as is this book. John T. Canfield of the University of Massachusetts has also compiled an extensive Bibliography on humanistic education with Harold Wells as co-author, *100 Ways to Enhance Self Concept in the Classroom,* to be published summer of 1973.

Abt, Clark C. *Serious Games.* New York: The Viking Press, 1970.

Agee, James. *Let Us Now Praise Famous Men.* New York: Ballantine Books, 1966.

Applegate, Mauree. *Helping Children Write.* Evanston, Illinois: Row, Peterson, 1954.

Ashton-Warner, Sylvia. *Teacher.* New York: Simon and Schuster, 1963.

Axline, Virginia. *Dibs: In Search of Self*. New York: Ballantine Books, 1969.

Bazeley, E. T. *Homer Lane and the Little Commonwealth*. New York: Schocken, 1969.

Beals, Alan R. *Culture in Process*. New York: Holt, Rinehart and Winston, 1967.

Beggs, Larry. *Huckleberry's for Runaways*. New York: Ballantine Books, 1969.

Berg, Ivan. *Education and Jobs: The Great Training Robbery*. Boston: Beacon Press, 1971.

Bettelheim, Bruno. *Love Is Not Enough*. New York: Collier Books, 1965.

Bloom, Benjamin. *Educational Evaluation: A Handbook*. New York: McGraw-Hill, 1970.

Borton, Terry. *Read, Touch and Teach*. New York: McGraw-Hill, 1970.

Boyd, Neva. *Handbook of Games*. Chicago, Illinois: H. G. Fitzsimmons, 1945.

Brand, Stewart. *Whole Earth Catalog*. Menlo Park, California: Portola Institute, 1971.

Brenton, Myron. *What's Happened to Teacher?* New York: Coward-McCann, 1970.

Brown, George I. *Human Teaching for Human Learning*. New York: The Viking Press, 1970.

Bruner, Jerome S. *The Process of Education*. New York: Vintage Books, 1960.

Buber, Martin. *I & Thou*. New York: Charles Scribner's Sons, 1958.

Bushnell, Don D., and Allen, Dwight W. *The Computer in American Education*. New York: John Wiley and Sons, 1967.

Button, Alan DeWitt. *The Authentic Child*. New York: Random House, 1969.

Channon, Gloria. *Homework: Required Reading for Teachers and Parents*. New York: Outerbridge and Dienstfrey, 1970.

Christensen, Francis. *Notes Toward a New Rhetoric*. New York: Harper and Row, 1967.

Clark, Kenneth. *Dark Ghetto*. New York: Harper and Row, 1965.

Cole, Larry. *Street Kids*. New York: Grossman Publishers, 1970.

Coles, Robert. *Children of Crisis*. Boston: Little Brown and Co., 1964.

————. *Dead End School*. Boston: Little Brown and Co., 1967.

Conant, J. B. *The Education of American Teachers*. New York: McGraw-Hill, 1963.

Cullum, Albert. *Push Back the Desks*. New York: Citation Press, 1967.

Dawson, Helaine S. *On the Outskirts of Hope*. New York: McGraw-Hill, 1968.

Decker, Sunny. *An Empty Spoon*. New York: Harper and Row, 1969.

Dennison, George. *The Lives of Children: The Story of the First Street School*. New York: Random House, 1969.

Dewey, John. *Art and Education*. Merion, Pennsylvania: The Barnes Foundation Press, 1947.

Dubos, René. *The Dreams of Reason*. New York: Columbia University Press, 1961.

Fader, Daniel. *The Naked Children*. New York: Macmillan, 1971.

————, and McNeil, Elton. *Hooked on Books: Program and Proof*. New York: Medallion Books, 1968.

Fantini, Mario; Gittell, Marilyn; and Magat, Richard. *Community Control and the Urban School*. New York: Frederick A. Praeger, 1970.

Fast, Julius. *Body Language*. New York: M. Evans and Company, 1970.

Featherstone, Joseph. "Experiments in Learning: Reading and Writing in British Junior Schools." *New Republic,* 159 (December 14, 1968) 23-25.

————. "How Children Learn: Primary School Reforms." *New Republic,* 157 (September 2, 1967) 17-21.

————. "Report Analysis: Children and Their Primary Schools." *Harvard Education Review,* 38 (Spring, 1968) 317-328.

————. "Schools for Children: What's Happening in British Classrooms." *New Republic,* 157 (August 19, 1967) 17-21.

————. "Schools for Learning: Further Report." *New Republic,* 159 (December 21, 1968) 17-20.

————. *Schools Where Children Learn*. New York: Liverwright, 1971.

————. "Teaching Children to Think; Primary School Reforms." *New Republic*, 157 (September 9, 1967) 15-19.

————. "Why So Few Good Schools?" *New Republic*, 160 (January 4, 1969) 18-21.

Fine, Benjamin. *Stretching Their Minds*. New York: Dutton, 1964.

Flesch, Rudolf. *Why Johnny Can't Read*. New York: Harper and Row, 1955.

Fraiberg, Selma H. *The Magic Years*. New York: Charles Scribner's Sons, 1959.

Freire, Paolo. *Pedagogy of the Oppressed*. New York: Herder and Herder, 1970.

Friendenberg, Edgar Z. *Coming of Age in America*. New York: Random House, 1965.

Fromm, Erich. *The Art of Loving*. New York: Harper and Row, 1956.

————. *Revolution of Hope*. New York: Harper and Row, 1968.

Fuchs, Estelle. *Teachers Talk, Views from Inside City Schools*. Garden City, New York: Doubleday and Company, 1969.

Fuller, Buckminster. *Education Automation*. Garden City, New York: Anchor Books, 1962.

Furth, Hans G. *Piaget for Teachers*. Englewood Cliffs, New Jersey: Prentice Hall Incorporated, 1970.

Gardner, D. E. M. *The Children's Play Center*. New York: Agathon Press, 1970.

Gardner, John W. *Self Renewal*. New York: Harper and Row, 1965.

Ginnot, Dr. Haim G. *Between Parent and Child*. New York: Avon Books, 1969.

Glasser, William. *Reality Therapy*. New York: Harper and Row, 1965.

————. *Schools Without Failure*. New York: Harper and Row, 1969.

Glazer, Nathan. *Remembering the Answers: Essays on the American Student Revolt*. New York: Basic Books, 1970.

Goodell, Carol; Dobbs, Dennis; and Hill, Robert. *Real World Learning: Educational Games and Simulations.* New York: Ballantine Books, 1973.

Goodman, Paul. *The New Reformation—Notes of a Neolithic Conservative.* New York: Dell Publishing Company, 1970.

Gordon, Alice. *Games for Growth.* Palo Alto, California: Science Research Associates, 1970.

Gordon, Julia Weber. *My Country School Diary.* New York: Dell Publishing Company, 1970.

Gordon, Ira J. *Baby Learning Through Baby Play.* New York: St. Martin's Press, 1970.

Graubard, Stephen R. (Editor) *Daedalus,* 94 (Spring 1965).

Green, Hannah. *I Never Promised You a Rose Garden.* New York: New American Library, 1964.

Gross, Ronald, and Oserman, Paul. *High School.* New York: Simon and Schuster, 1971.

Gross, Ronald, and Gross, Beatrice. *Radical School Reform.* New York: Simon and Schuster, 1970.

Halprin, Andrew. *Theory and Research in Administration.* New York: Macmillan, 1966.

Harris, Thomas A. *I'm OK—You're OK.* New York: Harper and Row, 1969.

Hart, Jane, and Jones, Beverly. *Where's Hannah?* New York: Hart Publishing Company, 1968.

Hart Publishing Company. *Summerhill: For and Against.* New York: Hart Publishing Company, 1970.

Hawkins, Frances. *The Logic of Action, From a Teacher's Notebook.* Boulder, Colorado: Elementary Science Advisory Center, University of Colorado.

Henderson, Davis; Christian, Barbara; and Walton, Carol. *Black Papers on Black Education.* Berkeley, California: Other Ways, 1968.

Hentoff, Nat. *Our Children Are Dying.* New York: Viking Compass Book, 1970.

Herndon, James. *How to Survive in Your Native Land.* New York: Simon and Schuster, 1971.

————. *The Way It Spozed to Be.* New York: Simon and Schuster, 1968.

Holt, John. *Freedom and Beyond.* New York: E. P. Dutton and Company, 1972.

————. *How Children Fail*. New York: Dell Publishing Company, 1964.

————. *How Children Learn*. New York: Pitman Publishing Company, 1967.

————. *The Underachieving School*. New York: Pitman Publishing Company, 1969.

————. *What Do I Do Monday?* New York: Dutton, 1970.

Hostetler, John A., and Huntington, Gertrude E. *Children in Amish Society*. New York: Holt, Rinehart and Winston, 1971.

Hudson, Virginia Cary. *O Ye Jigs and Juleps!* New York: MacFadden Books, 1962.

Huizinga, Johan. *Homo Ludens: A Study of the Play Element in Culture*. London, England: Routledge and Kegan Paul, 1949.

Ilg, Frances, and Ames, Louise. *Child Behavior from Birth to Ten*. New York: Harper and Row, 1955.

Illich, Ivan D. *Celebration of Awareness*. Garden City, New York: Doubleday and Company, 1970.

————. *Deschooling Society*. New York: Harper and Row, 1970.

James, Deborah. *The Taming, A Teacher Speaks*. New York: McGraw-Hill, 1969.

Jencks, Christopher, et al. *Inequality*.

Jones, R. M. *Contemporary Approaches to Education*. New York: New York University Press, 1970.

Jones, W. Ron. *Finding Community*. Palo Alto, California: James E. Freel and Associates, 1971.

Joseph, S. M. *The Me Nobody Knows*. Cleveland, Ohio: World Publishing, 1969.

Kaufman, Bel. *Up The Down Staircase*. New York: Avon, 1964.

Kay, Harry; Dodd, Bernard; and Sime, Max. *Teaching Machines and Programmed Instruction*. New York: Penguin Books, 1968.

Kellogg, Rhoda, and O'Dell, Scott. *The Psychology of Children's Art*. New York: Random House, 1967.

Koch, Kenneth. *Wishes, Lies and Dreams*. New York: Chelsea House, 1970.

Kohl, Herbert R. *The Open Classroom*. New York: The New American Library, 1969.

————. *36 Children.* New York: The New American Library, 1967.

Kozol, Jonathan. *Death at an Early Age.* Boston, Massachusetts: Houghton Mifflin Company, 1967.

Krishnamurti, Jiddu. *Education and the Significance of Life.* New York: Harper and Row, 1953.

Laing, R. D. *The Politics of Experience.* New York: Pantheon Books, 1967.

Lauter, Paul, and Howe, Florence. *The Conspiracy of the Young.* New York: World Publishing Company, 1970.

Lederman, Janet. *Anger and The Rocking Chair.* New York: McGraw-Hill, 1969.

Leonard, George. *Education and Ecstasy.* New York: Dell Publishing Company, 1968.

Lessinger, Leon. *Every Kid A Winner.* New York: Simon and Schuster, 1970.

Lurie, Ellen. *How To Change the Schools: A Parents' Action Handbook on How to Fight the System.* New York: Random House, 1970.

McCarthy, Mary. *The Groves of Academe.* New York: Harcourt, Brace and World, 1951.

McLuhan, Marshall. *The Medium Is the Massage.* New York: Random House, 1967.

————. *Understanding Media: The Extensions of Man.* New York: McGraw-Hill, 1964.

Madsen, William. *The Mexican-Americans of South Texas.* New York: Holt, Rinehart and Winston, 1964.

Mager, Robert F. *Developing Attitude Toward Learning.* Palo Alto, California: Fearon, 1968.

Marin, Peter, and Cohen, Allen Y. *Understanding Drug Use.* New York: Harper and Row, 1972.

Maslow, Abraham. *Motivation and Personality.* Revised edition. Harper and Row, 1970.

Matterson, E. M. *Play and Playthings for the Preschool Child.* Baltimore, Maryland: Penguin Books, 1965.

Mayer, Martin. *The Schools.* Garden City, New York: Doubleday and Company, 1963.

Montaigne, Michel Eyquem de. *Montaigne, The Education of Children.* New York: D. Appleton and Company, 1899.

Montessori, Maria. *Montessori's Own Handbook.* New York: Schocken Books, 1965.

————. *The Absorbent Mind*. New York: Holt, Rinehart and Winston, 1967.

Moustakas, Clark E. *The Authentic Teacher*. Cambridge, Massachusetts: H. A. Doyle Publishing Company, 1966.

————. *Psychotherapy With Children*. New York: Ballantine, 1959.

Neill, A. S. *Freedom—Not License*. New York: Hart Publishing Company, 1966.

————. *Summerhill*. New York: Hart Publishing Company, 1960.

O'Gorman, Ned. *The Storefront*. New York: Harper and Row, 1970.

O'Neill, William F. *Selected Educational Heresies*. Glenview, Illinois: Scott Foresman and Company, 1969.

Opie, Iona, and Opie, Peter. *Children's Games in Street and Playground*. London, England: Oxford University Press, 1969.

Patterson, Gerald R., and Gullion, M. Elizabeth. *Living With Children*. Champaign, Illinois: Research Press, 1968.

Pateerson, Marion. *Alternatives—Educational Innovations in San Mateo County Schools*. San Mateo County Schools, Spring 1968.

Patton, Francis Grey. *Good Morning, Miss Dove*. New York: Pocket Books, 1956.

Peddiwell, J. Abner. *The Saber-Tooth Curriculum*. New York: McGraw-Hill, 1939.

Peterson, Houstan. *Great Teachers*. New York: Random House, 1946.

Piaget, Jean. *The Origins of Intelligence in Children*. New York: W. W. Norton and Company, 1963.

Plowdon, Lady. *Children and Their Primary Schools*. New York: British Information Services, 1967.

Poirier, Gerard. *Students as Partners in Team Learning*. Berkeley, California: Center of Team Learning, 1970.

Postman, Neil, and Weingartner, Charles. *Teaching as a Subversive Activity*. New York: Delacorte Press, 1969.

————. *The Soft Revolution*, New York: Delacorte Press, 1971.

Pratt, Caroline. *I Learn From Children*. New York: Simon and Schuster, 1948.

Prescott, Peter S. *A World of Our Own.* New York: Coward-McCann, 1970.

Rafferty, Max Lewis. *Suffer The Little Children.* New York: Devin-Adair, 1962.

Rambush, Nancy. *Learning How to Learn.* Baltimore, Maryland: Helicorn Press, 1963.

Rasberry, Salli, and Greenway, Robert. *The Rasberry Exercises: How to Start Your Own School and Make a Book.* Sebastopol, California: Freestone Publishing Company, 1970.

Raths, Louis; Harmin, Merrill; and Simon, Sidney. *Values and Teaching: Working with Values in the Classroom.* Columbus: Charles E. Merrill, 1966.

Read, Sir Herbert Edward. *The Redemption of the Robot.* New York: Trident Press, 1966.

Reich, Charles. *The Greening of America.* New York: Random House, 1970.

Rogers, Carl Ransom. *Freedom To Learn.* Columbus, Ohio: C. E. Merrill Publishing Company, 1969.

————. *On Becoming a Person.* Boston, Massachusetts: Houghton Mifflin Company, 1961.

Rosenthal, Robert, and Jacobson, Lenore. *Pygmalion In the Classroom.* New York: Holt, Rinehart and Winston, 1968.

Schmuck, Richard A., and Miles, Matthew. *Organizational Development in the Schools.* Palo Alto, California: National Press, 1971.

Schoolboys of Barbiana. *Letter to a Teacher.* New York: Random House, 1970.

Sears, Pauline S., and Sherman, Vivian S. *In Pursuit of Self Esteem.* Belmont, California: Wadsworth Publishing Company, 1964.

Schrank, Jeffrey. *Teaching Human Beings 101 Subversive Activities for the Classroom.* Boston: Beacon Press, 1972.

Shaftel, Fannie Raskin, and Shaftel, George. *Role Playing for Social Values.* New Jersey: Prentice-Hall, 1967.

Shears, Lloyda, and Bowers, Eli, eds. *Play and Games in Human Development.* Springfield, Illinois: Charles Thomas Publishers, 1973.

Shostrom, Everett L. *Man, the Manipulator.* New York: Bantam Books, 1968.

Shuttlesworth, Dorothy Edwards. *Exploring Nature with Your Child*. New York: Greystone Press, 1952.

Silberman, Charles. *Crisis in the Classroom*. New York: Random House, 1970.

Skinner, B. F. *Walden Two*. New York: Macmillian Company, 1967.

————. *Beyond Freedom and Dignity*. Bantam Books, 1971.

Smith, Lillian H. *The Unreluctant Years*. New York: Viking Press, 1953.

Spindler, George. *Education and Culture*. New York: Holt, Rinehart and Winston, 1956.

Spiro, M. E. *Children of the Kibbutz*. New York: Schocken Books, 1967.

Spolin, Viola. *Improvisation for the Teacher*. Evanston, Illinois: Northwestern University Press, 1963.

Stanford, Gene, and Stanford, Barbara Dodds, *Learning Discussion Skills Through Games*. Englewood Cliffs, New Jersey: Citation Press, 1969.

Stein, Susan M., and Lottick, Sarah T. *Three, Four, Open the Door*. Chicago: Follett Publishing Company, 1971.

Terry, Mark. *Teaching for Survival*. New York: Ballantine, 1971.

Tolstoy, Leo. *Tolstoy on Education*. Translated by Leo Weiner. Chicago, Illinois: Chicago Press, 1967.

Uchendu, Victor C. *The Igbo of Southeast Nigeria*. New York: Holt, Rinehart and Winston, 1965.

University of Washington. *Precision Teaching*. Seattle, Washington: University of Washington Press.

Van Doren, Mark. *Liberal Education*. Boston, Massachusetts: Beacon Press, 1959.

Van Lawick Goodall, Jane. *In the Shadow of Man*. New York: Dell, 1972.

Von Hilsheimer, George. *How to Live with Your Special Child*. Acropolis Books, 1970.

Weaver, Kitty D. *Lenin's Grandchildren*. New York: Simon and Schuster, 1971.

Weber, Lillian. *The English Infant School and Informal Education*. New York: Prentice-Hall, 1971.

Williams, Sylvia Berry. *Hassling: Two Years in a Suburban High School*. Boston, Massachusetts: Little Brown, 1970.

Wright, Nathan Jr. *What Black Educators Are Saying.* New York: Hawthorne Books, Incorporated, 1970.

Wurman, Richard Saul, ed. *Yellow Pages of Learning Resources.* Boston, Massachusetts: MIT Press, 1972.

"Stop managing—and start enjoying—your children!"
A revolutionary approach to parenting

JOHN HOLT
ESCAPE FROM CHILDHOOD

is about
freedom...everybody's freedom!

What if children had the right to equal treatment under the law...the right to be legally responsible for their lives and acts...the right to work for money...the right to travel, live away from home, choose or make their own homes ...the right to do, in general, what any adult may legally do?

"Astonishingly cogent. John Holt's book is touching in its beautiful respect for children and its insistence on their dignity."
—New York Times

$1.75

▼ **Available at your local bookstore or mail the coupon below** ▼